VOLUME 1

JUSTIN JORDAN
writer

TYASSETA
artist

SARAH STERN
colorist

RACHEL DEERING
letterer · production

DARK HORSE BOOKS

DARK HORSE TEAM

PRESIDENT AND PUBLISHER	MIKE RICHARDSON
EDITOR	DANIEL CHABON
ASSISTANT EDITOR	CHUCK HOWITT
DESIGNER	BRENNAN THOME
DIGITAL ART TECHNICIAN	JASON RICKERD

Neil Hankerson Executive Vice President • Tom Weddle Chief Financial Officer • Randy Stradley Vice President of Publishing • Nick McWhorter Chief Business Development Officer • Dale LaFountain Chief Information Officer • Matt Parkinson Vice President of Marketing • Vanessa Todd-Holmes Vice President of Production and Scheduling • Mark Bernardi Vice President of Book Trade and Digital Sales • Ken Lizzi General Counsel • Dave Marshall Editor in Chief • Davey Estrada Editorial Director • Chris Warner Senior Books Editor • Cary Grazzini Director of Specialty Projects • Lia Ribacchi Art Director • Matt Dryer Director of Digital Art and Prepress • Michael Gombos Senior Director of Licensed Publications • Kari Yadro Director of Custom Programs • Kari Torson Director of International Licensing • Sean Brice Director of Trade Sales

Published by Dark Horse Books / A division of Dark Horse Comics LLC / 10956 SE Main Street / Milwaukie, OR 97222

First edition: March 2021 / Trade paperback ISBN: 978-1-50672-441-6

10 9 8 7 6 5 4 3 2 1
Printed in China

Comic Shop Locator Service: comicshoplocator.com

BREAKLANDS SEASON ONE

This volume collects *Breaklands* #1-#5.

Library of Congress Cataloging-in-Publication Data

Names: Jordan, Justin, writer. | Tyasseta, artist. | Stern, Sarah (Colorist), colourist. | Deering, Rachel, 1983- letterer.
Title: Breaklands / Justin Jordan, writer ; Tyasseta Tyasseta, artist ; Sarah Stern, colorist ; Rachel Deering, letterer.
Description: First edition. | Milwaukie, OR : Dark Horse Books, 2021. | "This volume collects Breaklands #1-#5"
Identifiers: LCCN 2020038816 | ISBN 9781506724416 (trade paperback)
Subjects: LCSH: Comic books, strips, etc.
Classification: LCC PN6728.B674 J67 2021 | DDC 741.5/973--dc23
LC record available at https://lccn.loc.gov/2020038816

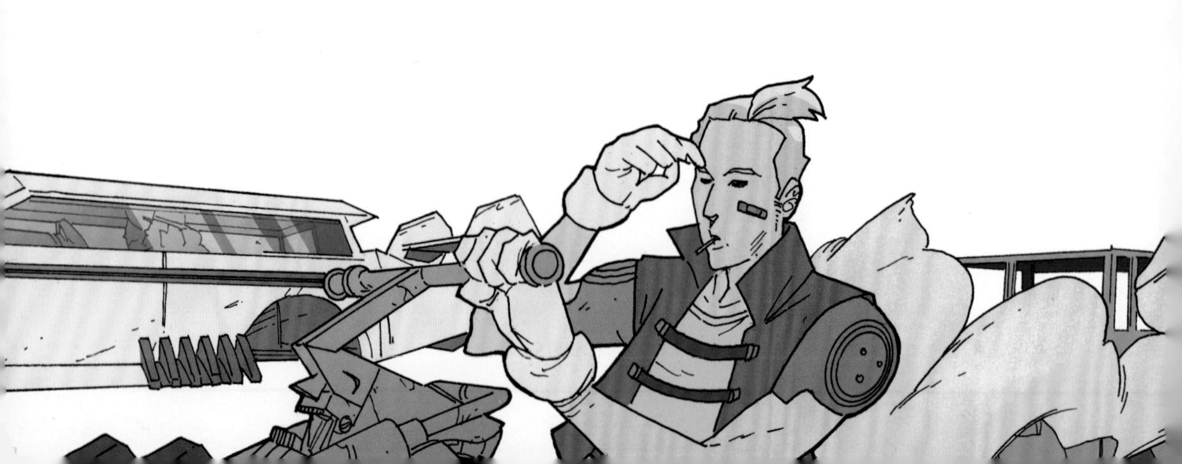

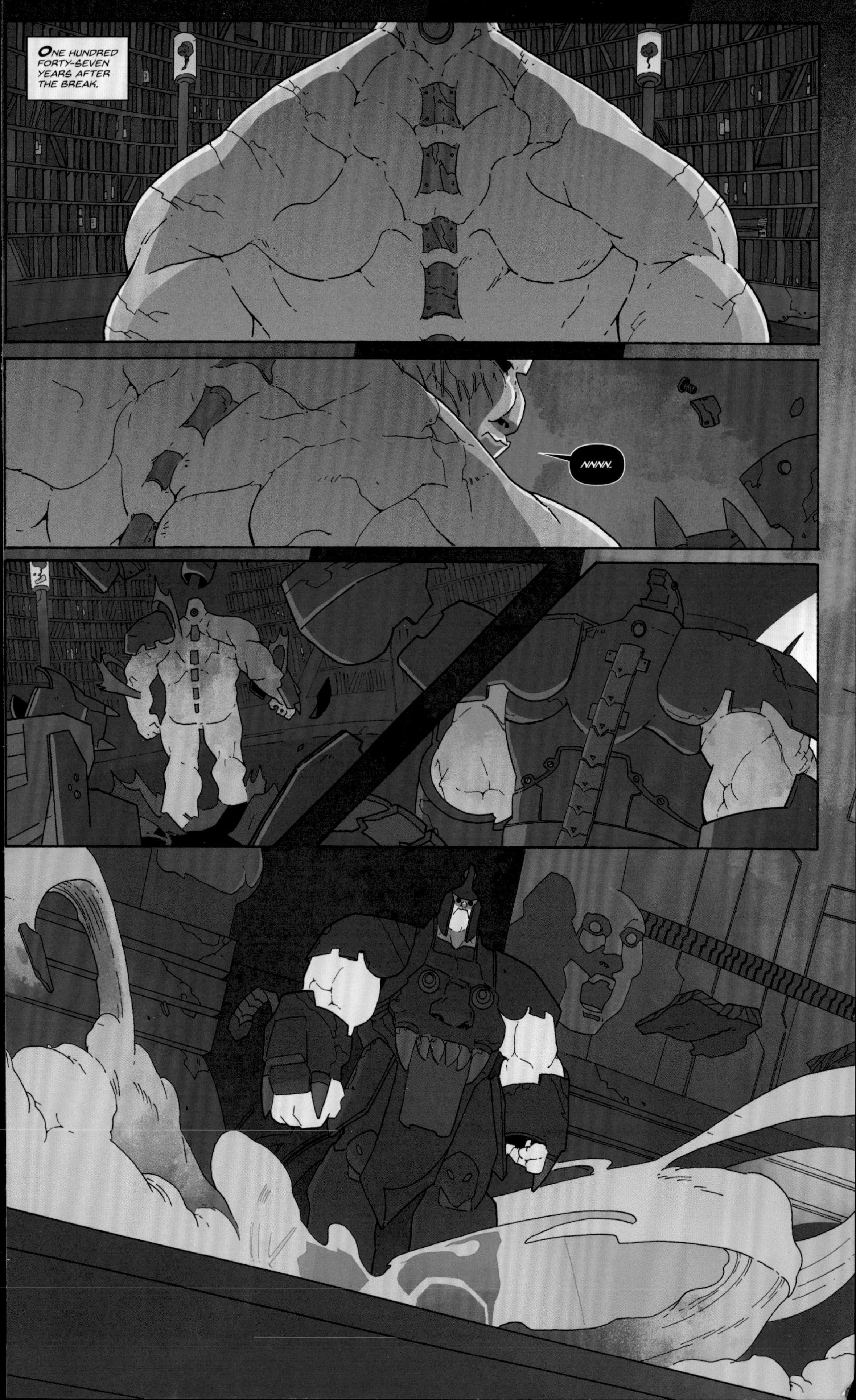
ONE HUNDRED FORTY-SEVEN YEARS AFTER THE BREAK.
NNNN.

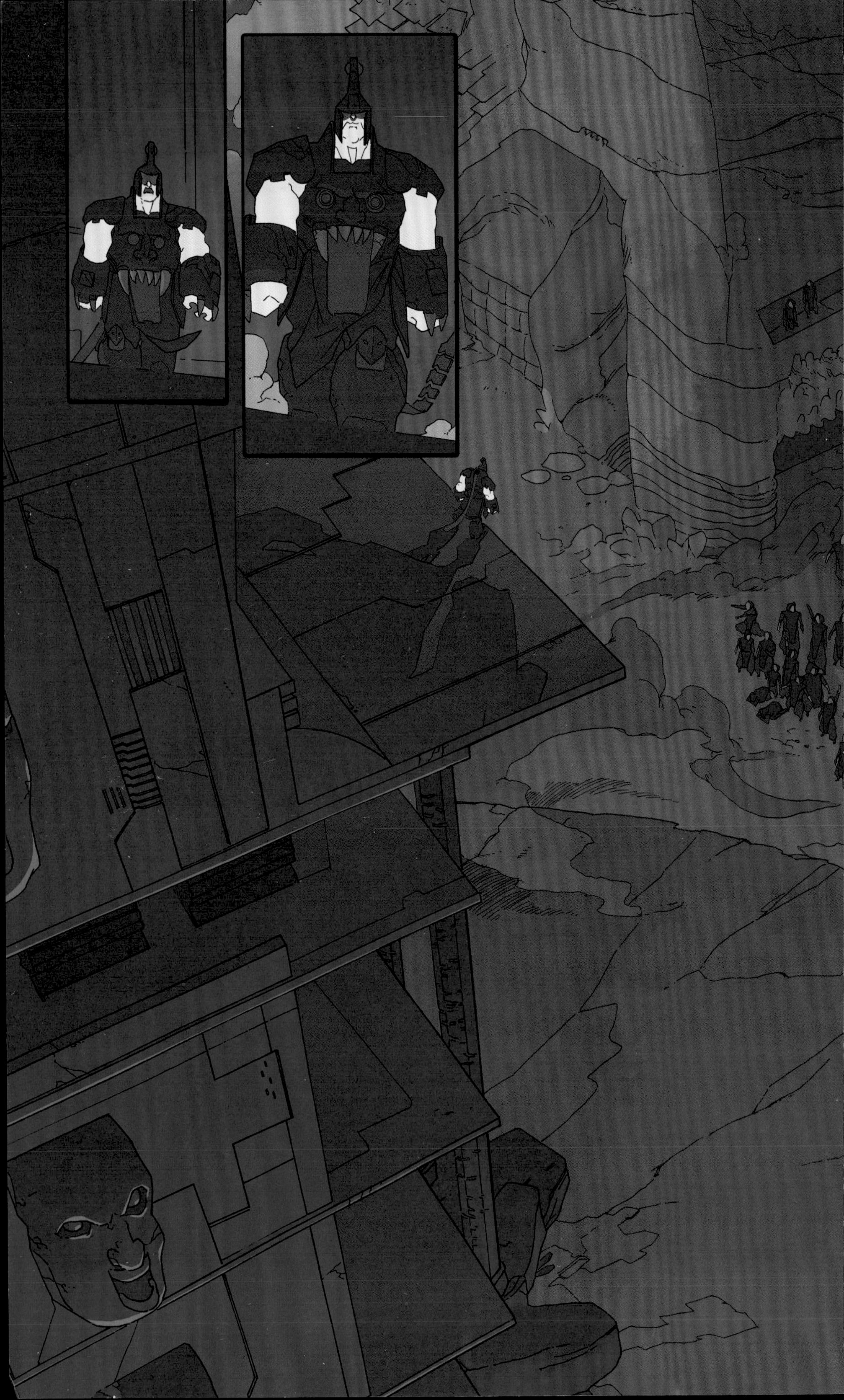

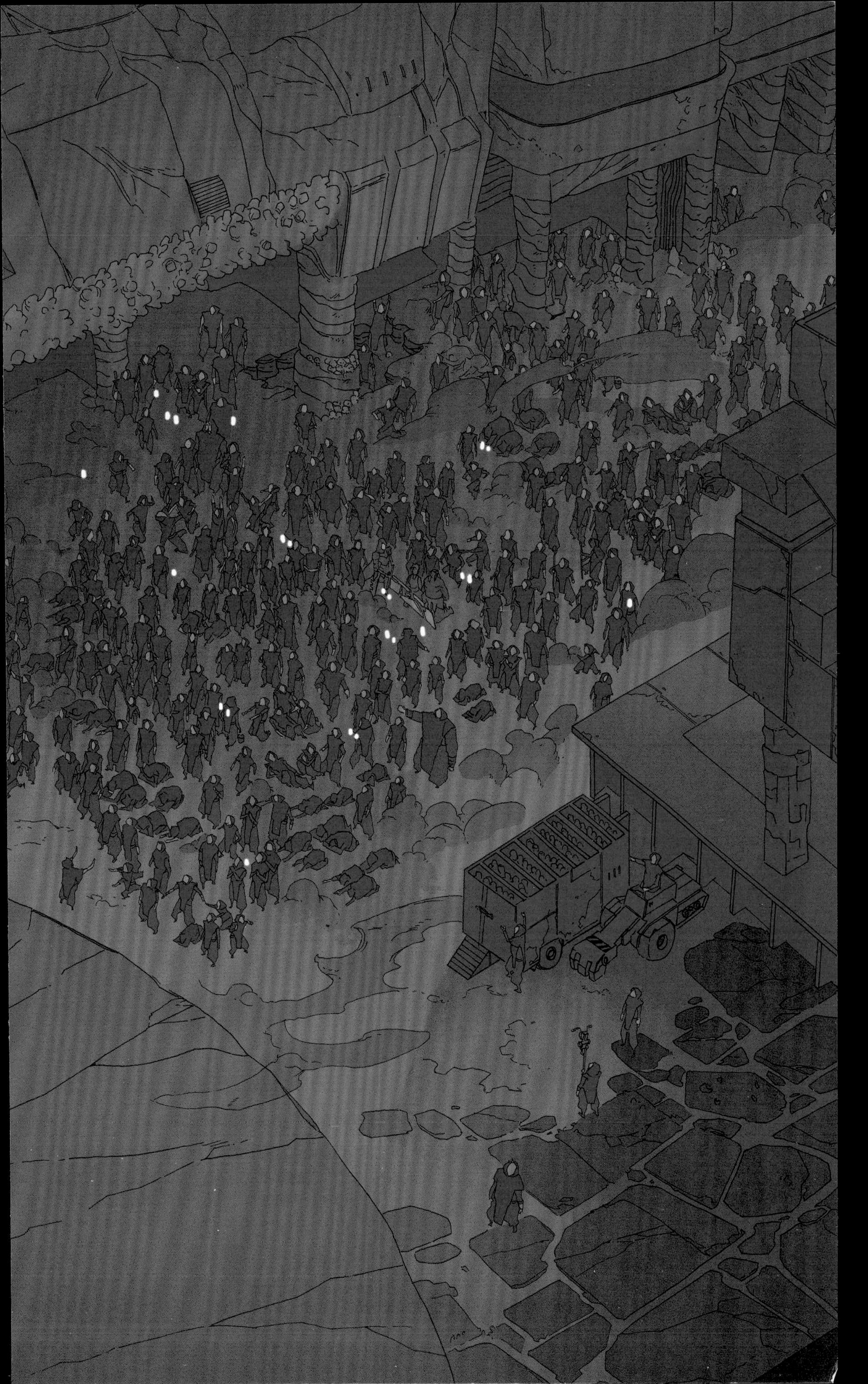

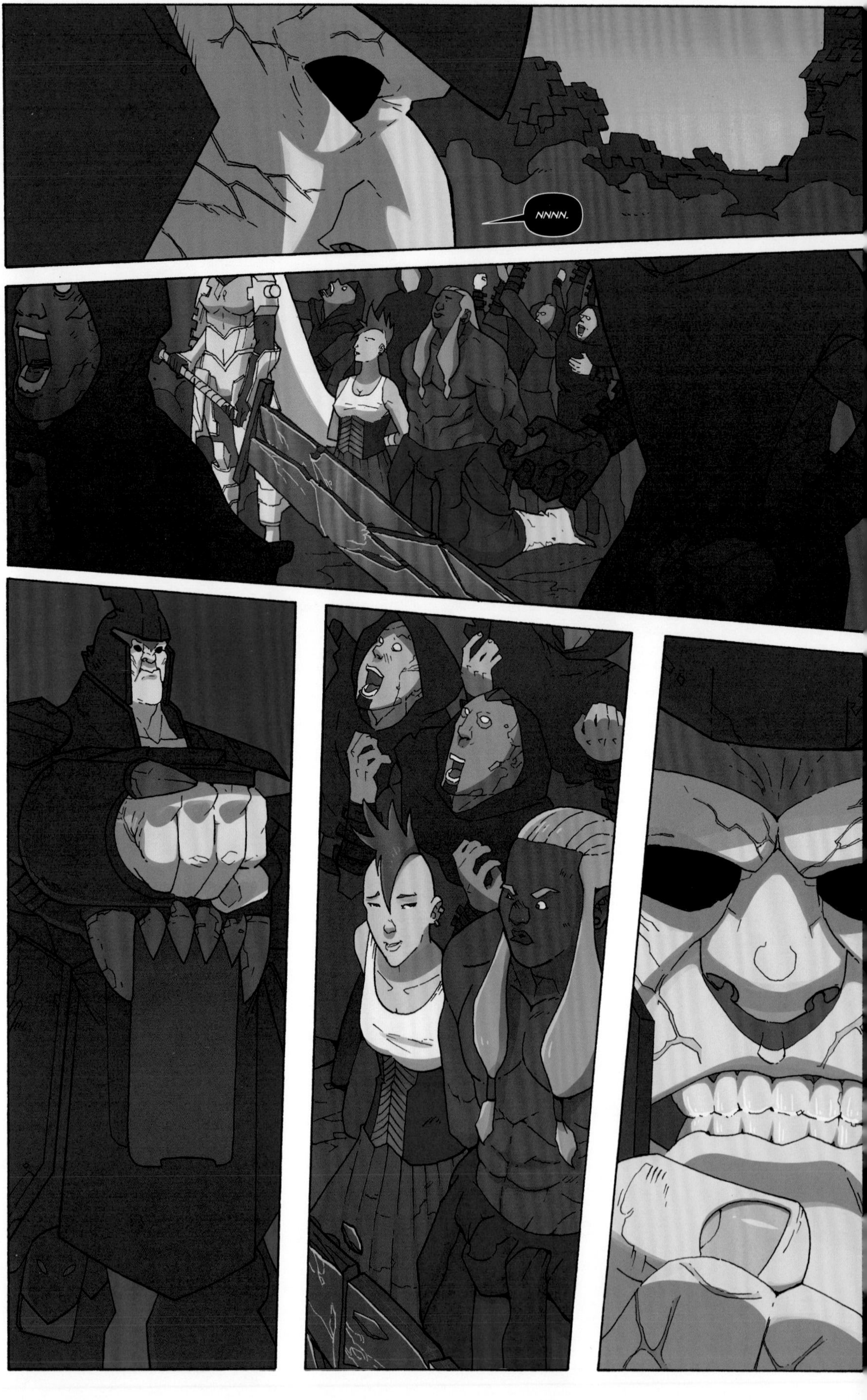
NNNN.

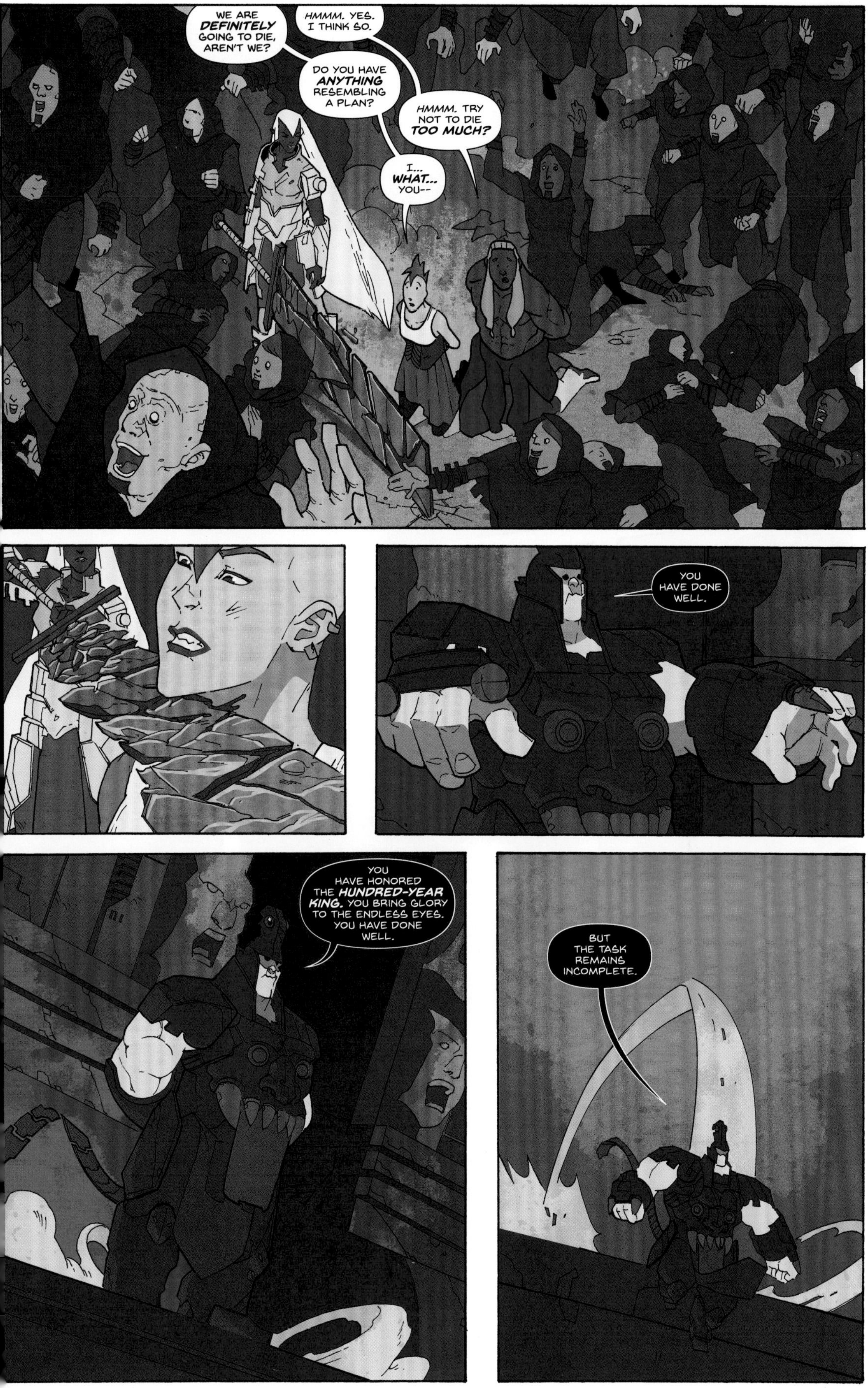
WE ARE DEFINITELY GOING TO DIE, AREN'T WE?
HMMM. YES. I THINK SO.
DO YOU HAVE ANYTHING RESEMBLING A PLAN?
HMMM. TRY NOT TO DIE TOO MUCH?
I... WHAT... YOU--
YOU HAVE DONE WELL.
YOU HAVE HONORED THE HUNDRED-YEAR KING. YOU BRING GLORY TO THE ENDLESS EYES. YOU HAVE DONE WELL.
BUT THE TASK REMAINS INCOMPLETE.

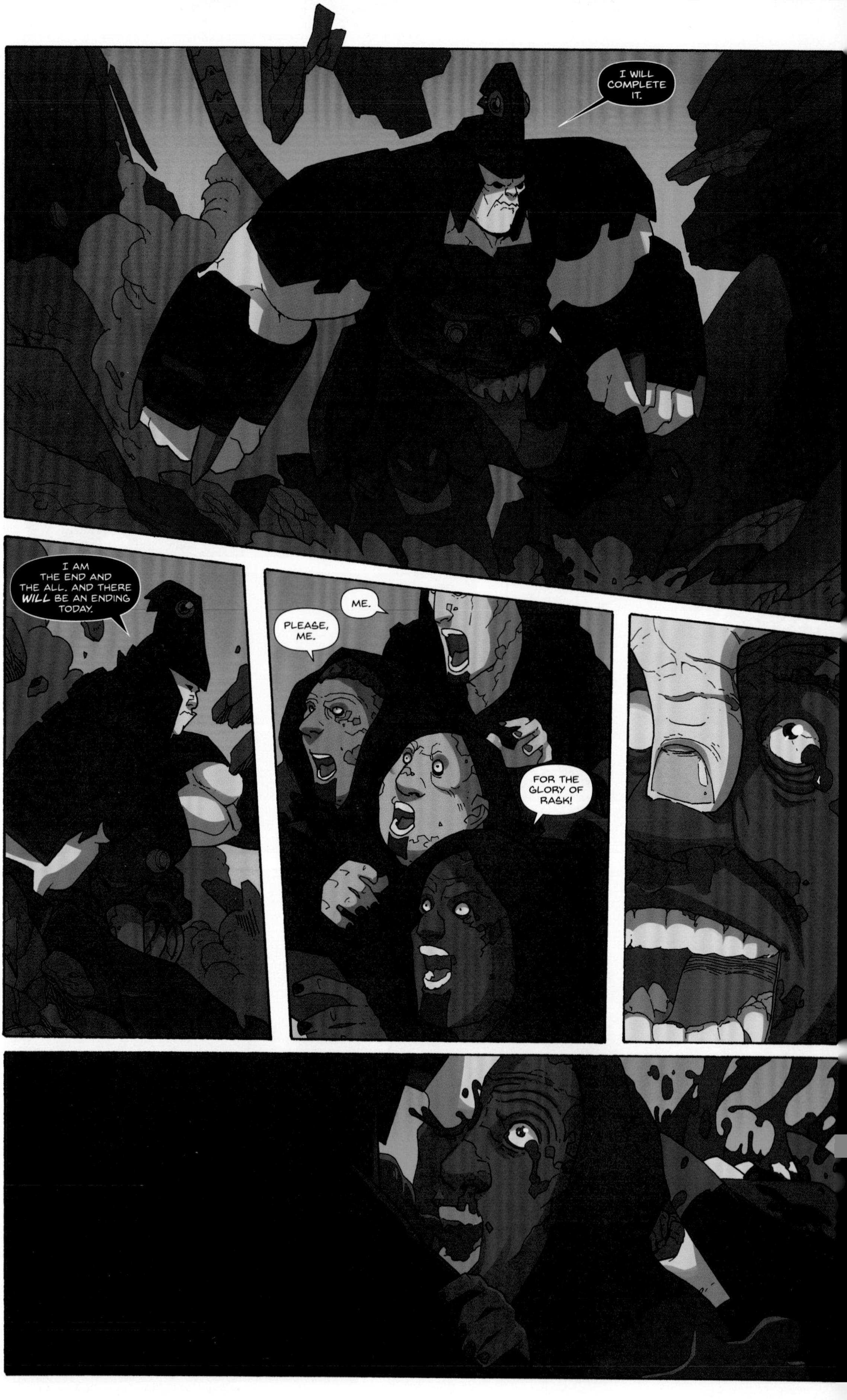
I WILL COMPLETE IT.
I AM THE END AND THE ALL. AND THERE WILL BE AN ENDING TODAY.
ME.
PLEASE, ME.
FOR THE GLORY OF RASK!

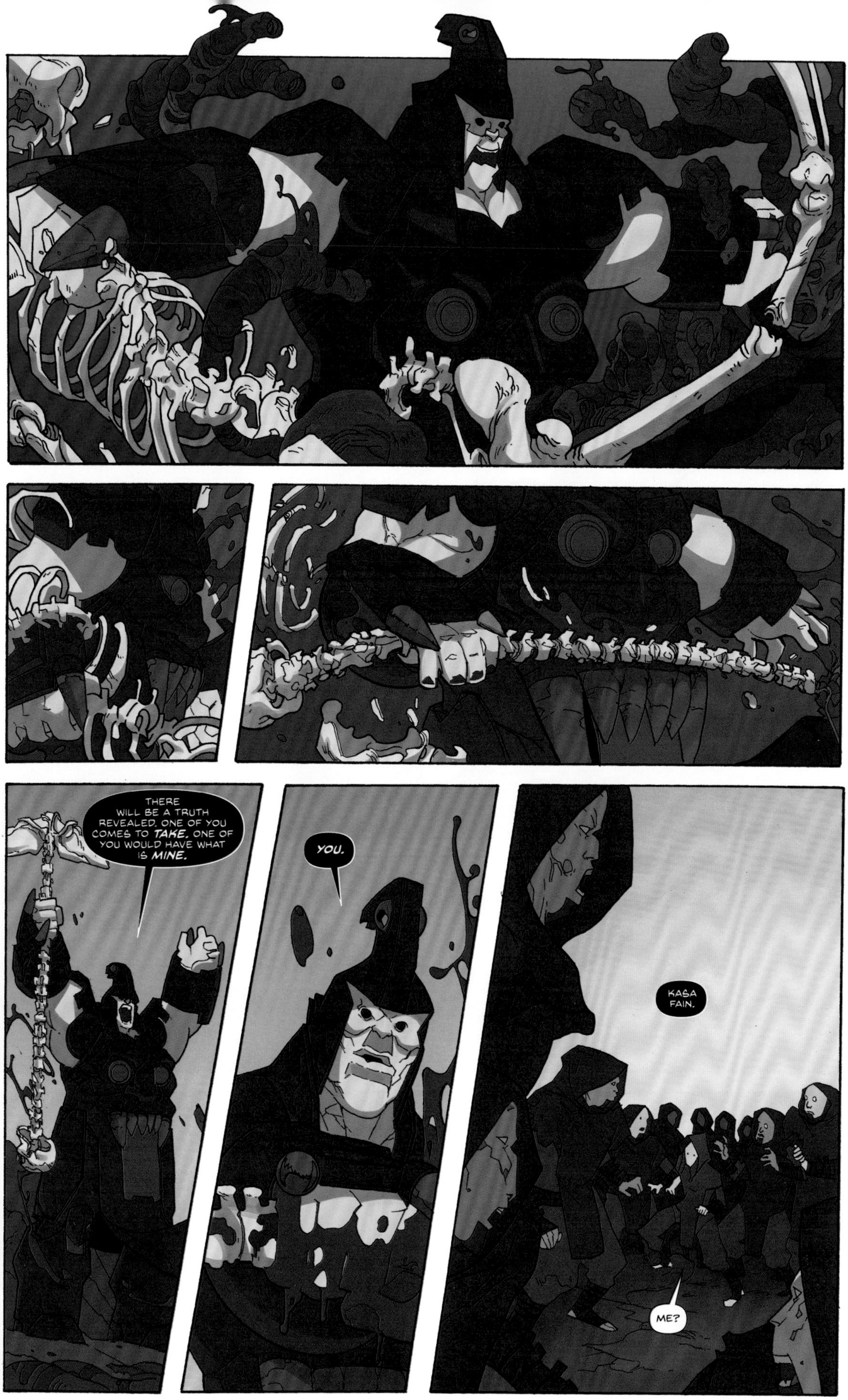
THERE WILL BE A TRUTH REVEALED. ONE OF YOU COMES TO *TAKE.* ONE OF YOU WOULD HAVE WHAT IS *MINE.*
YOU.
KASA FAIN.
ME?

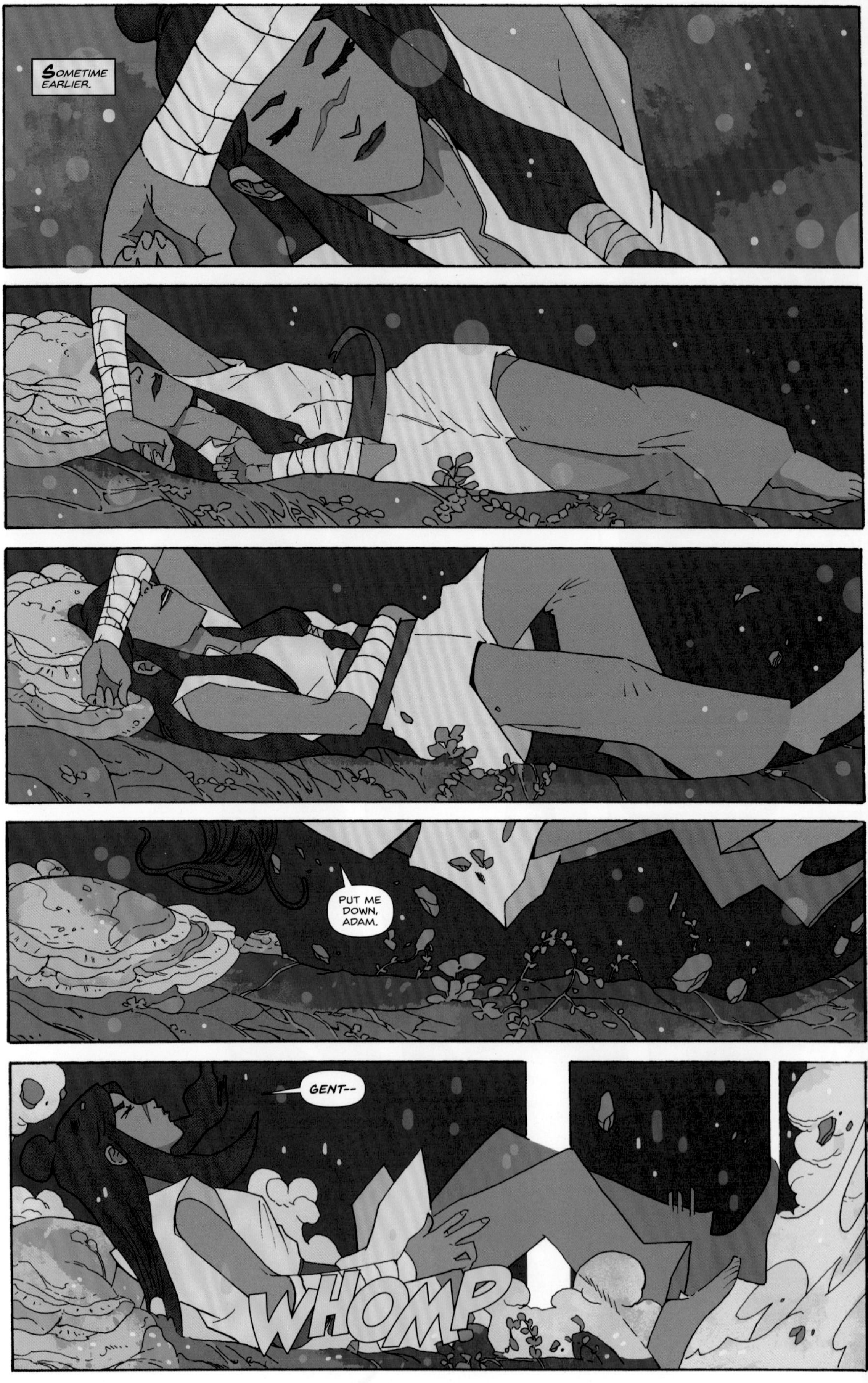
SOMETIME EARLIER.
PUT ME DOWN, ADAM.
GENT--
WHOMP

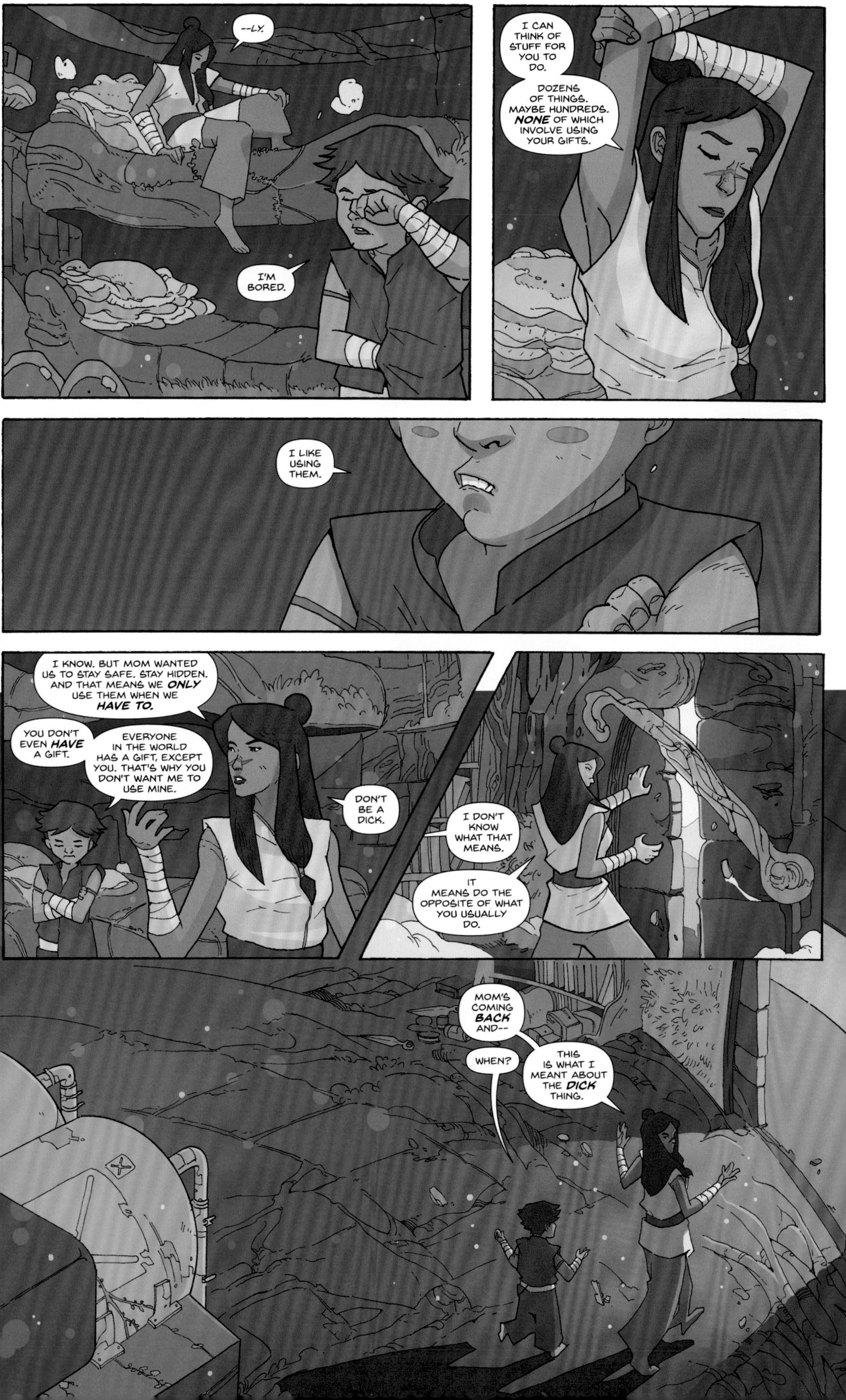
--LY.
I'M BORED.
I CAN THINK OF STUFF FOR YOU TO DO.
DOZENS OF THINGS. MAYBE HUNDREDS. NONE OF WHICH INVOLVE USING YOUR GIFTS.
I LIKE USING THEM.
I KNOW. BUT MOM WANTED US TO STAY SAFE. STAY HIDDEN. AND THAT MEANS WE ONLY USE THEM WHEN WE HAVE TO.
YOU DON'T EVEN HAVE A GIFT.
EVERYONE IN THE WORLD HAS A GIFT, EXCEPT YOU. THAT'S WHY YOU DON'T WANT ME TO USE MINE.
DON'T BE A DICK.
I DON'T KNOW WHAT THAT MEANS.
IT MEANS DO THE OPPOSITE OF WHAT YOU USUALLY DO.
MOM'S COMING BACK AND--
WHEN?
THIS IS WHAT I MEANT ABOUT THE DICK THING.

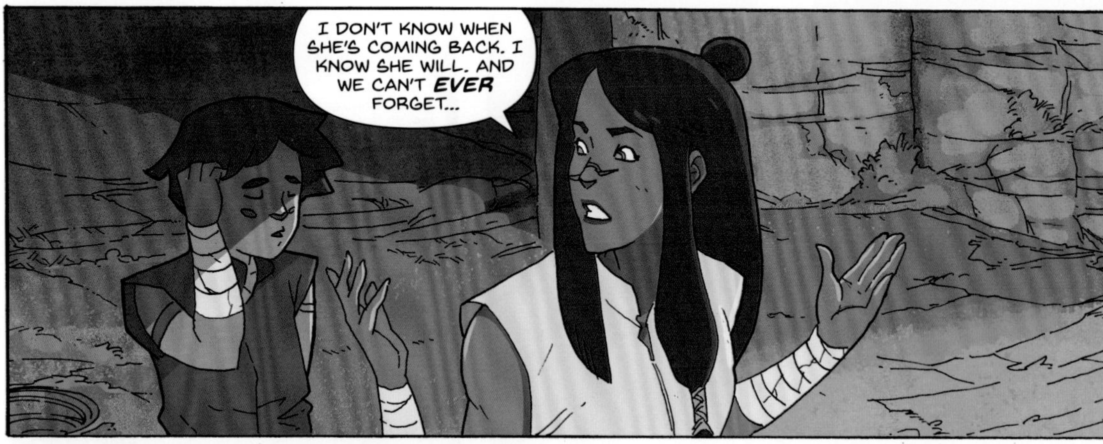
I DON'T KNOW WHEN SHE'S COMING BACK. I KNOW SHE WILL. AND WE CAN'T ***EVER*** FORGET...

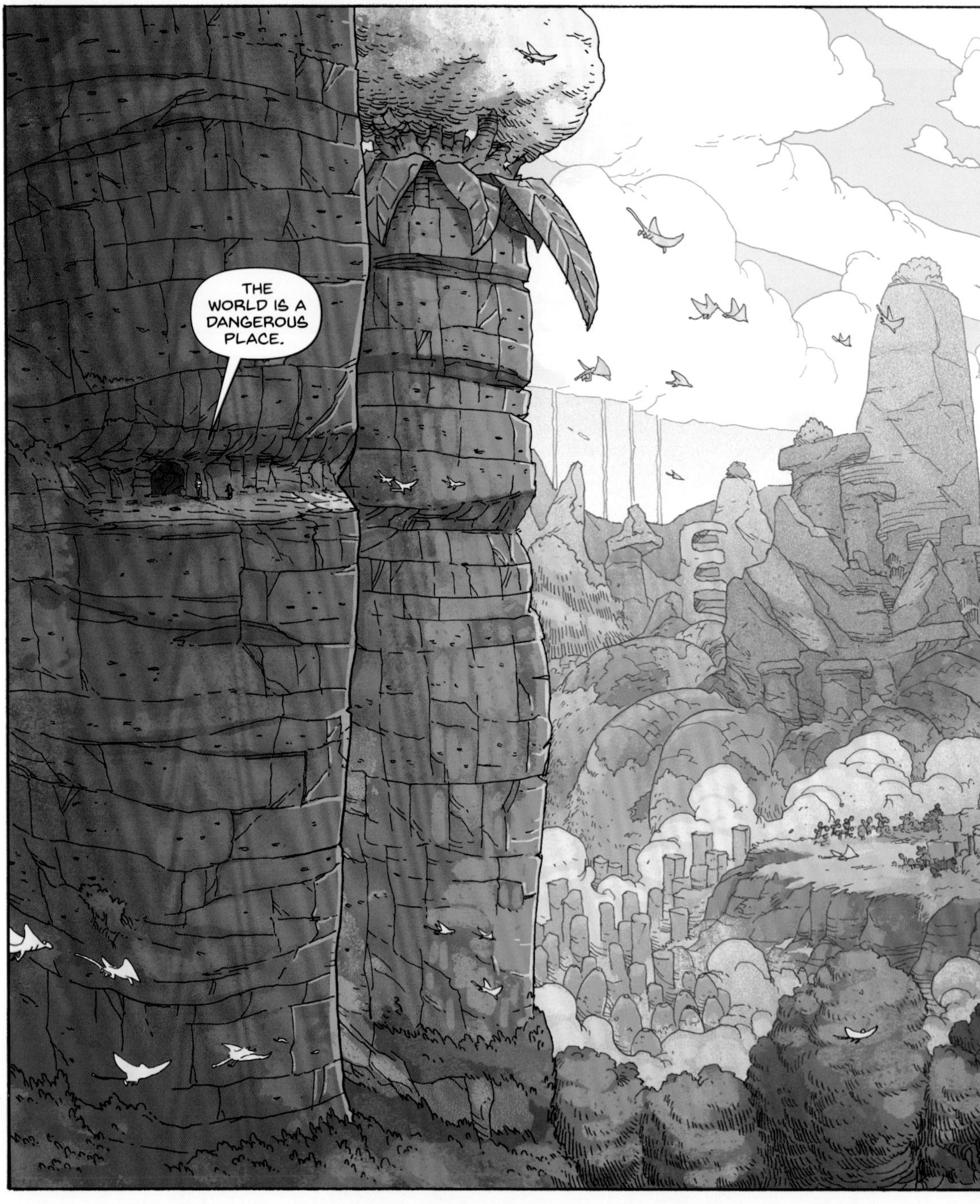
THE WORLD IS A DANGEROUS PLACE.

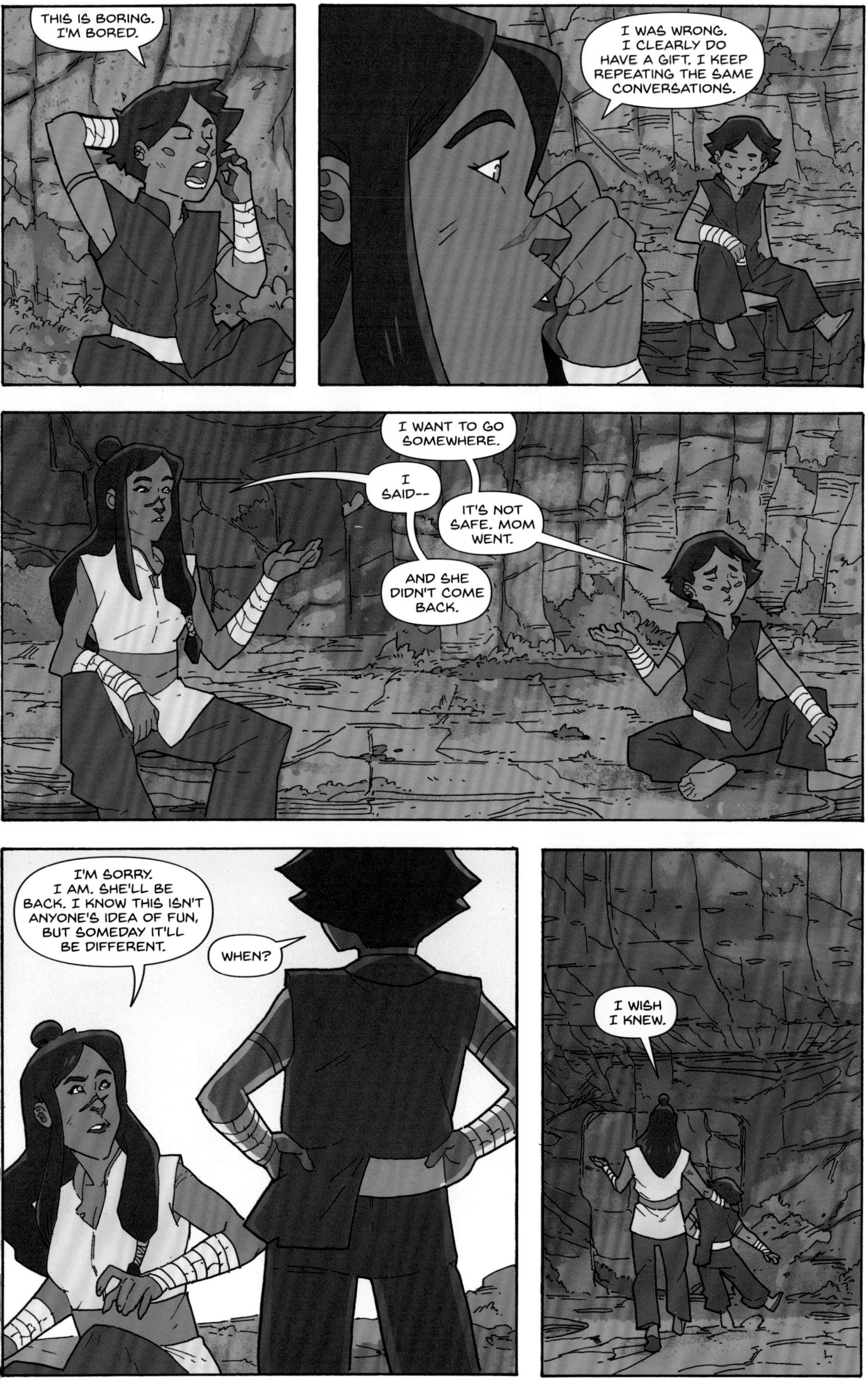
THIS IS BORING. I'M BORED.
I WAS WRONG. I CLEARLY DO HAVE A GIFT. I KEEP REPEATING THE SAME CONVERSATIONS.
I WANT TO GO SOMEWHERE.
I SAID--
IT'S NOT SAFE. MOM WENT.
AND SHE DIDN'T COME BACK.
I'M SORRY. I AM. SHE'LL BE BACK. I KNOW THIS ISN'T ANYONE'S IDEA OF FUN, BUT SOMEDAY IT'LL BE DIFFERENT.
WHEN?
I WISH I KNEW.

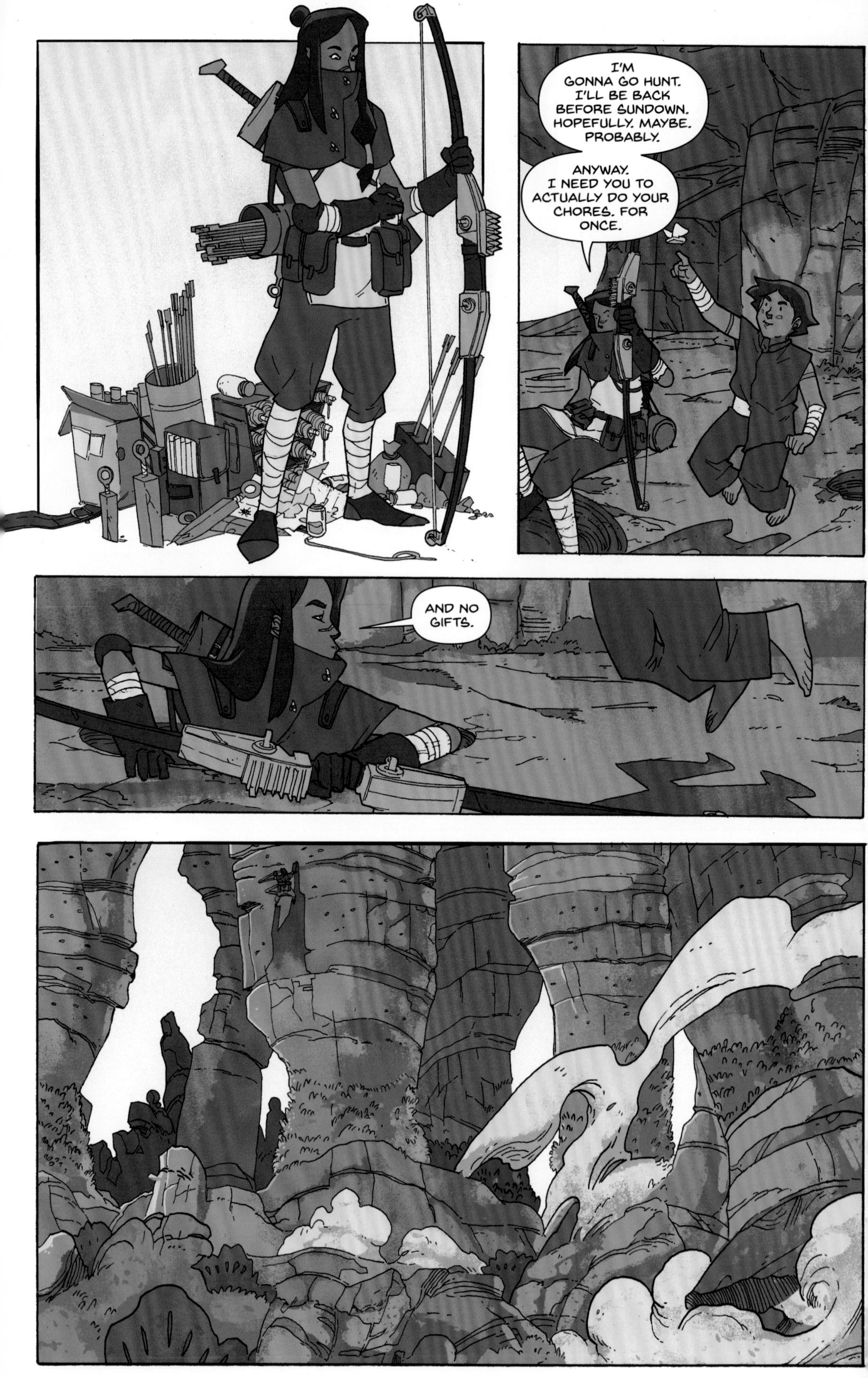
I'M GONNA GO HUNT. I'LL BE BACK BEFORE SUNDOWN. HOPEFULLY. MAYBE. PROBABLY.
ANYWAY. I NEED YOU TO ACTUALLY DO YOUR CHORES. FOR ONCE.
AND NO GIFTS.

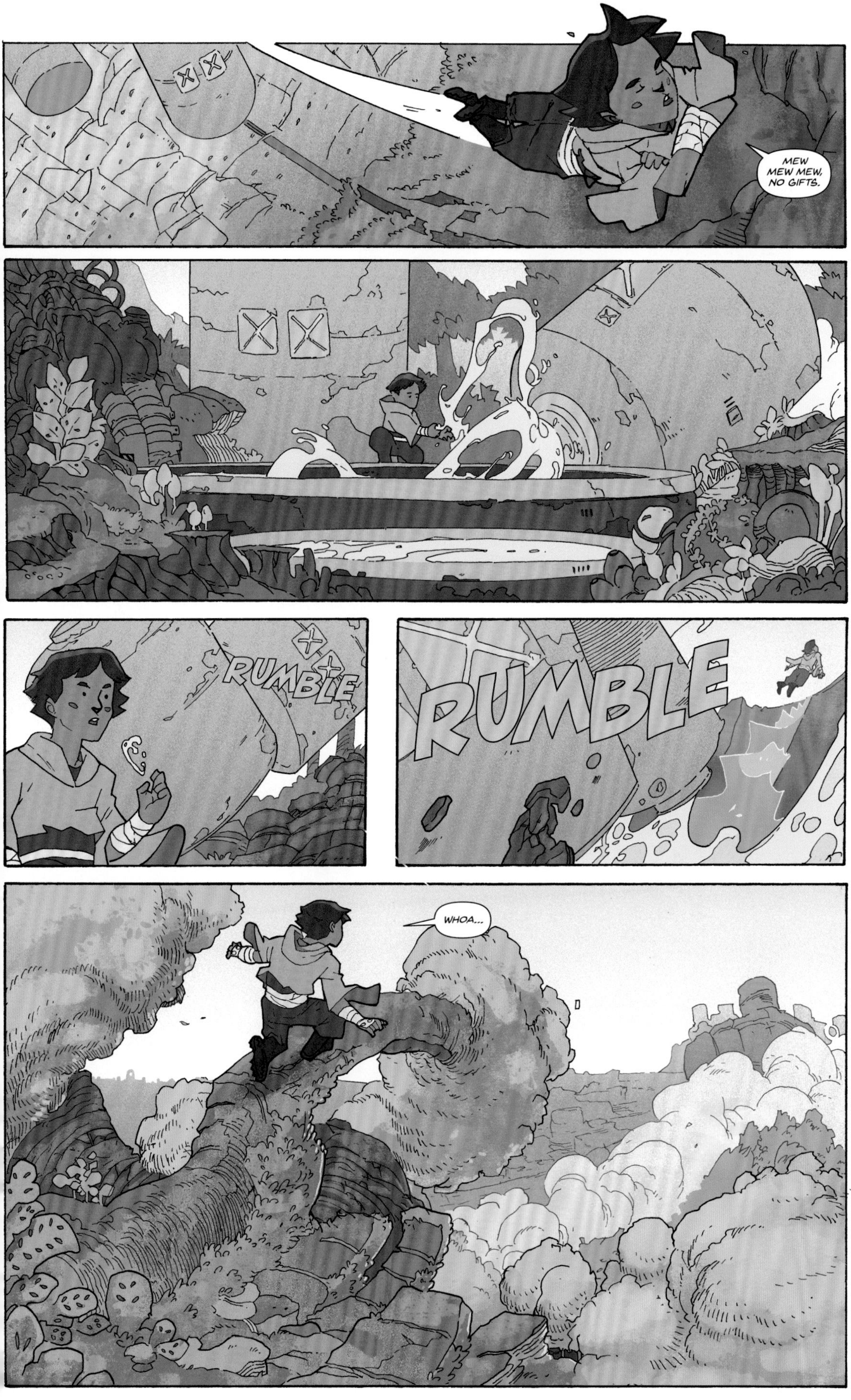
MEW MEW MEW, NO GIFTS.
RUMBLE
RUMBLE
WHOA...

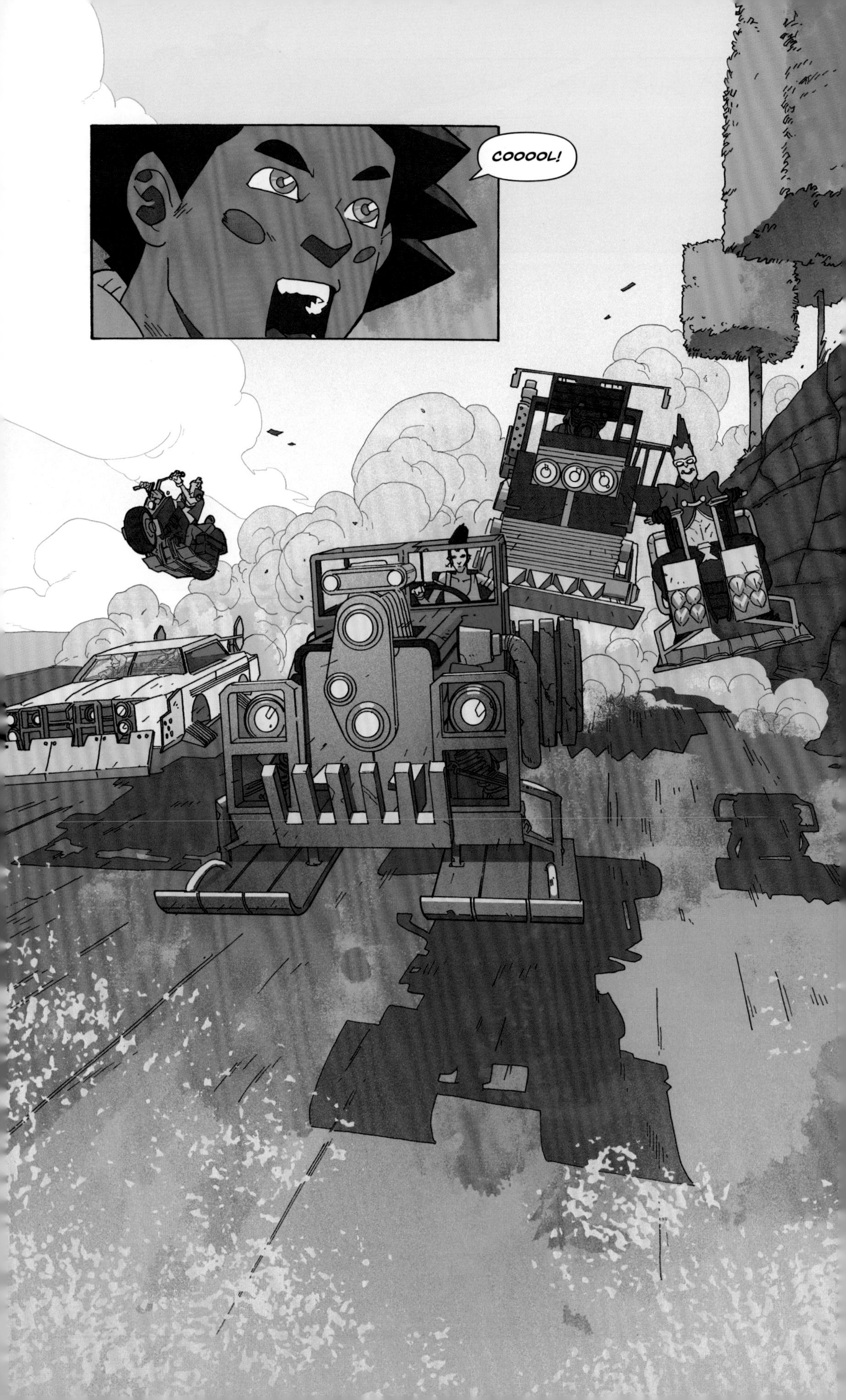
COOOOL!

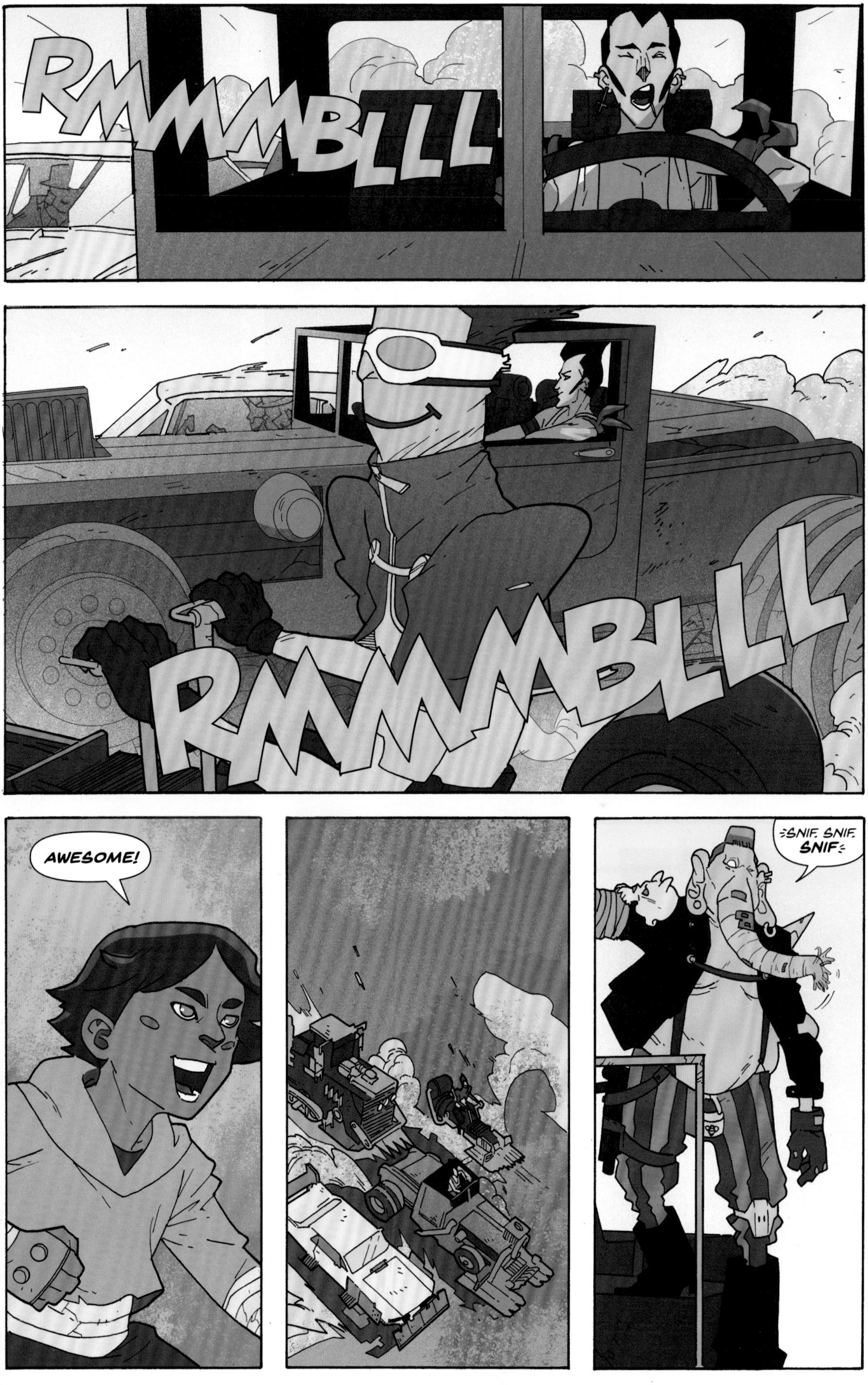
RMMMBLLL
RMMMBLLL
AWESOME!
SNIF. SNIF.
SNIF

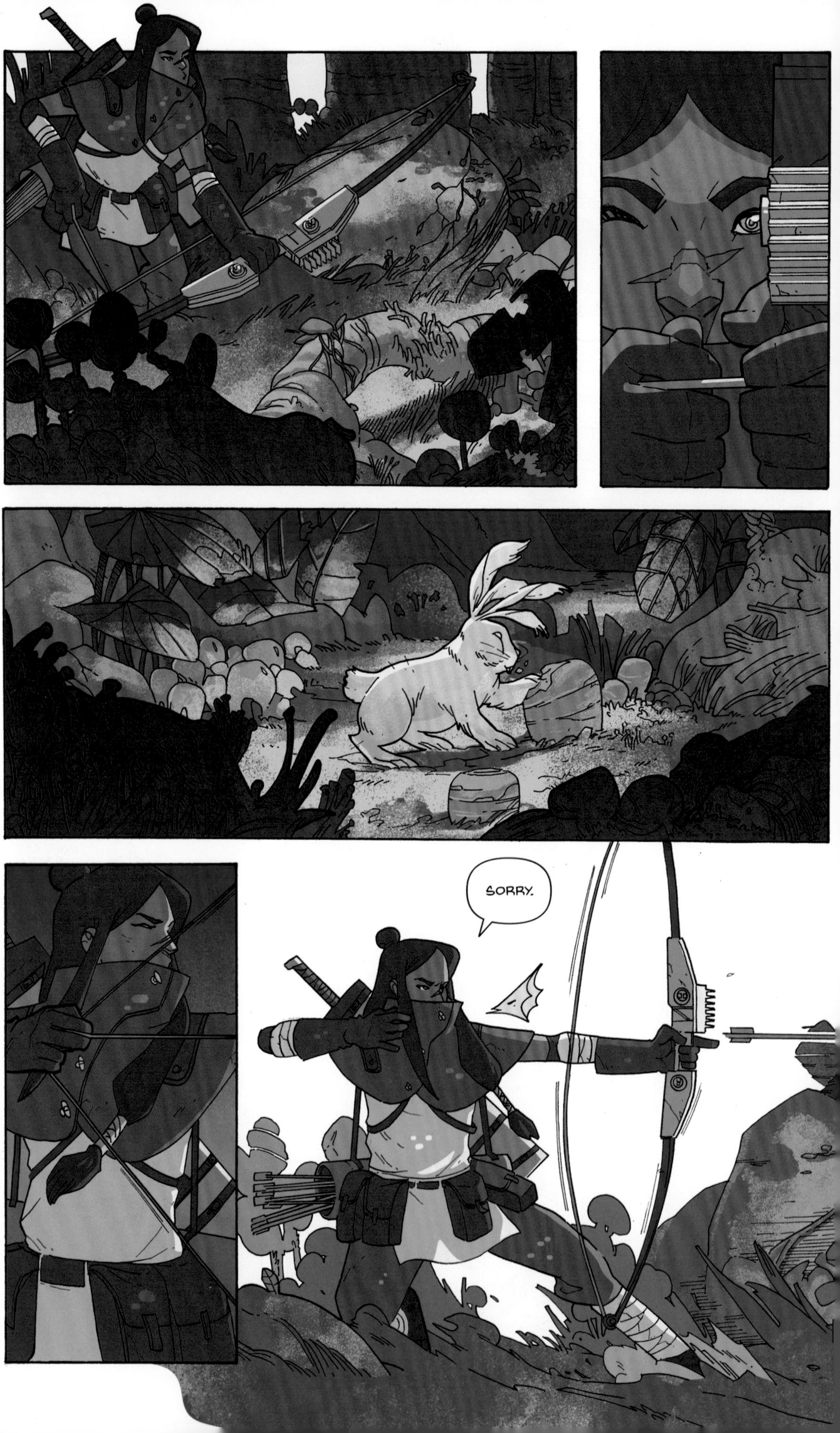
SORRY.

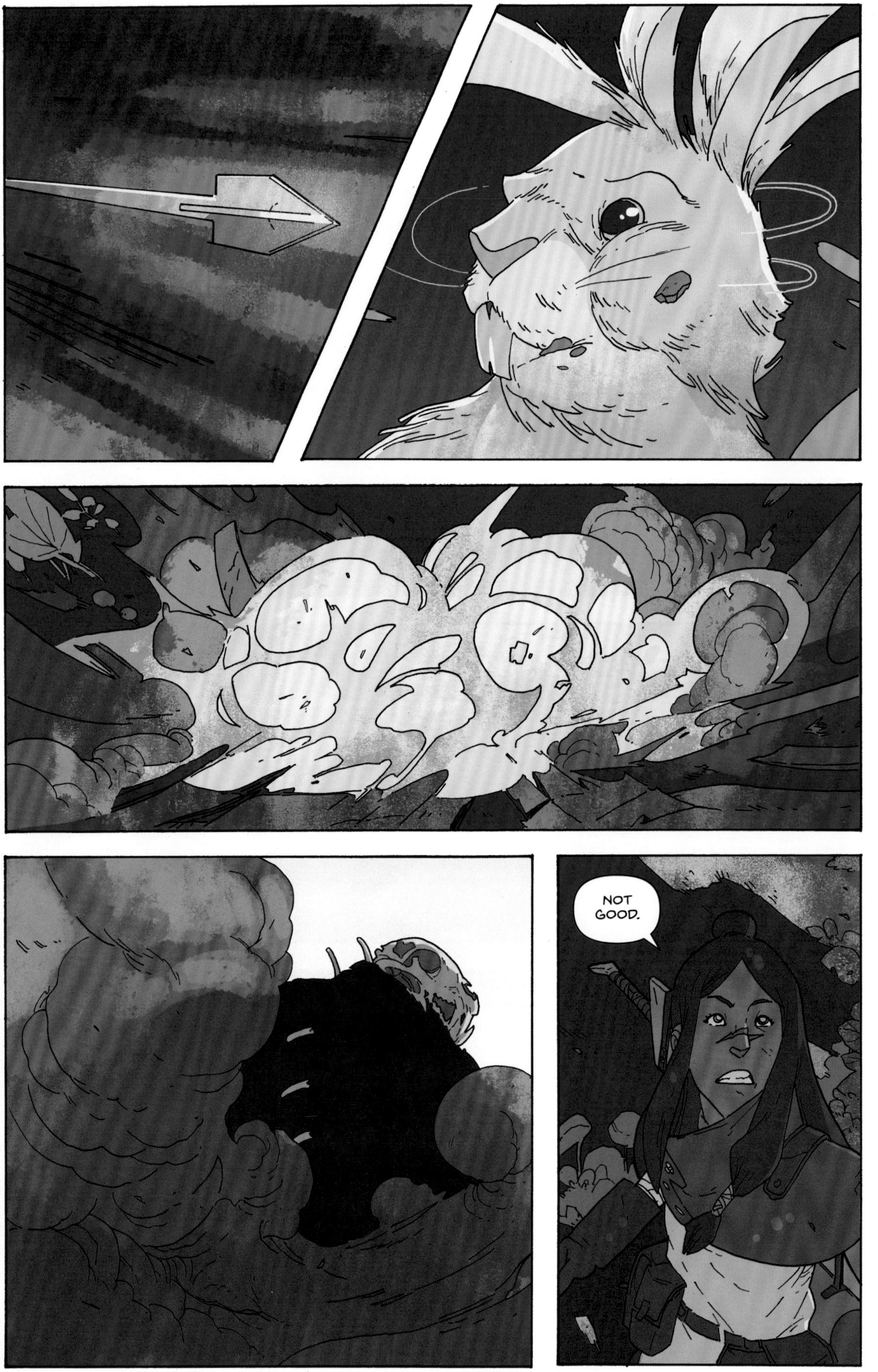
NOT GOOD.

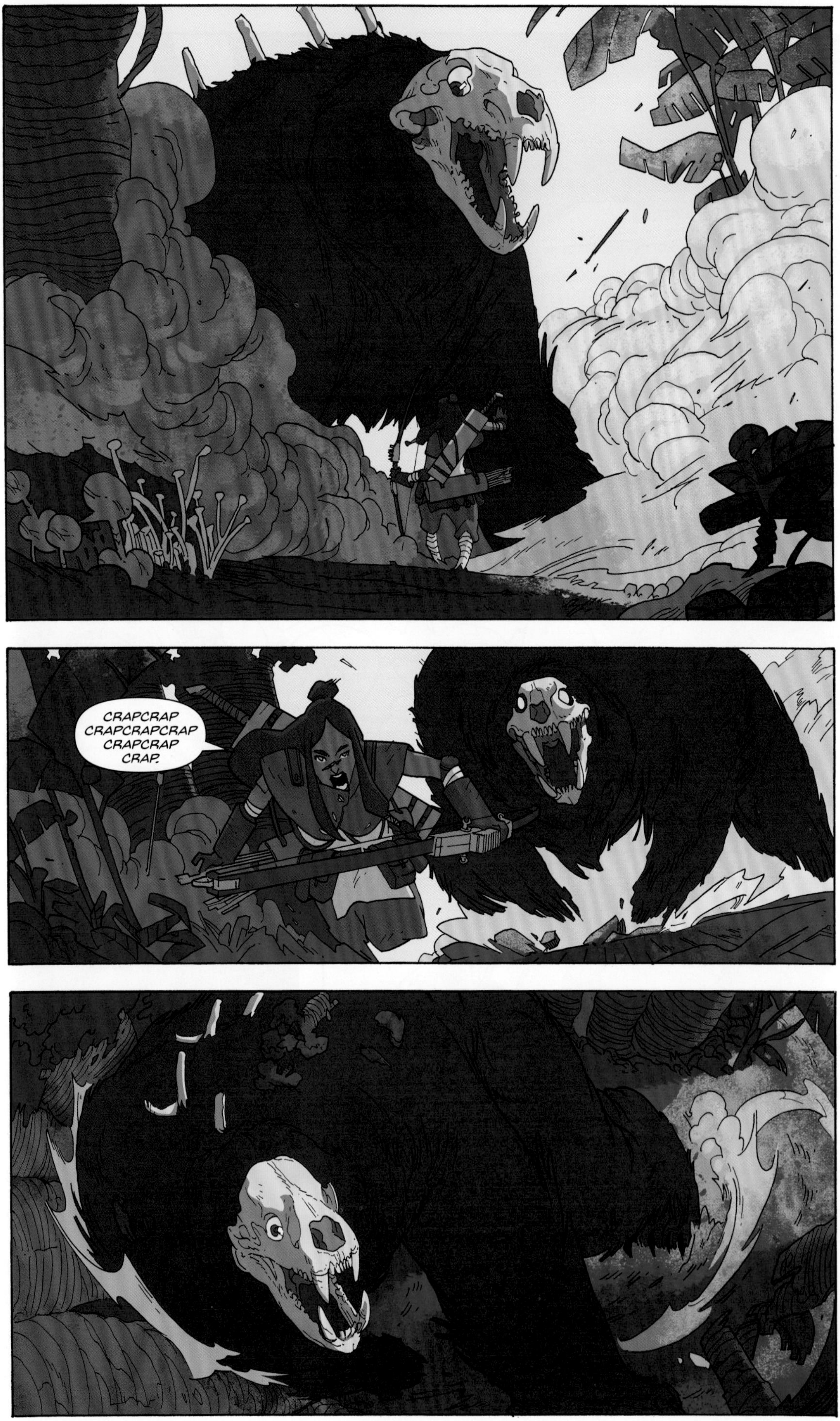
CRAPCRAP CRAPCRAPCRAP CRAPCRAP CRAP.

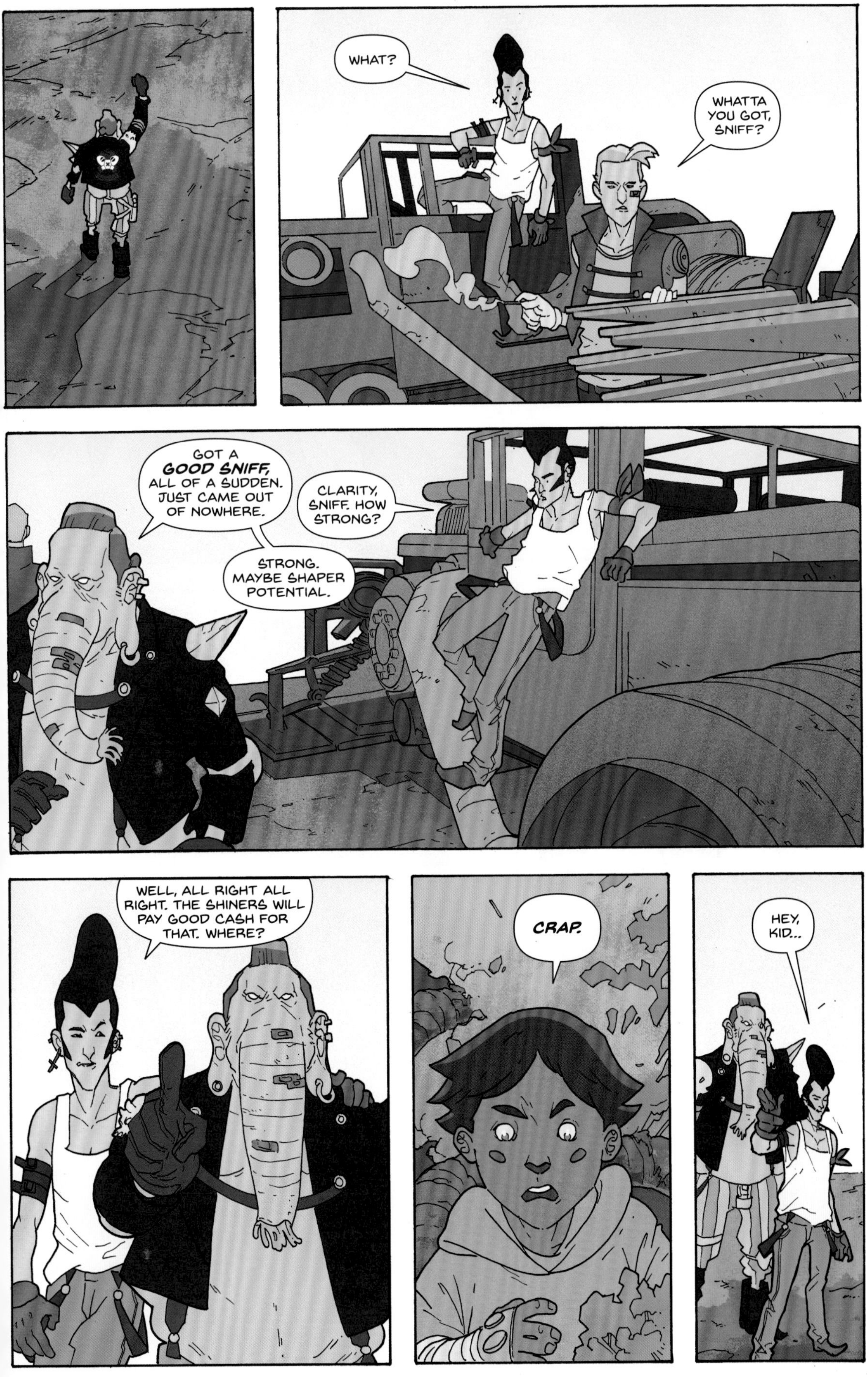
WHAT?
WHATTA YOU GOT, SNIFF?
GOT A **GOOD SNIFF,** ALL OF A SUDDEN. JUST CAME OUT OF NOWHERE.
CLARITY, SNIFF. HOW STRONG?
STRONG. MAYBE SHAPER POTENTIAL.
WELL, ALL RIGHT ALL RIGHT. THE SHINERS WILL PAY GOOD CASH FOR THAT. WHERE?
CRAP.
HEY, KID...

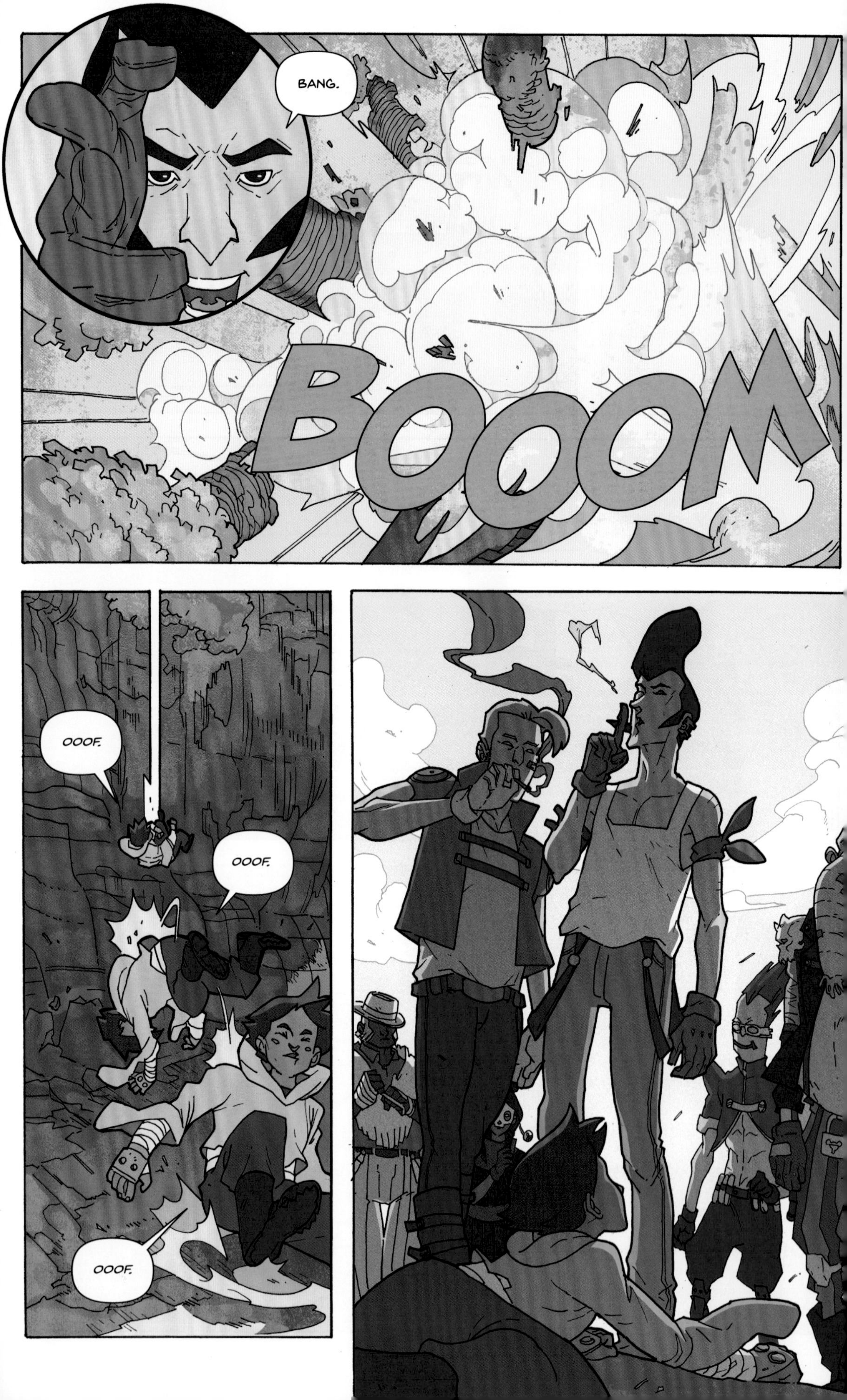
BANG.
BOOOM
OOOF.
OOOF.
OOOF.

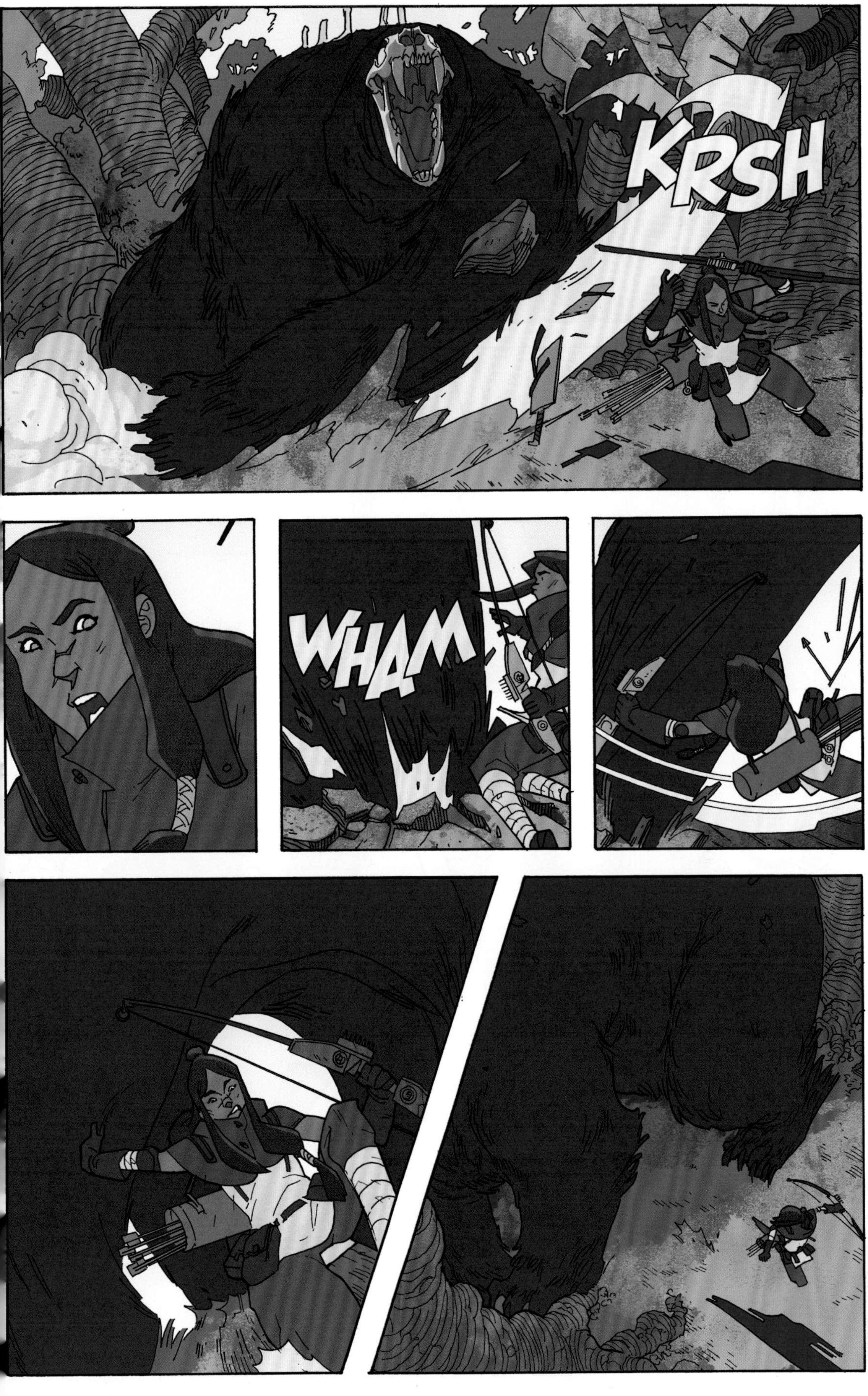
KRSH
WHAM

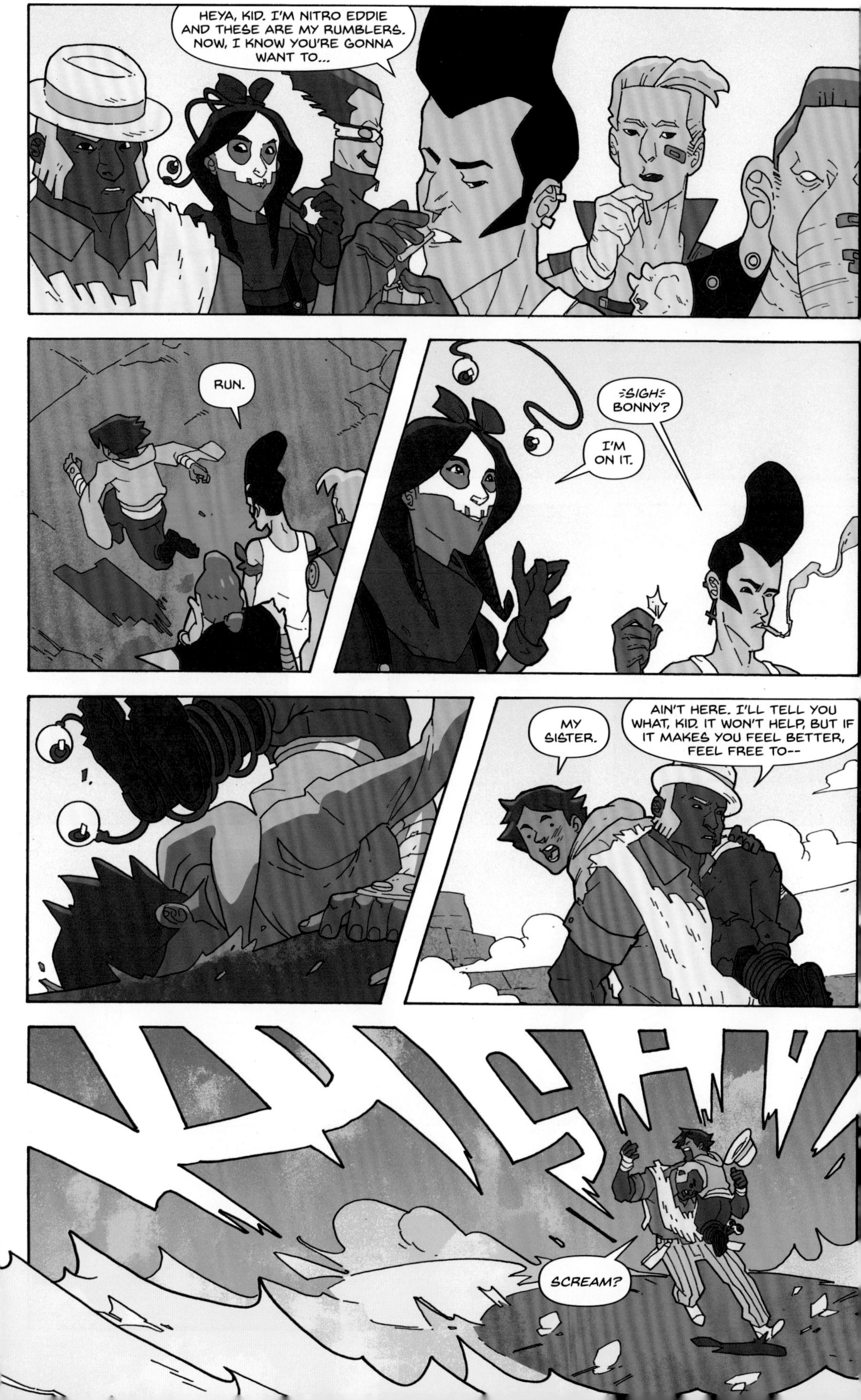
HEYA, KID. I'M NITRO EDDIE AND THESE ARE MY RUMBLERS. NOW, I KNOW YOU'RE GONNA WANT TO...
RUN.
SIGH BONNY?
I'M ON IT.
MY SISTER.
AIN'T HERE. I'LL TELL YOU WHAT, KID. IT WON'T HELP, BUT IF IT MAKES YOU FEEL BETTER, FEEL FREE TO--
SCREAM?

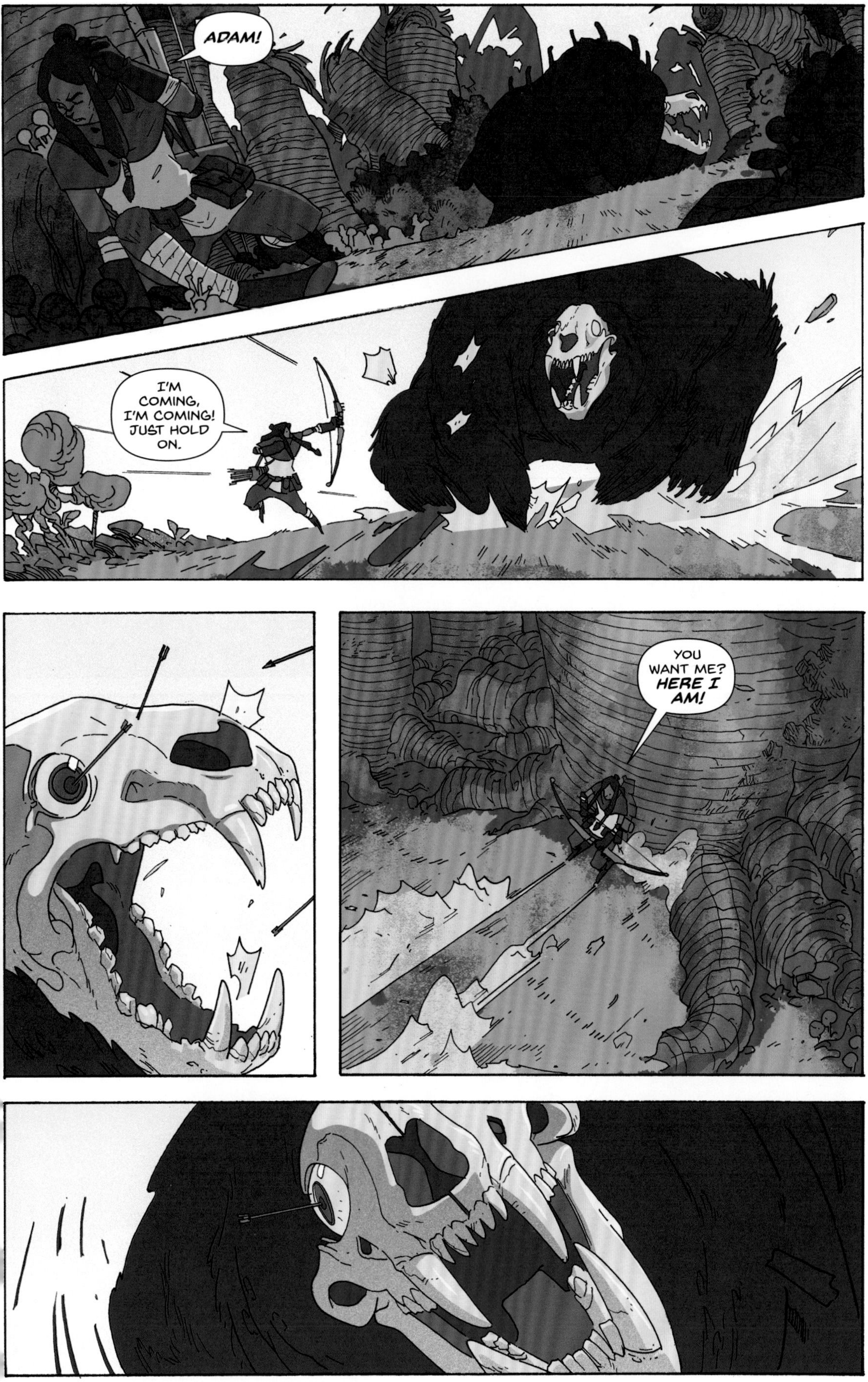
ADAM!
I'M COMING, I'M COMING! JUST HOLD ON.
YOU WANT ME? HERE I AM!

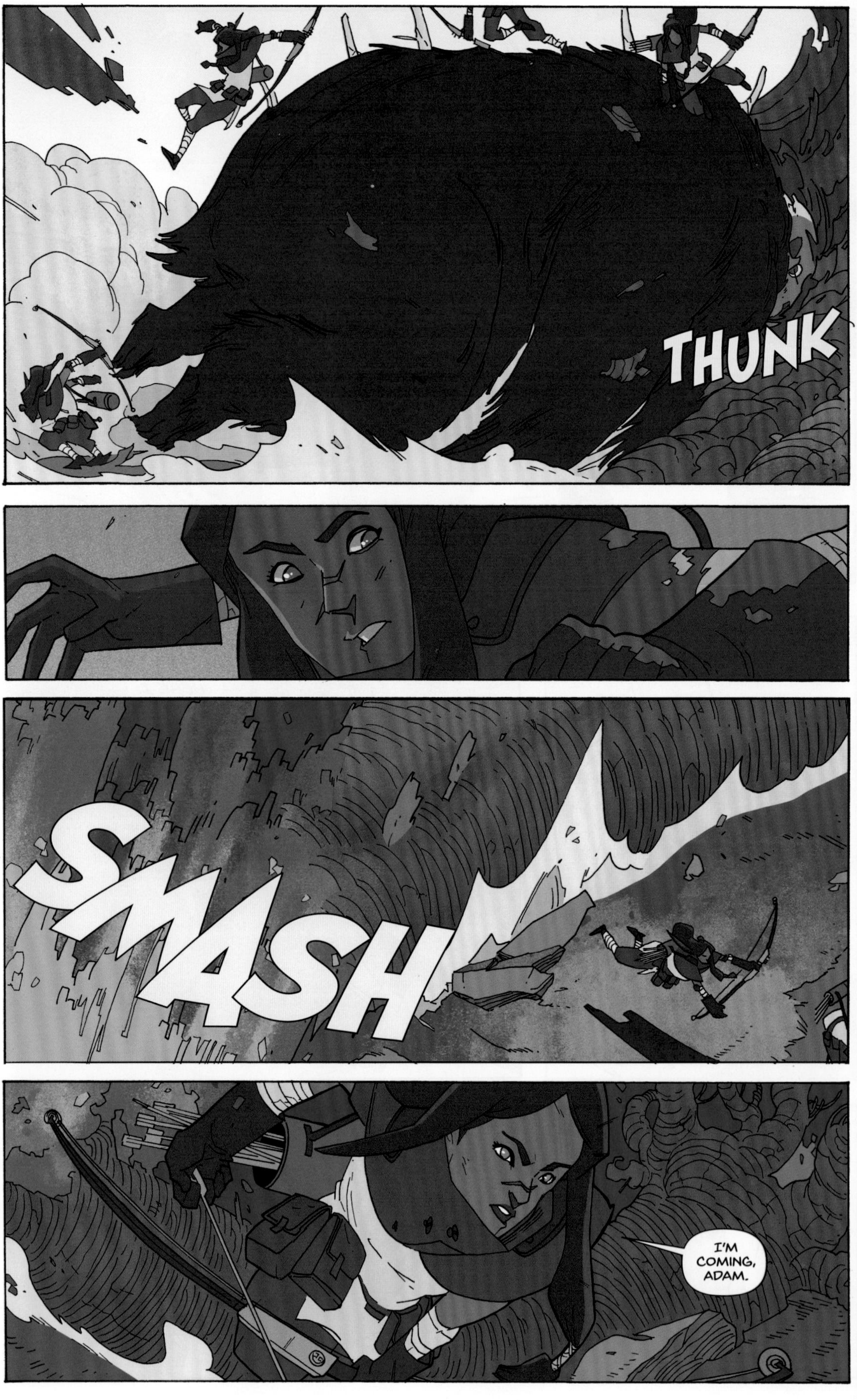
THUNK
SMASH
I'M COMING, ADAM.

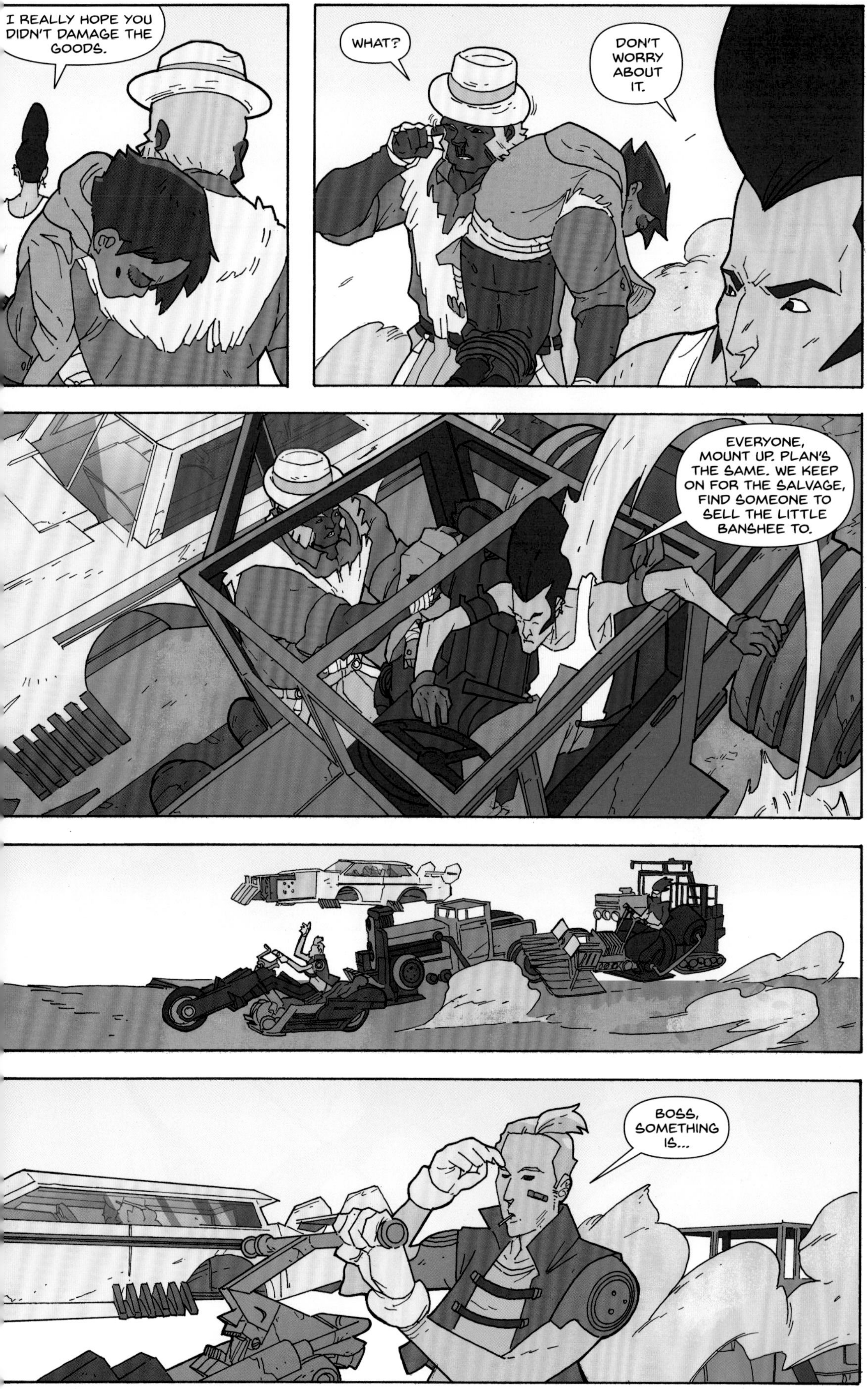
I REALLY HOPE YOU DIDN'T DAMAGE THE GOODS.
WHAT?
DON'T WORRY ABOUT IT.
EVERYONE, MOUNT UP. PLAN'S THE SAME. WE KEEP ON FOR THE SALVAGE, FIND SOMEONE TO SELL THE LITTLE BANSHEE TO.
BOSS, SOMETHING IS...

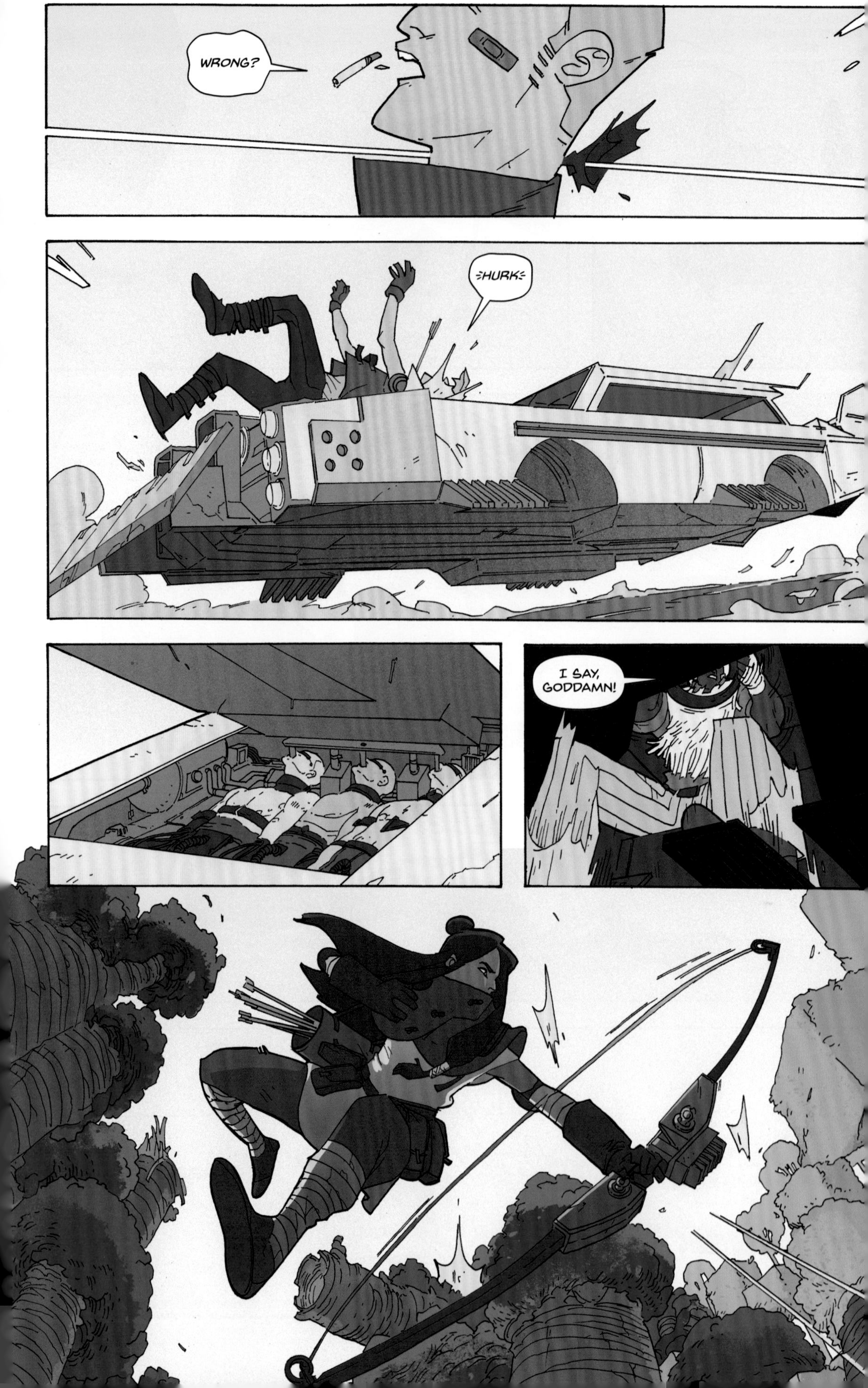
WRONG?
HURK
I SAY, GODDAMN!

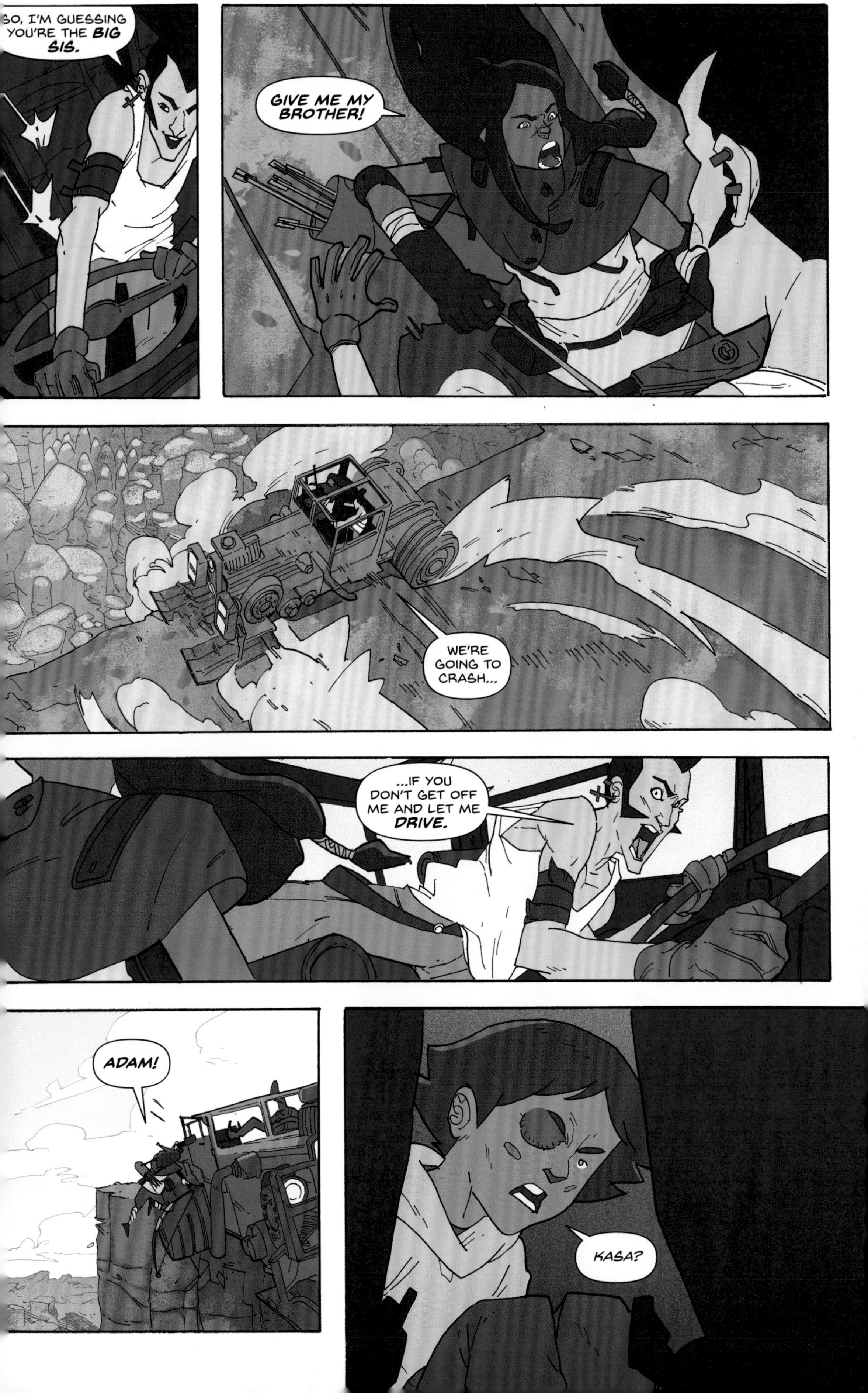
SO, I'M GUESSING YOU'RE THE BIG SIS.
GIVE ME MY BROTHER!
WE'RE GOING TO CRASH...
...IF YOU DON'T GET OFF ME AND LET ME DRIVE.
ADAM!
KASA?

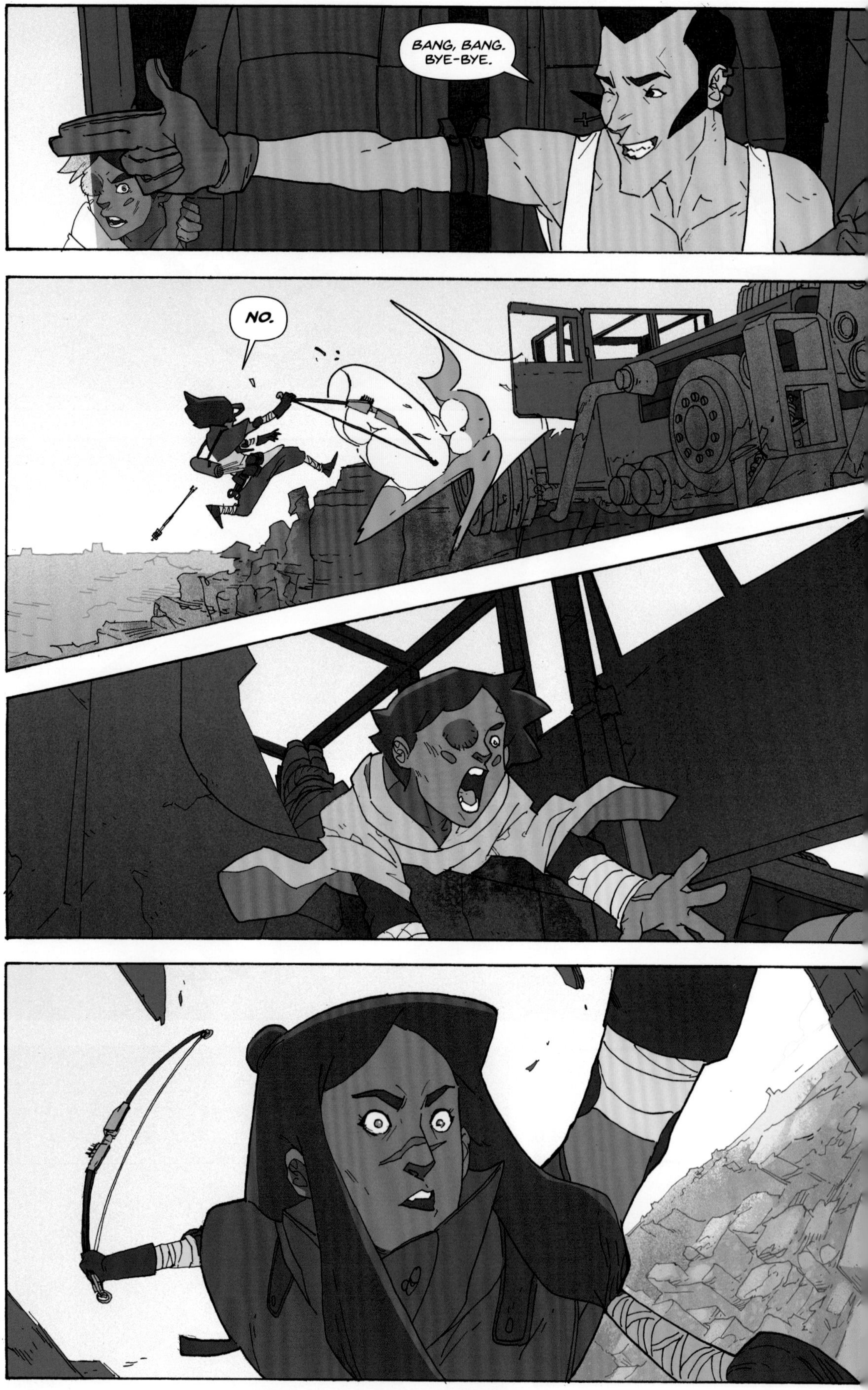
BANG, BANG. BYE-BYE.
NO.

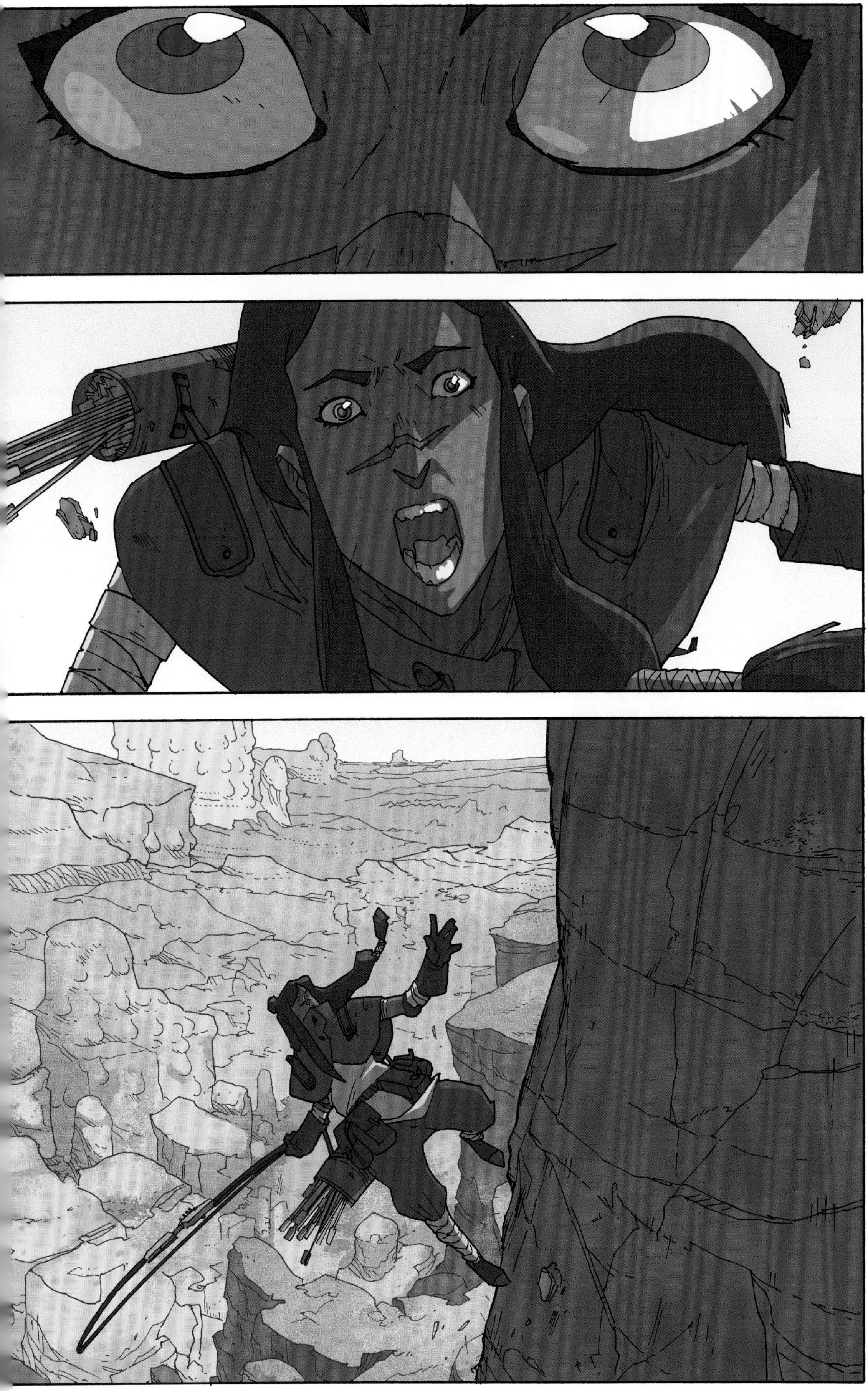

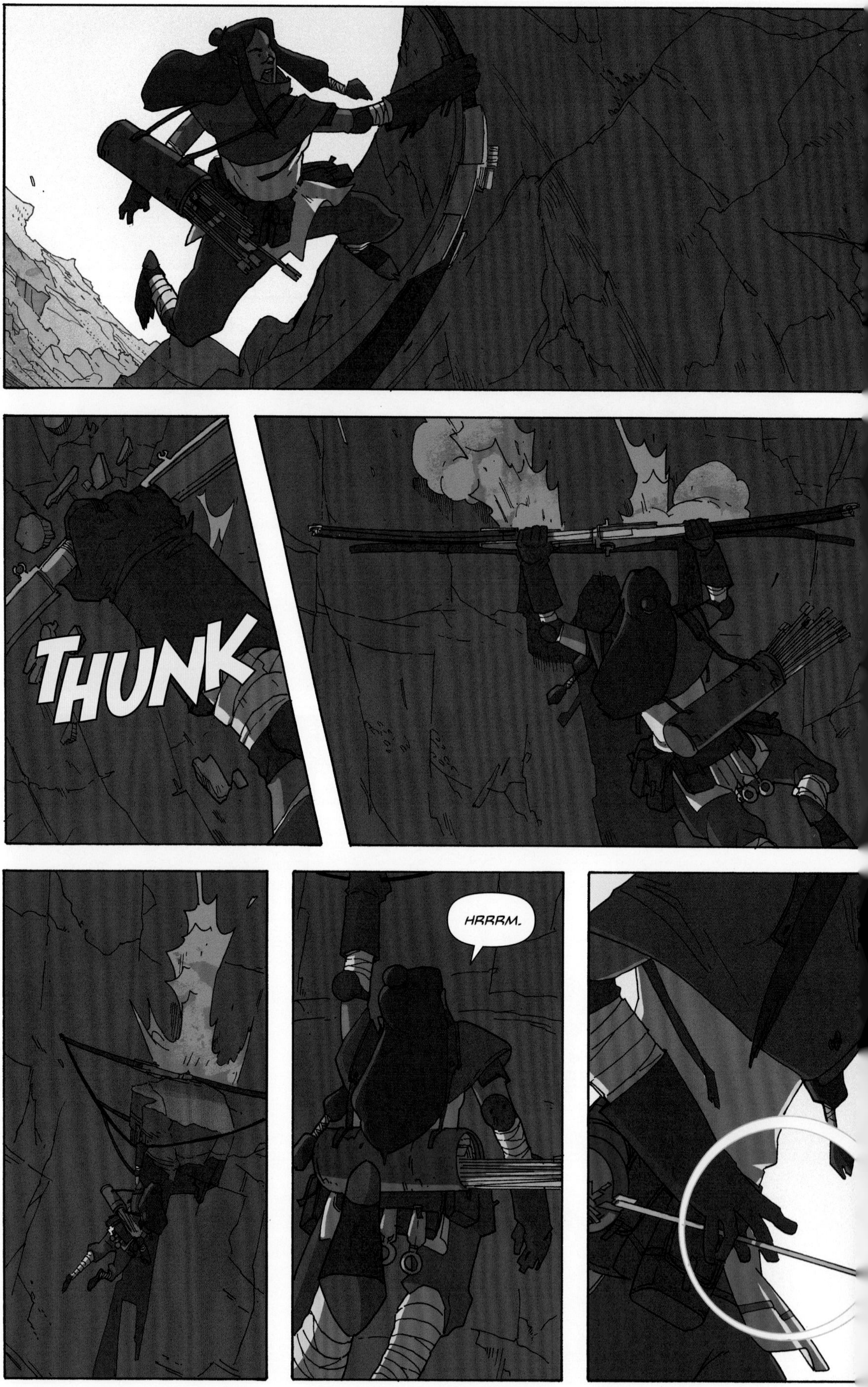
THUNK
HRRRM.

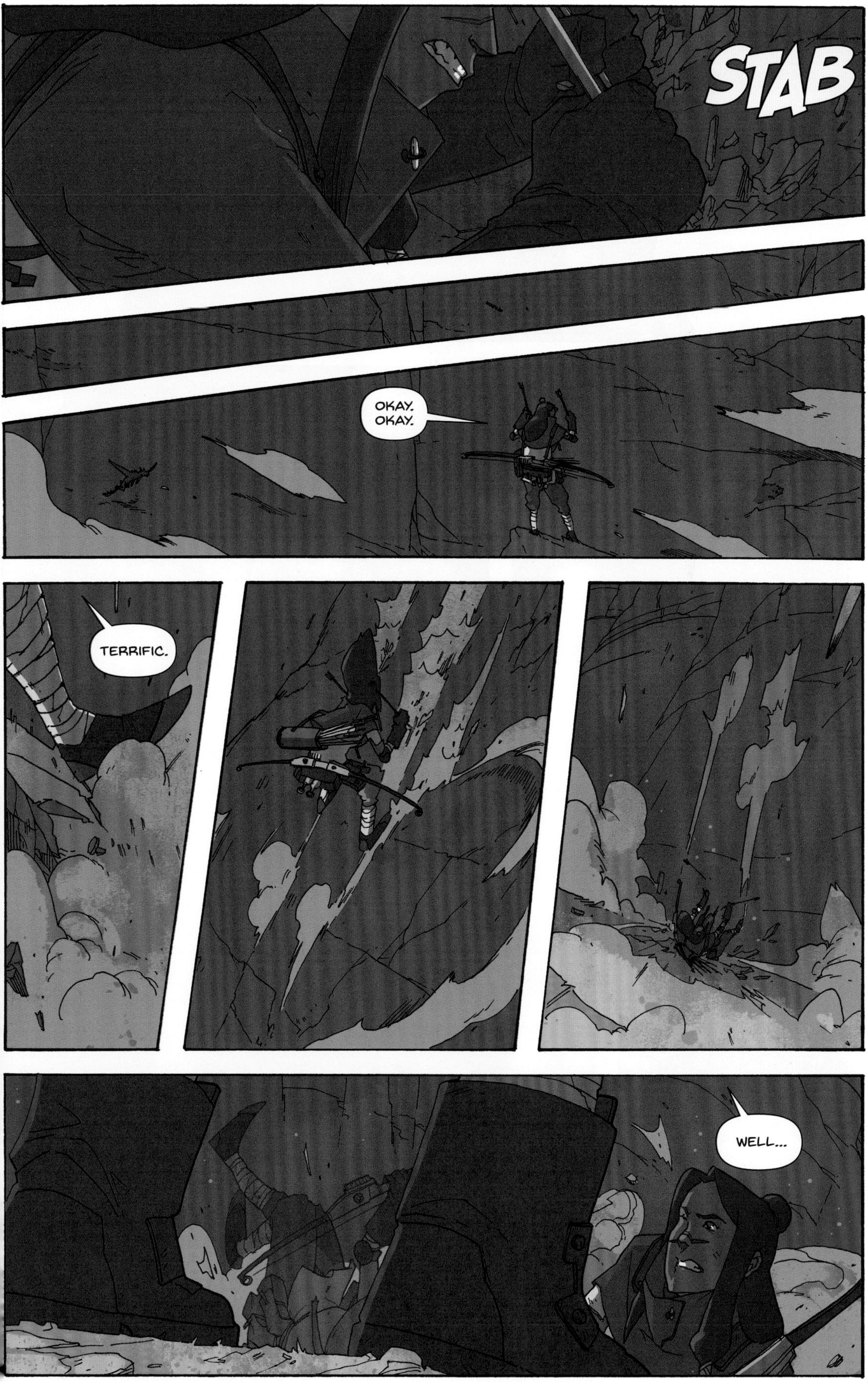
STAB
OKAY.
OKAY.
TERRIFIC.
WELL...

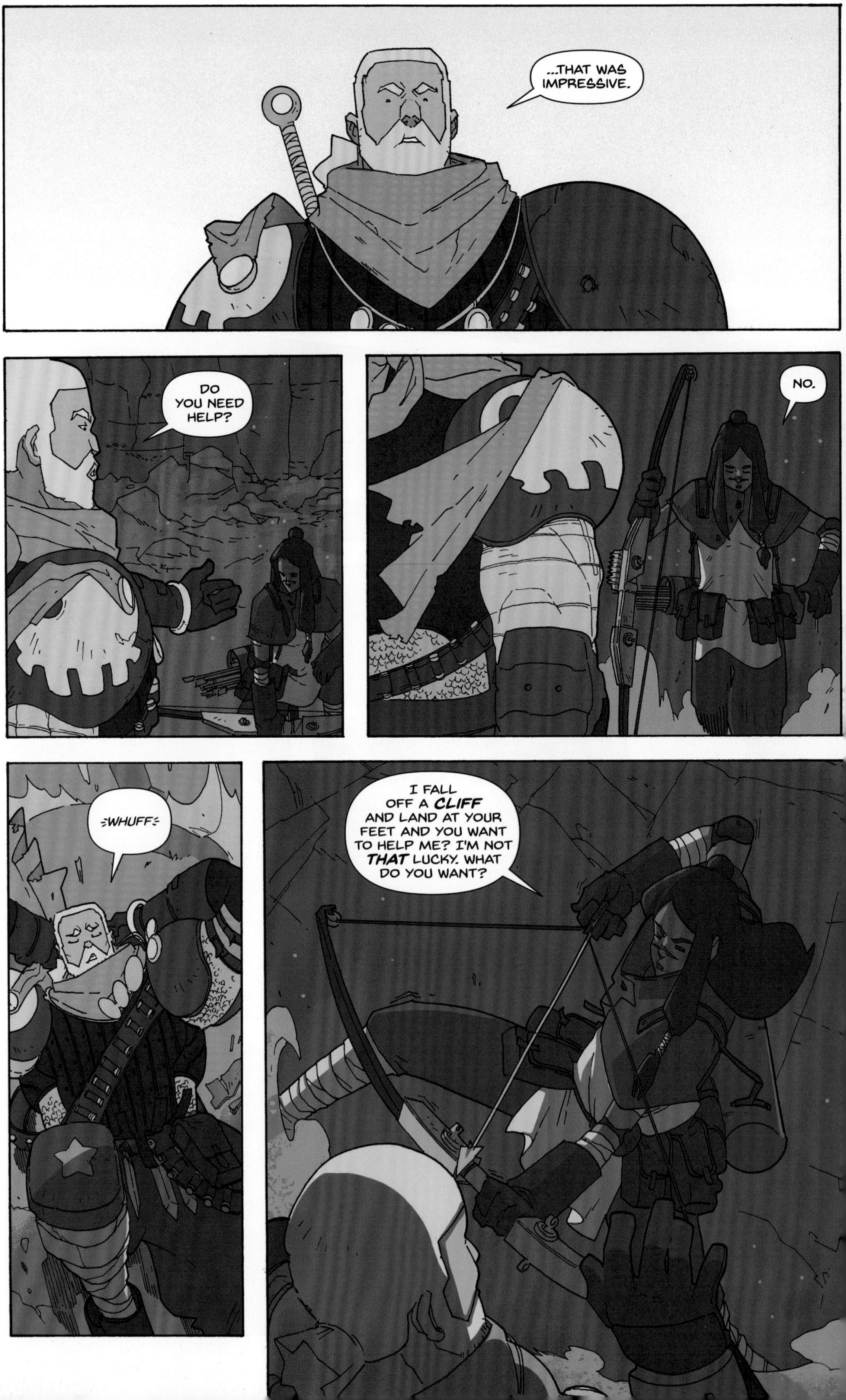
...THAT WAS IMPRESSIVE.
DO YOU NEED HELP?
NO.
WHUFF
I FALL OFF A CLIFF AND LAND AT YOUR FEET AND YOU WANT TO HELP ME? I'M NOT THAT LUCKY. WHAT DO YOU WANT?

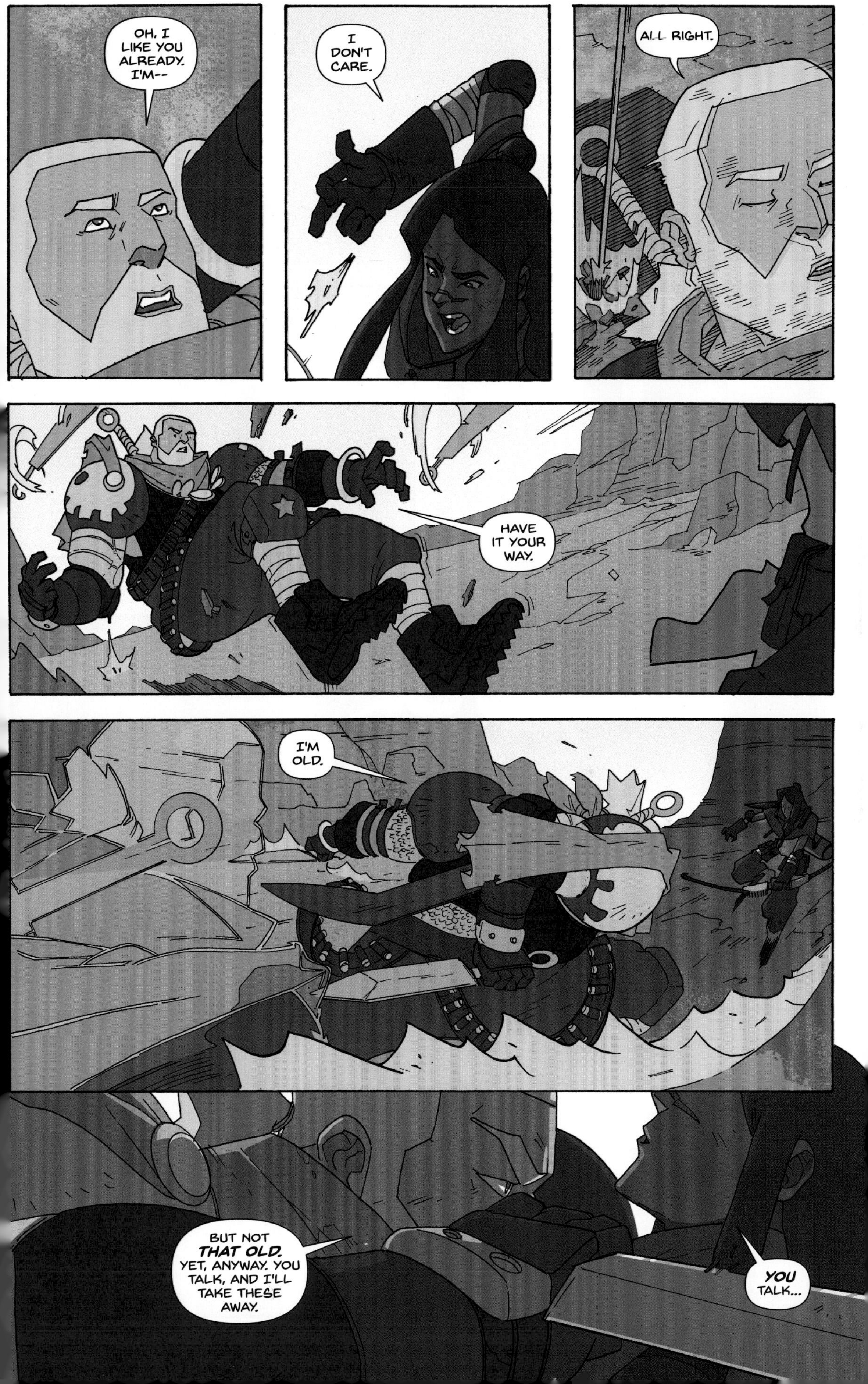
OH, I LIKE YOU ALREADY. I'M--
I DON'T CARE.
ALL RIGHT.
HAVE IT YOUR WAY.
I'M OLD.
BUT NOT **THAT OLD.** YET, ANYWAY. YOU TALK, AND I'LL TAKE THESE AWAY.
YOU TALK...

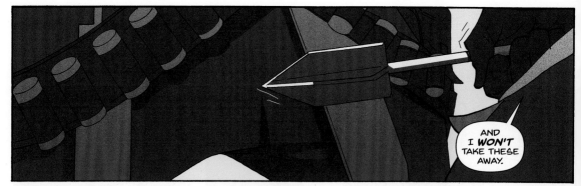

AND I **WON'T** TAKE THESE AWAY.

CALL IT A **DRAW?** I--

TOO OLD FOR THIS. WAY TOO OLD.

IF YOU STILL WANT TO PUT AN ARROW IN ME, NOW WOULD BE THE TIME.

ARE YOU--

THAT'S YOUR TALENT.

I'M JUST **OLD.** THERE'S A COST TO SPEEDING MYSELF UP LIKE THAT. HEAVIER AND HEAVIER AS TIME GOES BY.

ONE OF THEM. I CAN'T SENSE YOU. YOUR TALENT.

DON'T HAVE ONE.

EVERYONE HAS ONE. THAT'S HOW THE WORLD GOT THIS WAY.

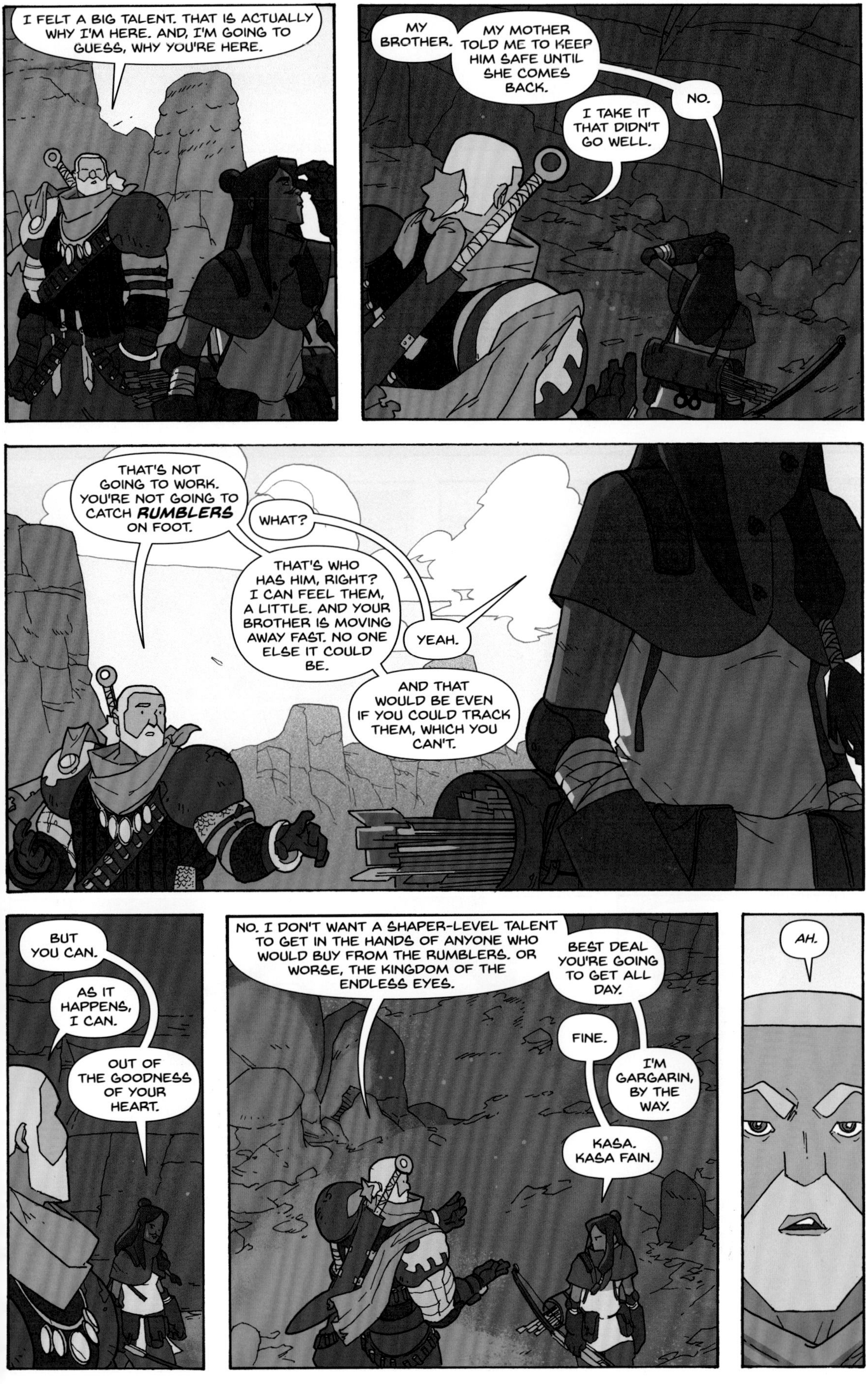
I FELT A BIG TALENT. THAT IS ACTUALLY WHY I'M HERE. AND, I'M GOING TO GUESS, WHY YOU'RE HERE.
MY BROTHER.
MY MOTHER TOLD ME TO KEEP HIM SAFE UNTIL SHE COMES BACK.
NO.
I TAKE IT THAT DIDN'T GO WELL.
THAT'S NOT GOING TO WORK. YOU'RE NOT GOING TO CATCH RUMBLERS ON FOOT.
WHAT?
THAT'S WHO HAS HIM, RIGHT? I CAN FEEL THEM, A LITTLE. AND YOUR BROTHER IS MOVING AWAY FAST. NO ONE ELSE IT COULD BE.
YEAH.
AND THAT WOULD BE EVEN IF YOU COULD TRACK THEM, WHICH YOU CAN'T.
BUT YOU CAN.
AS IT HAPPENS, I CAN.
OUT OF THE GOODNESS OF YOUR HEART.
NO. I DON'T WANT A SHAPER-LEVEL TALENT TO GET IN THE HANDS OF ANYONE WHO WOULD BUY FROM THE RUMBLERS. OR WORSE, THE KINGDOM OF THE ENDLESS EYES.
BEST DEAL YOU'RE GOING TO GET ALL DAY.
FINE.
I'M GARGARIN, BY THE WAY.
KASA. KASA FAIN.
AH.

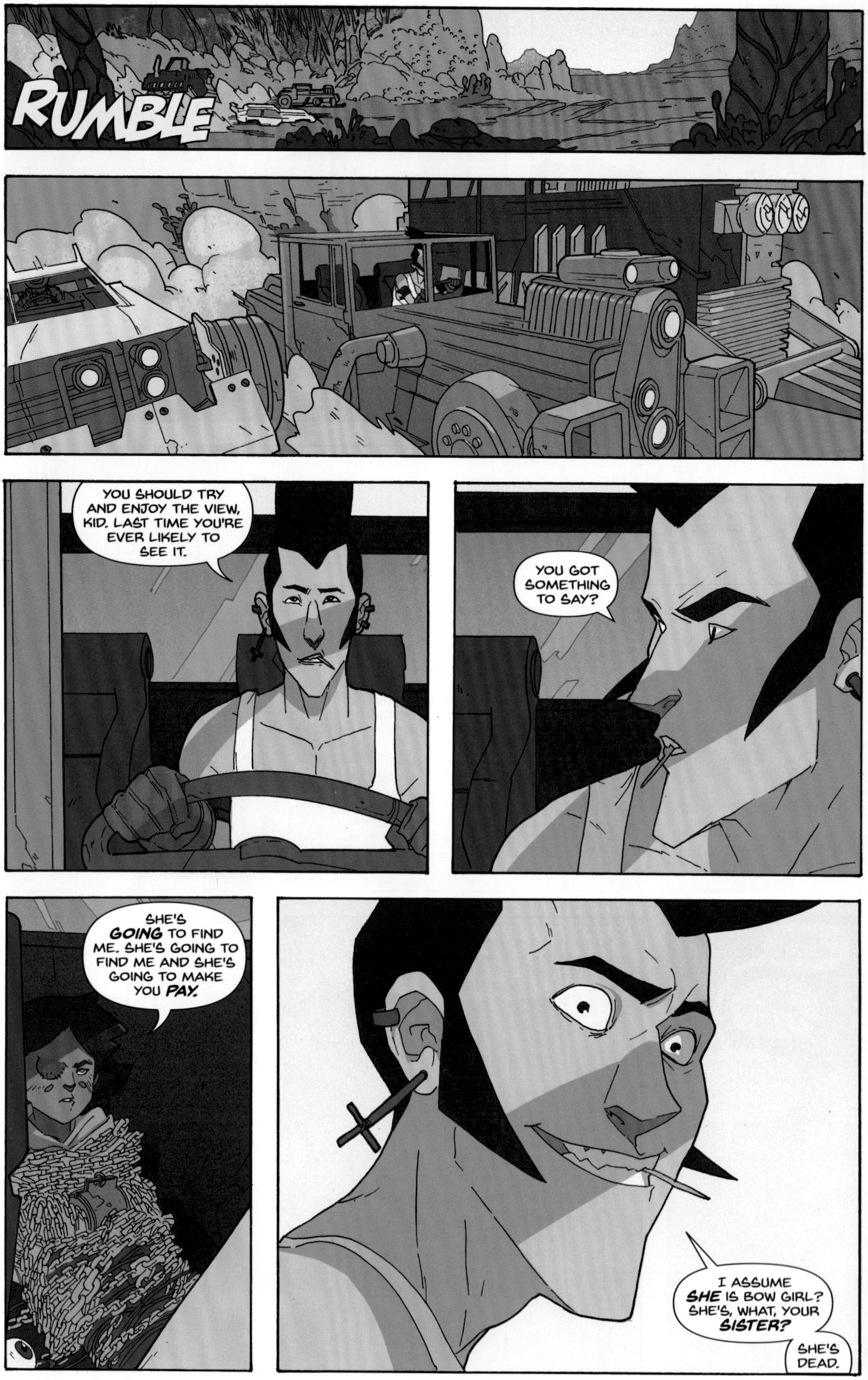
RUMBLE
YOU SHOULD TRY AND ENJOY THE VIEW, KID. LAST TIME YOU'RE EVER LIKELY TO SEE IT.
YOU GOT SOMETHING TO SAY?
SHE'S GOING TO FIND ME. SHE'S GOING TO FIND ME AND SHE'S GOING TO MAKE YOU PAY.
I ASSUME SHE IS BOW GIRL? SHE'S, WHAT, YOUR SISTER?
SHE'S DEAD.

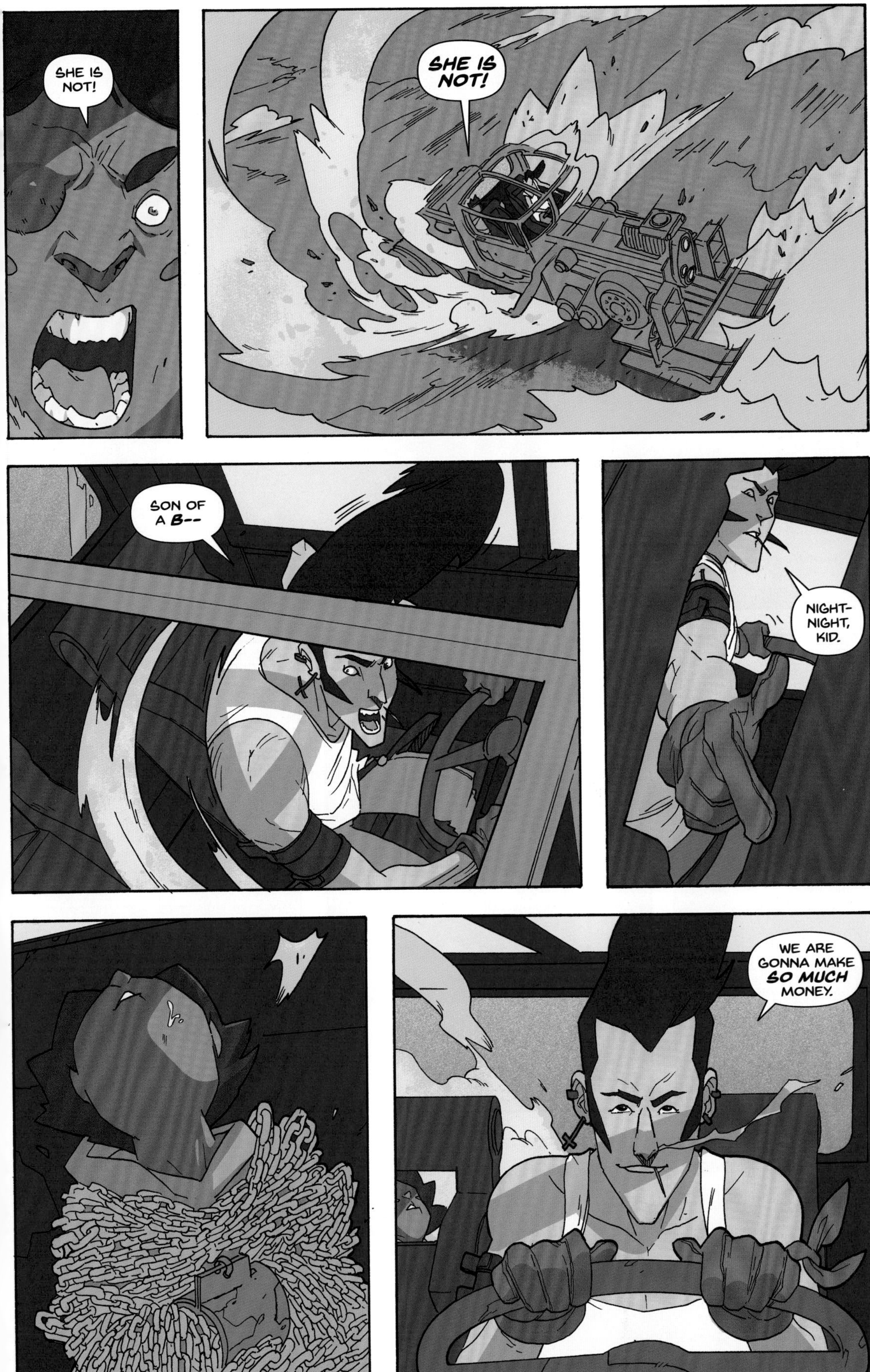
SHE IS NOT!
SHE IS NOT!
SON OF A B--
NIGHT-NIGHT, KID.
WE ARE GONNA MAKE SO MUCH MONEY.

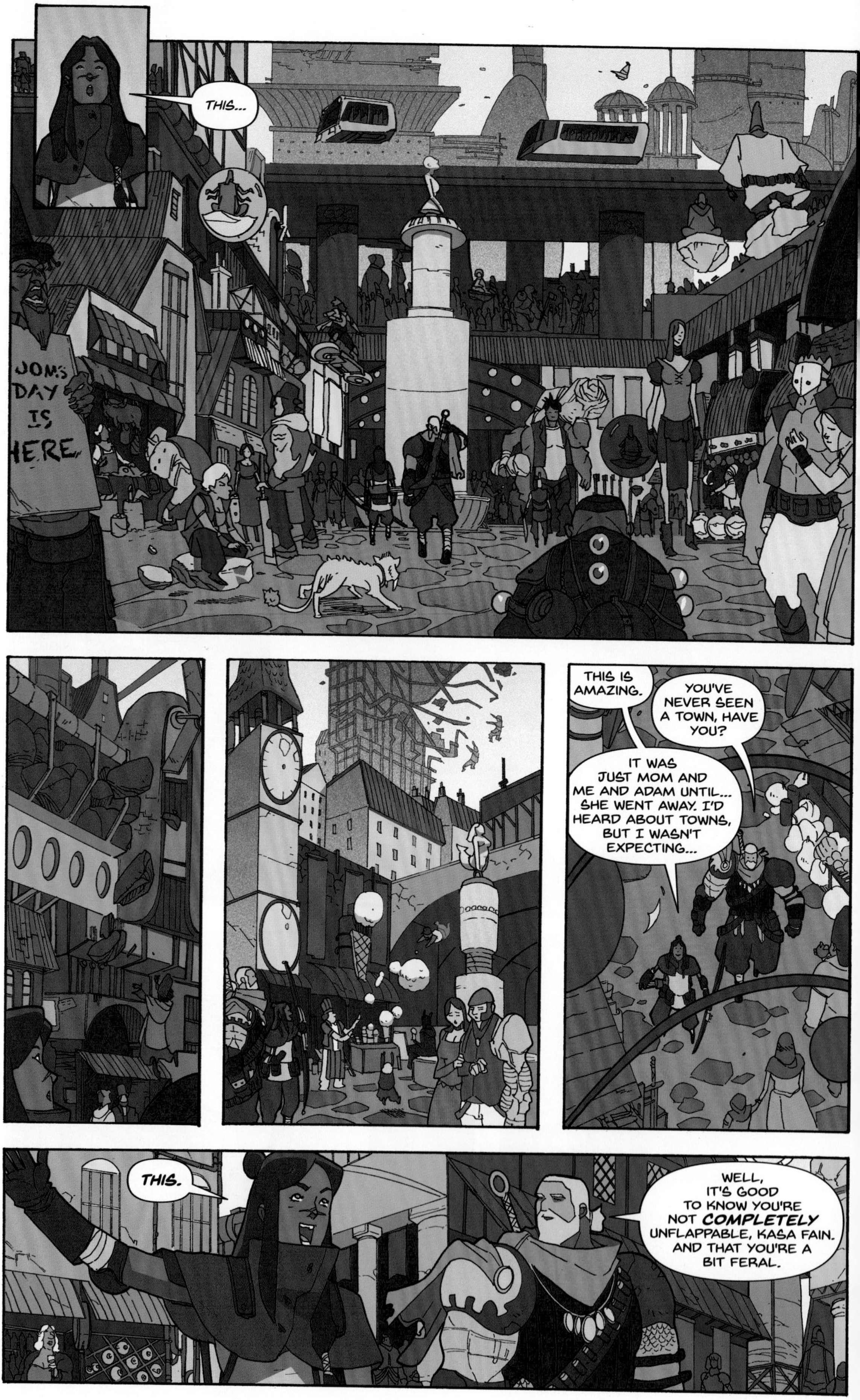
THIS...
DAY IS HERE
THIS IS AMAZING.
YOU'VE NEVER SEEN A TOWN, HAVE YOU?
IT WAS JUST MOM AND ME AND ADAM UNTIL... SHE WENT AWAY. I'D HEARD ABOUT TOWNS, BUT I WASN'T EXPECTING...
THIS.
WELL, IT'S GOOD TO KNOW YOU'RE NOT *COMPLETELY* UNFLAPPABLE, KASA FAIN. AND THAT YOU'RE A BIT FERAL.

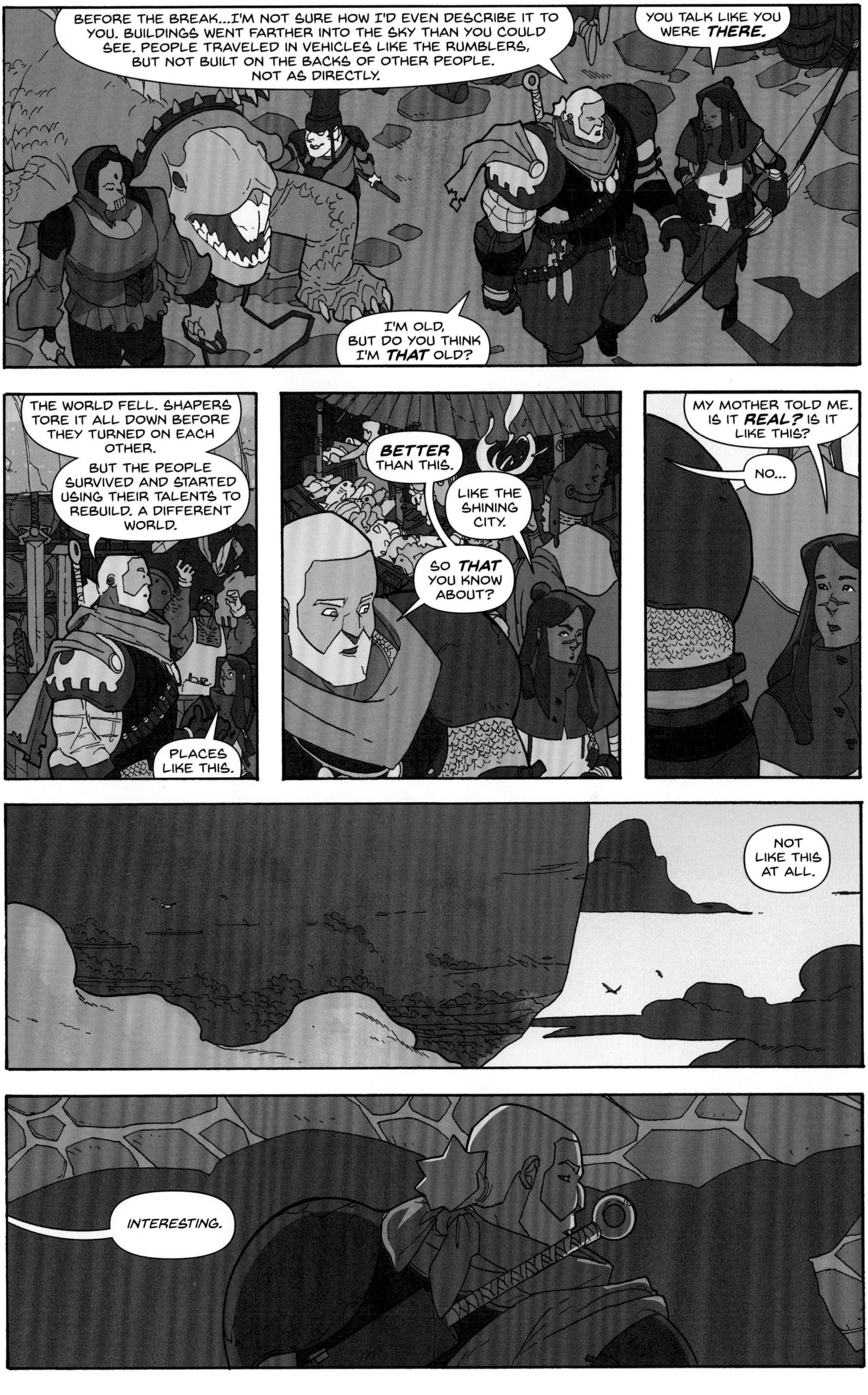
BEFORE THE BREAK...I'M NOT SURE HOW I'D EVEN DESCRIBE IT TO YOU. BUILDINGS WENT FARTHER INTO THE SKY THAN YOU COULD SEE. PEOPLE TRAVELED IN VEHICLES LIKE THE RUMBLERS, BUT NOT BUILT ON THE BACKS OF OTHER PEOPLE. NOT AS DIRECTLY.
YOU TALK LIKE YOU WERE THERE.
I'M OLD, BUT DO YOU THINK I'M THAT OLD?
THE WORLD FELL. SHAPERS TORE IT ALL DOWN BEFORE THEY TURNED ON EACH OTHER.
BUT THE PEOPLE SURVIVED AND STARTED USING THEIR TALENTS TO REBUILD. A DIFFERENT WORLD.
PLACES LIKE THIS.
BETTER THAN THIS.
LIKE THE SHINING CITY.
SO THAT YOU KNOW ABOUT?
MY MOTHER TOLD ME. IS IT REAL? IS IT LIKE THIS?
NO...
NOT LIKE THIS AT ALL.
INTERESTING.

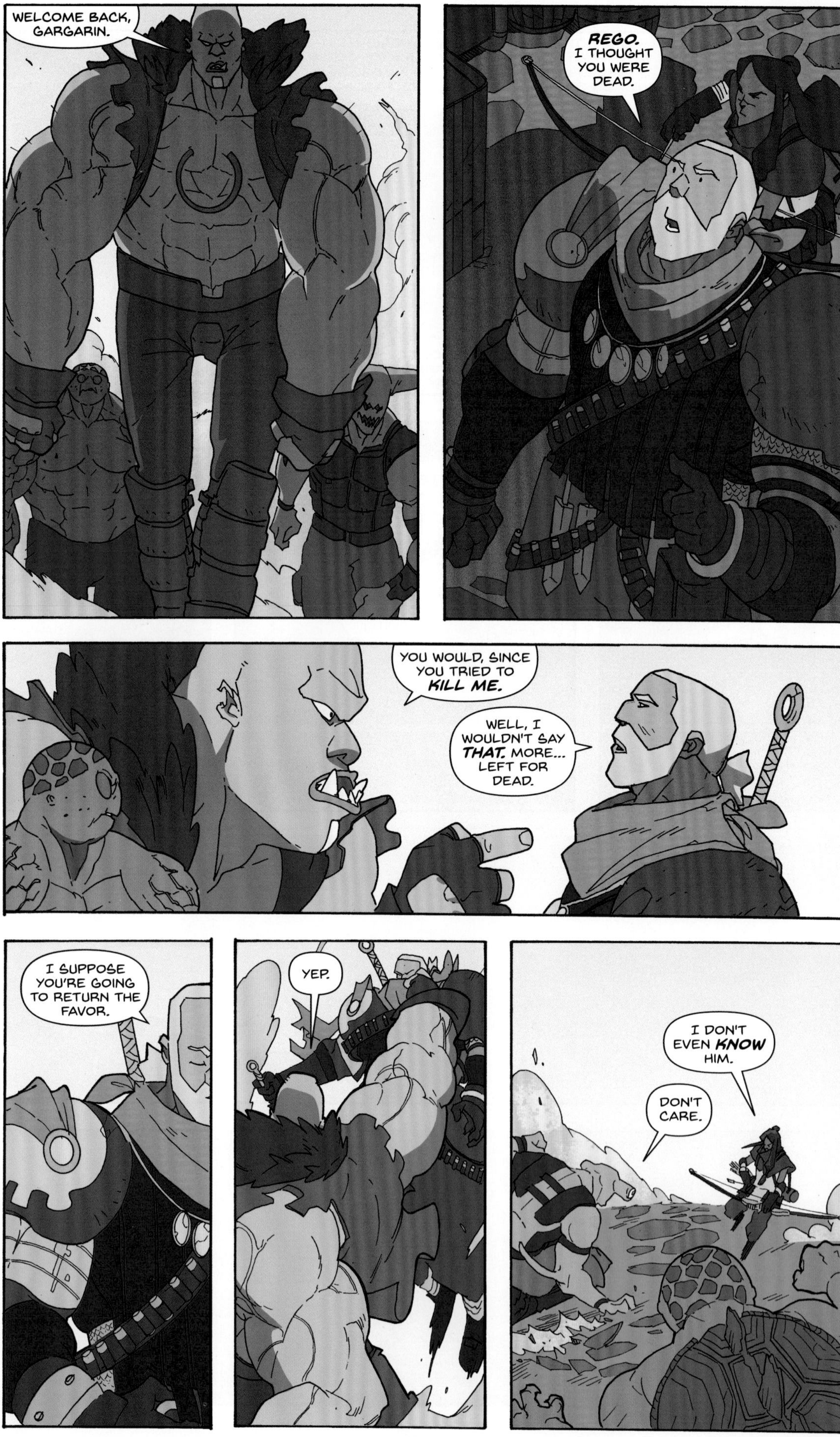
WELCOME BACK, GARGARIN.
REGO. I THOUGHT YOU WERE DEAD.
YOU WOULD, SINCE YOU TRIED TO KILL ME.
WELL, I WOULDN'T SAY THAT. MORE... LEFT FOR DEAD.
I SUPPOSE YOU'RE GOING TO RETURN THE FAVOR.
YEP.
I DON'T EVEN KNOW HIM.
DON'T CARE.

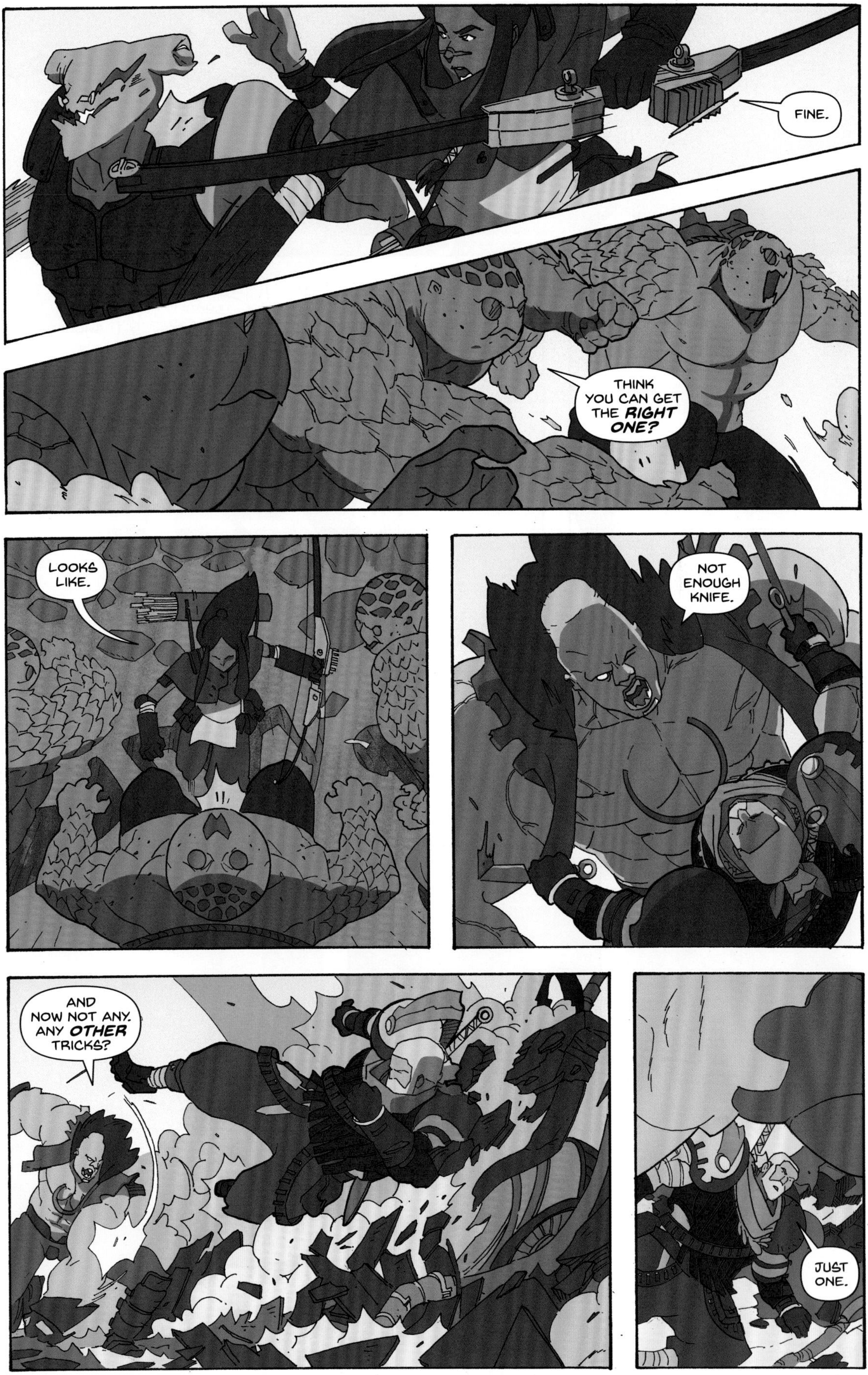
FINE.
THINK YOU CAN GET THE RIGHT ONE?
LOOKS LIKE.
NOT ENOUGH KNIFE.
AND NOW NOT ANY. ANY OTHER TRICKS?
JUST ONE.

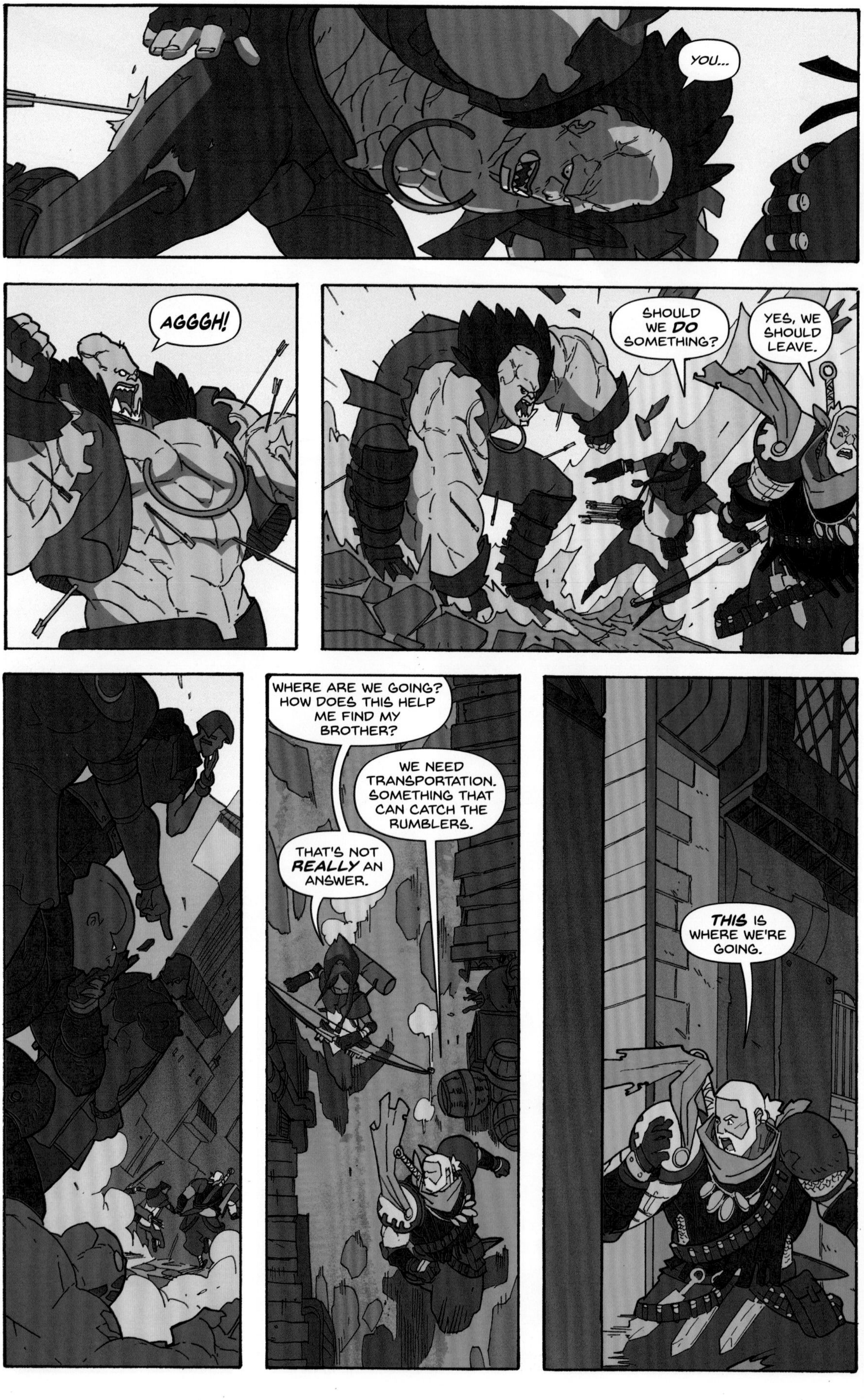
YOU...
AGGGH!
SHOULD WE DO SOMETHING?
YES, WE SHOULD LEAVE.
WHERE ARE WE GOING? HOW DOES THIS HELP ME FIND MY BROTHER?
WE NEED TRANSPORTATION. SOMETHING THAT CAN CATCH THE RUMBLERS.
THAT'S NOT REALLY AN ANSWER.
THIS IS WHERE WE'RE GOING.

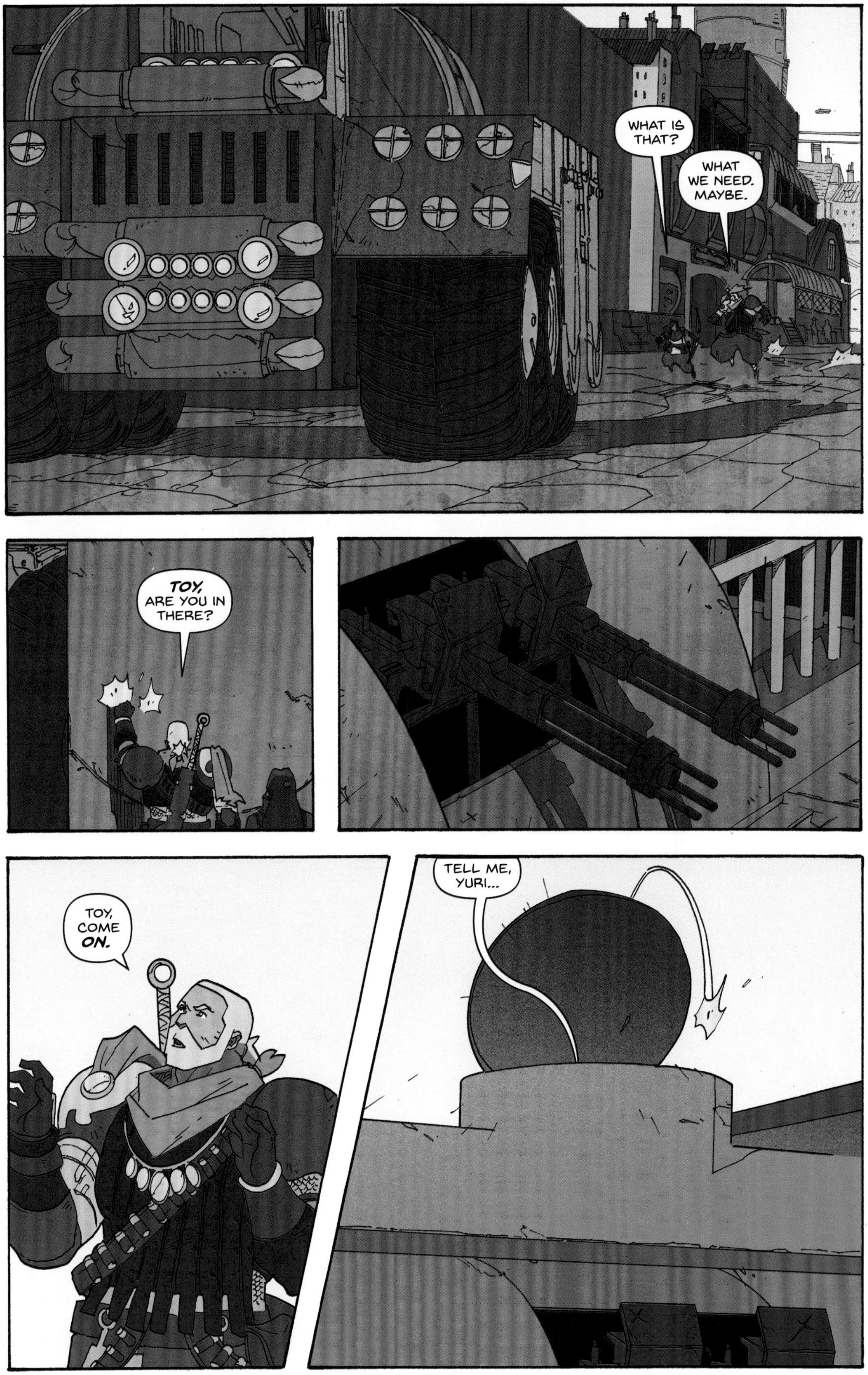
WHAT IS THAT?
WHAT WE NEED. MAYBE.
TOY, ARE YOU IN THERE?
TOY, COME ON.
TELL ME, YURI...

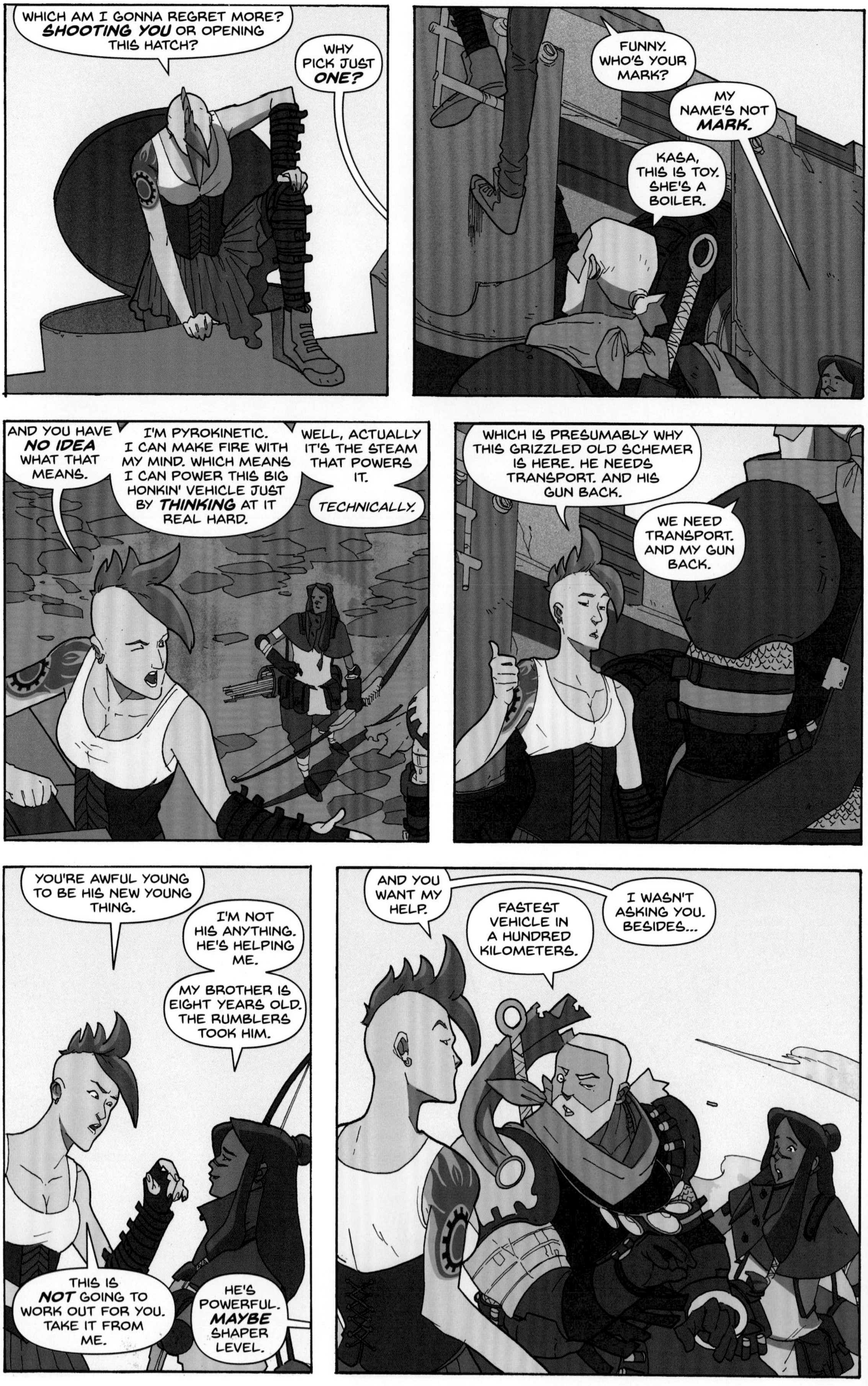
WHICH AM I GONNA REGRET MORE? SHOOTING YOU OR OPENING THIS HATCH?
WHY PICK JUST ONE?
FUNNY. WHO'S YOUR MARK?
MY NAME'S NOT MARK.
KASA, THIS IS TOY. SHE'S A BOILER.
AND YOU HAVE NO IDEA WHAT THAT MEANS.
I'M PYROKINETIC. I CAN MAKE FIRE WITH MY MIND. WHICH MEANS I CAN POWER THIS BIG HONKIN' VEHICLE JUST BY THINKING AT IT REAL HARD.
WELL, ACTUALLY IT'S THE STEAM THAT POWERS IT.
TECHNICALLY.
WHICH IS PRESUMABLY WHY THIS GRIZZLED OLD SCHEMER IS HERE. HE NEEDS TRANSPORT. AND HIS GUN BACK.
WE NEED TRANSPORT. AND MY GUN BACK.
YOU'RE AWFUL YOUNG TO BE HIS NEW YOUNG THING.
I'M NOT HIS ANYTHING. HE'S HELPING ME.
MY BROTHER IS EIGHT YEARS OLD. THE RUMBLERS TOOK HIM.
THIS IS NOT GOING TO WORK OUT FOR YOU. TAKE IT FROM ME.
HE'S POWERFUL. MAYBE SHAPER LEVEL.
AND YOU WANT MY HELP.
FASTEST VEHICLE IN A HUNDRED KILOMETERS.
I WASN'T ASKING YOU. BESIDES...

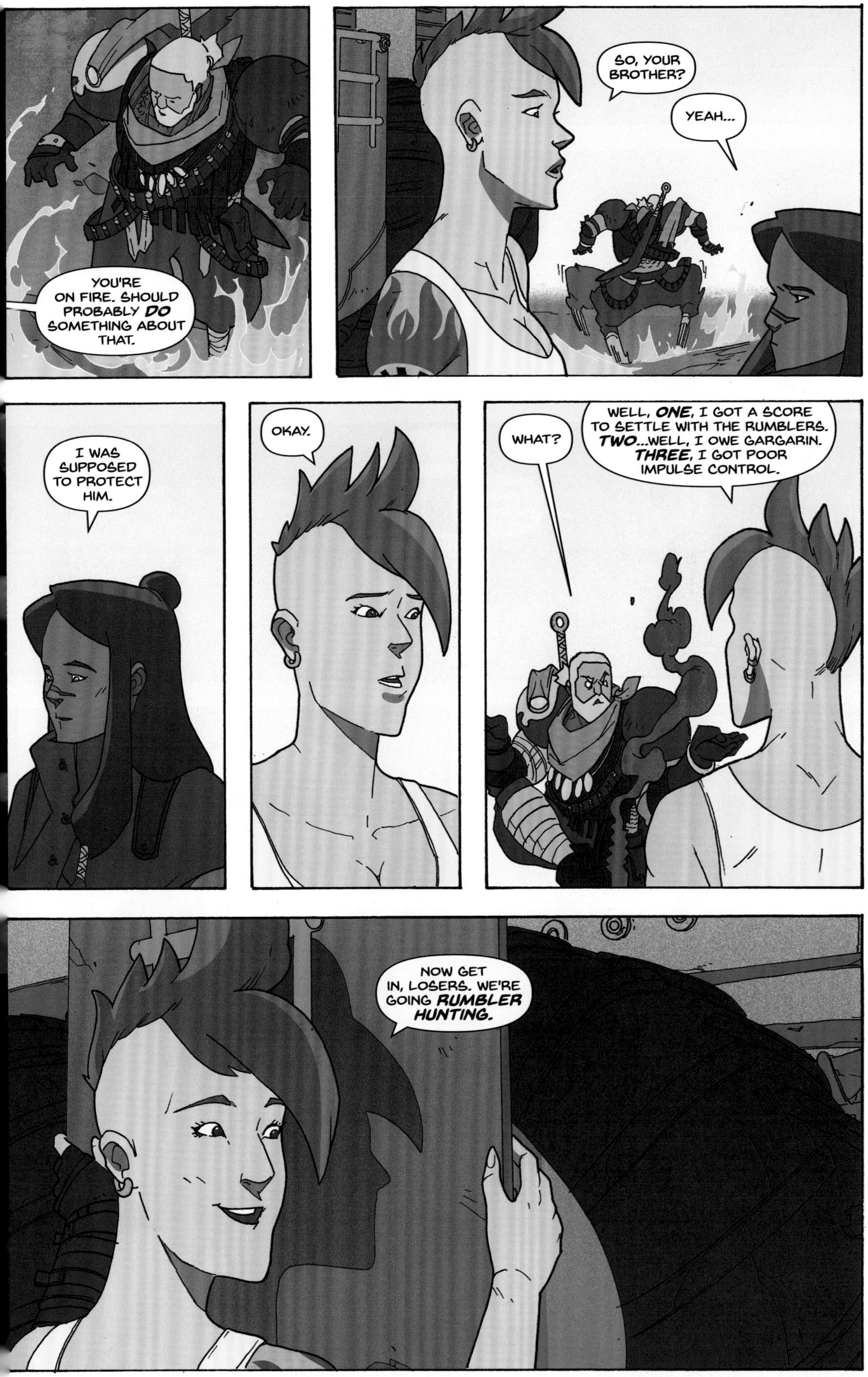

YOU'RE ON FIRE. SHOULD PROBABLY *DO* SOMETHING ABOUT THAT.
SO, YOUR BROTHER?
YEAH...
I WAS SUPPOSED TO PROTECT HIM.
OKAY.
WHAT?
WELL, *ONE*, I GOT A SCORE TO SETTLE WITH THE RUMBLERS. *TWO*...WELL, I OWE GARGARIN. *THREE*, I GOT POOR IMPULSE CONTROL.
NOW GET IN, LOSERS. WE'RE GOING *RUMBLER HUNTING.*

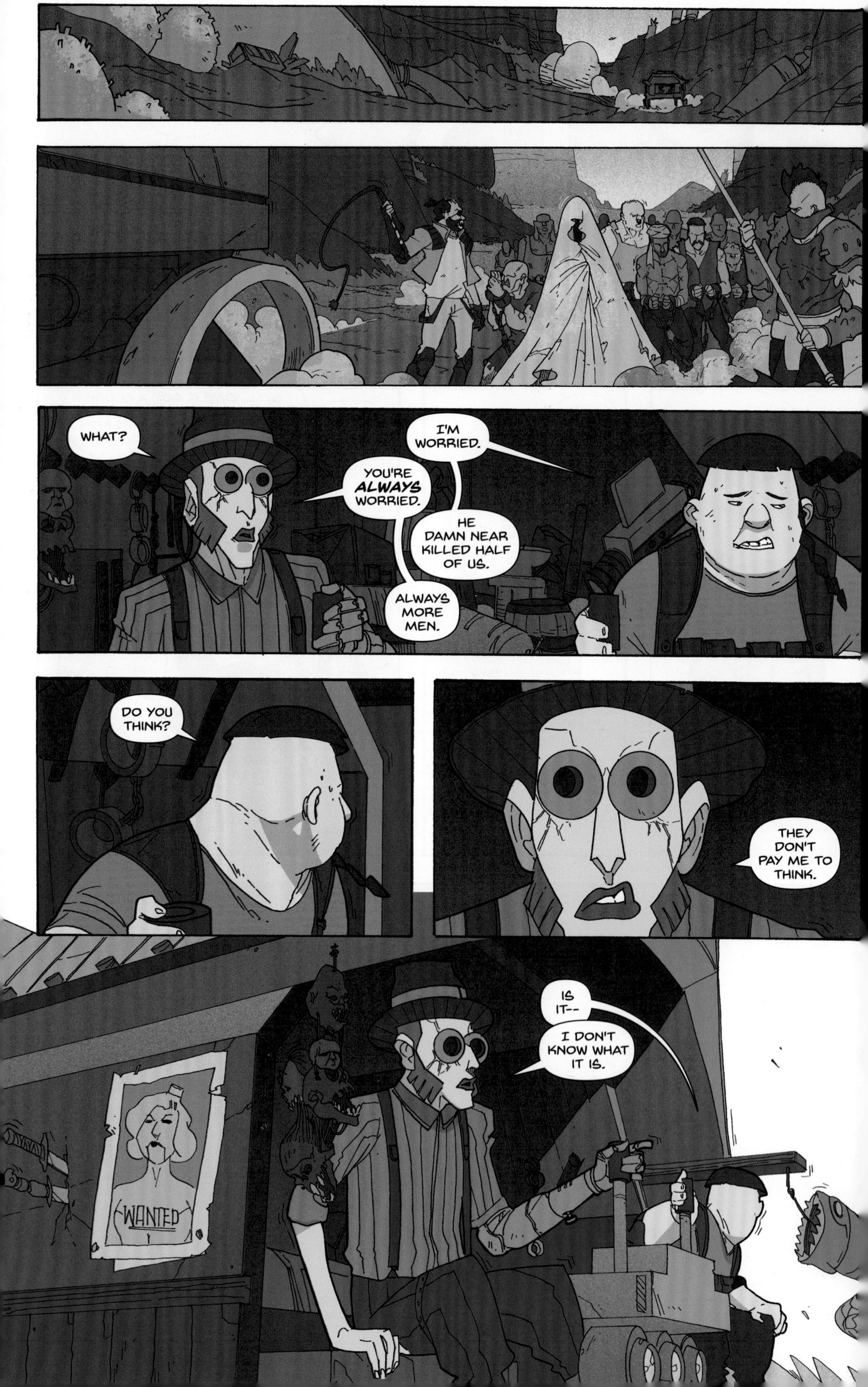
WHAT?
I'M WORRIED.
YOU'RE ALWAYS WORRIED.
HE DAMN NEAR KILLED HALF OF US.
ALWAYS MORE MEN.
DO YOU THINK?
THEY DON'T PAY ME TO THINK.
IS IT--
I DON'T KNOW WHAT IT IS.
WANTED

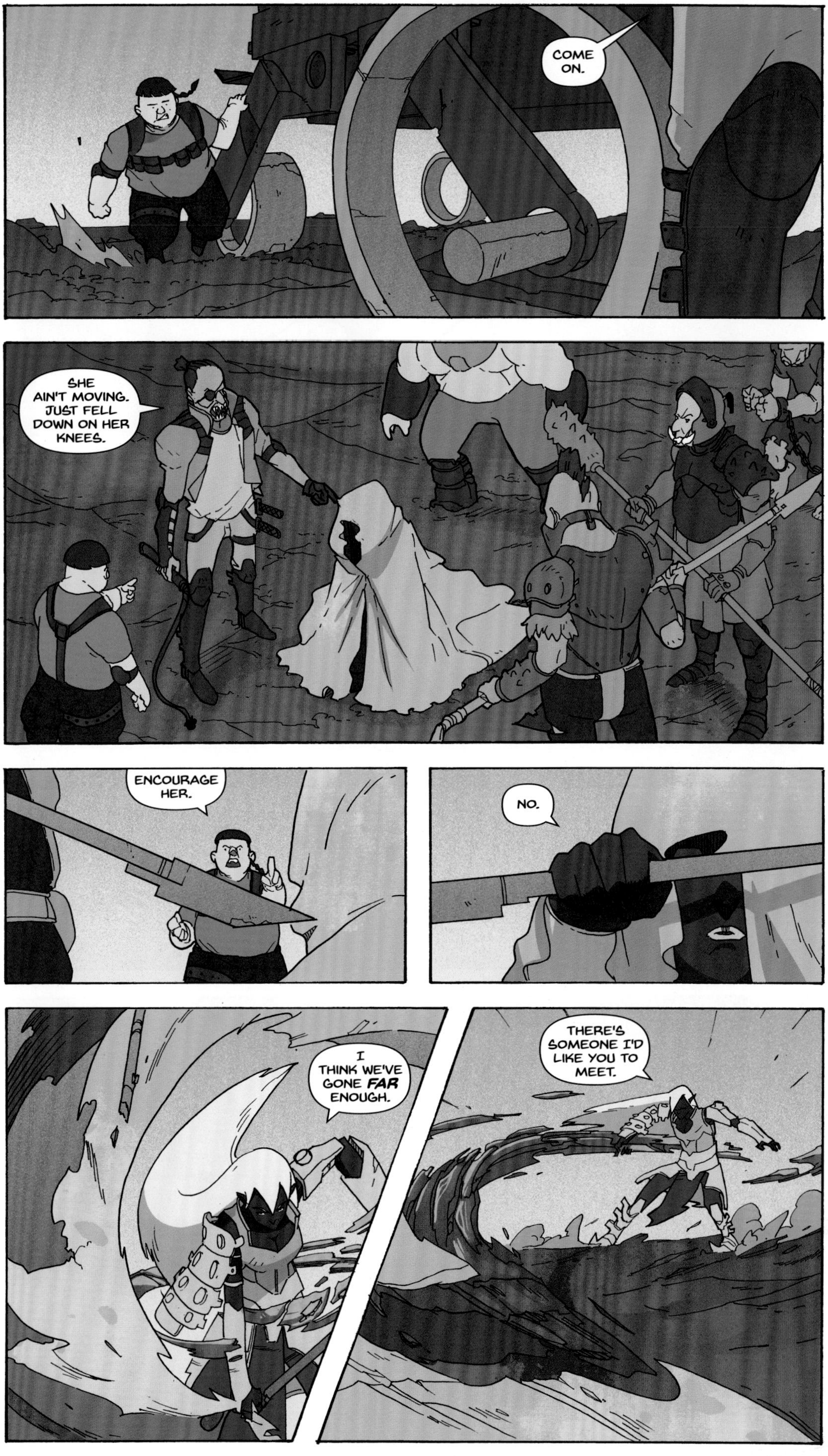
COME ON.
SHE AIN'T MOVING. JUST FELL DOWN ON HER KNEES.
ENCOURAGE HER.
NO.
I THINK WE'VE GONE FAR ENOUGH.
THERE'S SOMEONE I'D LIKE YOU TO MEET.

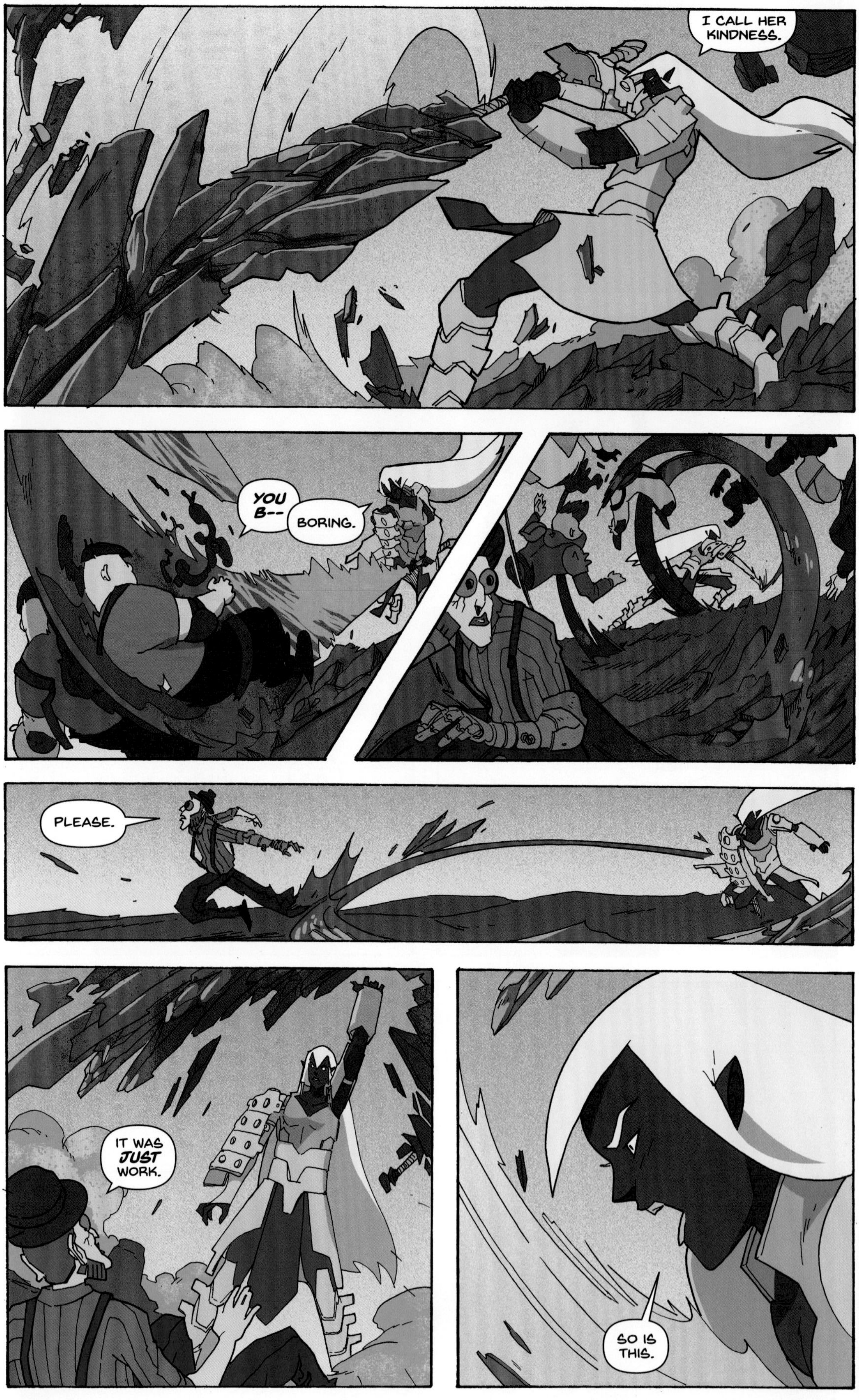
I CALL HER KINDNESS.
YOU B--
BORING.
PLEASE.
IT WAS JUST WORK.
SO IS THIS.

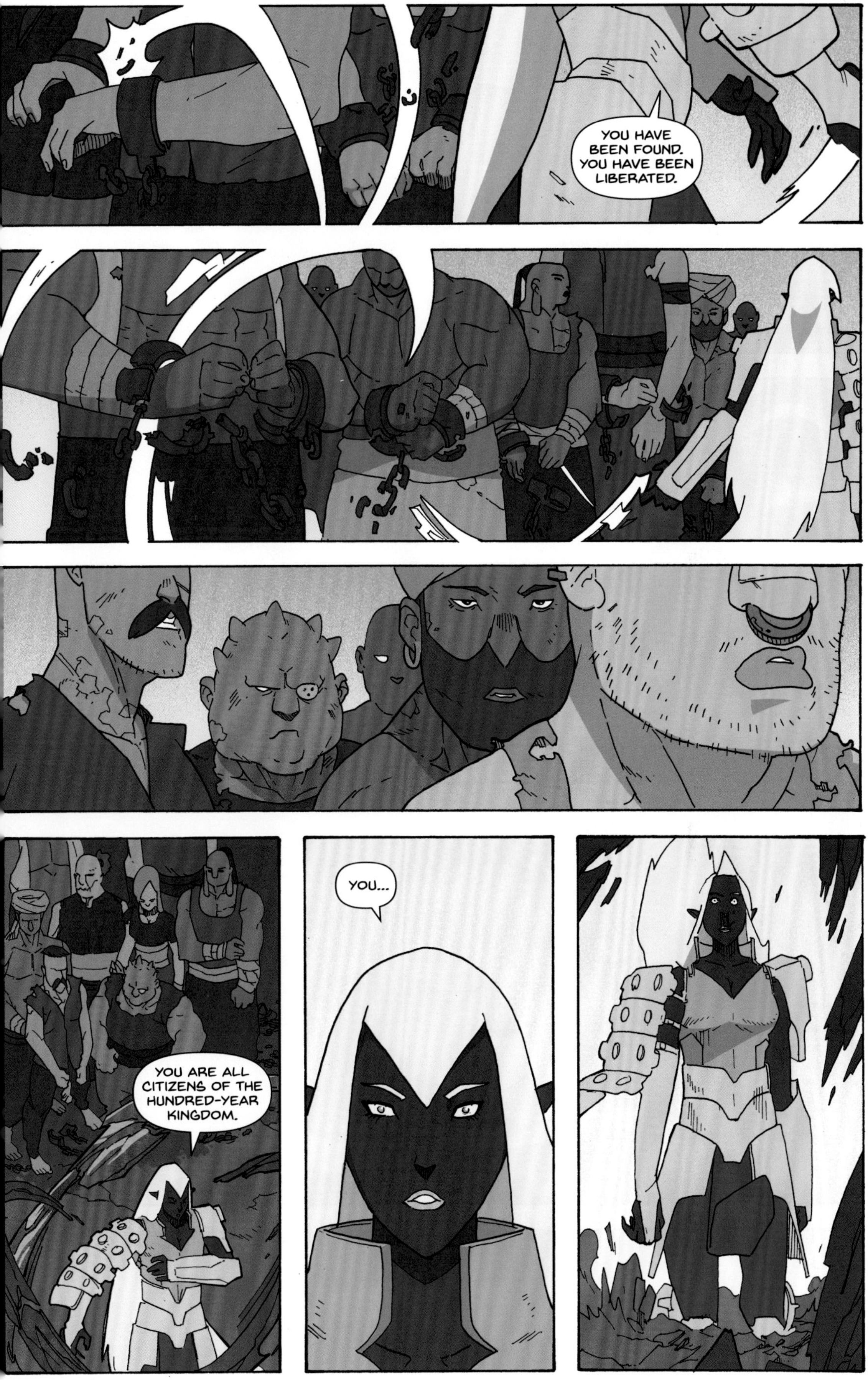
YOU HAVE BEEN FOUND. YOU HAVE BEEN LIBERATED.
YOU ARE ALL CITIZENS OF THE HUNDRED-YEAR KINGDOM.
YOU...

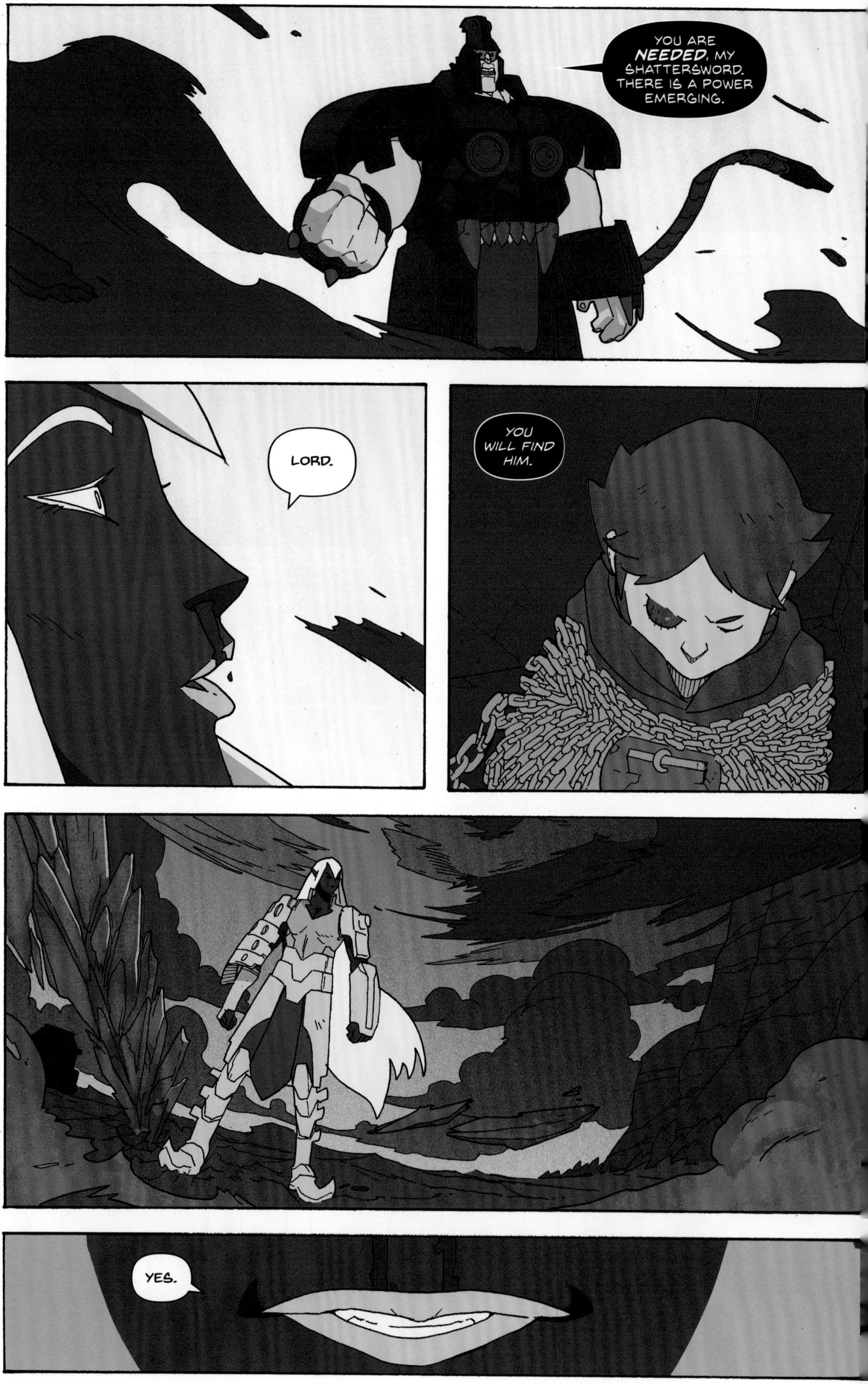
YOU ARE NEEDED, MY SHATTERSWORD. THERE IS A POWER EMERGING.
LORD.
YOU WILL FIND HIM.
YES.

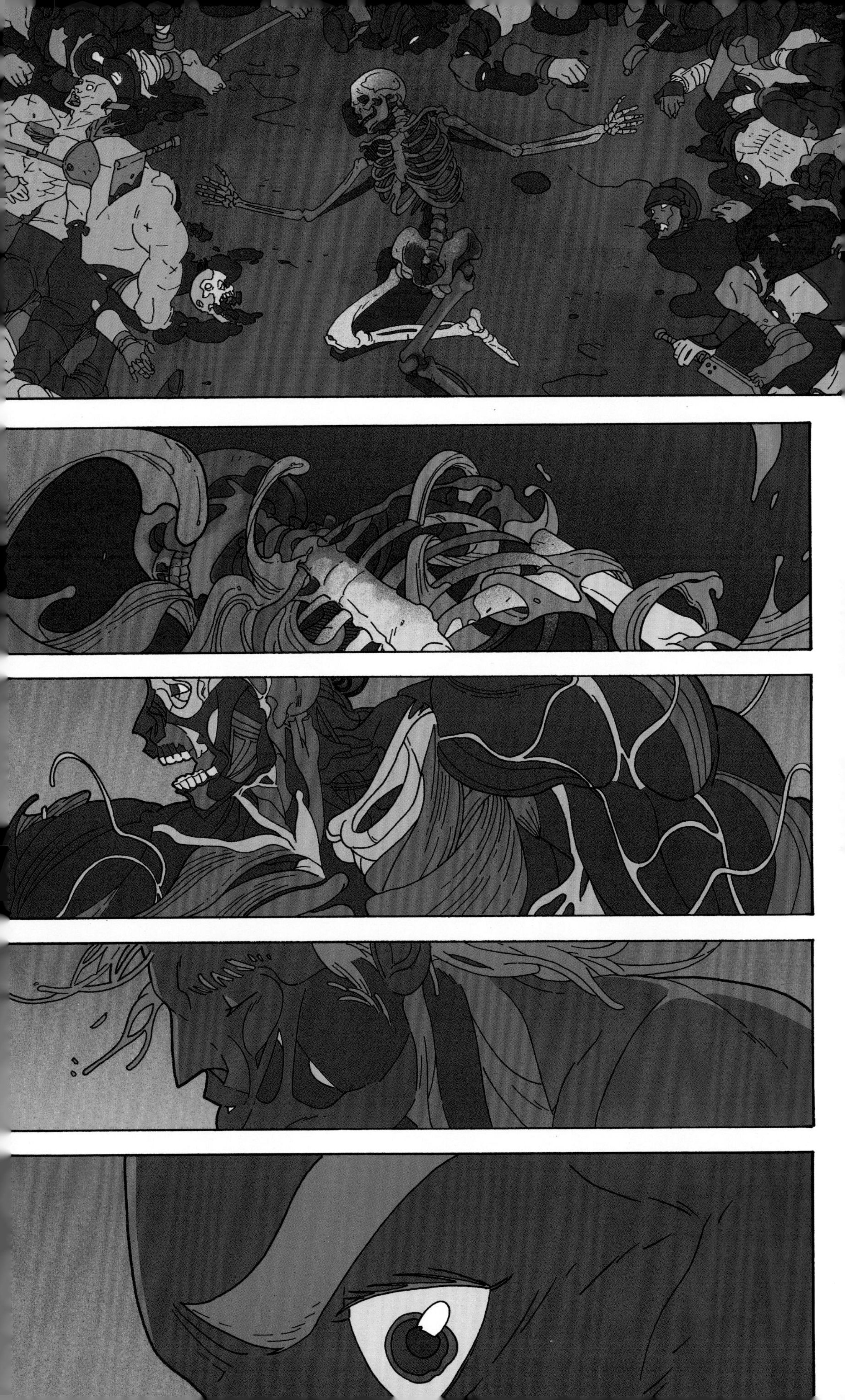

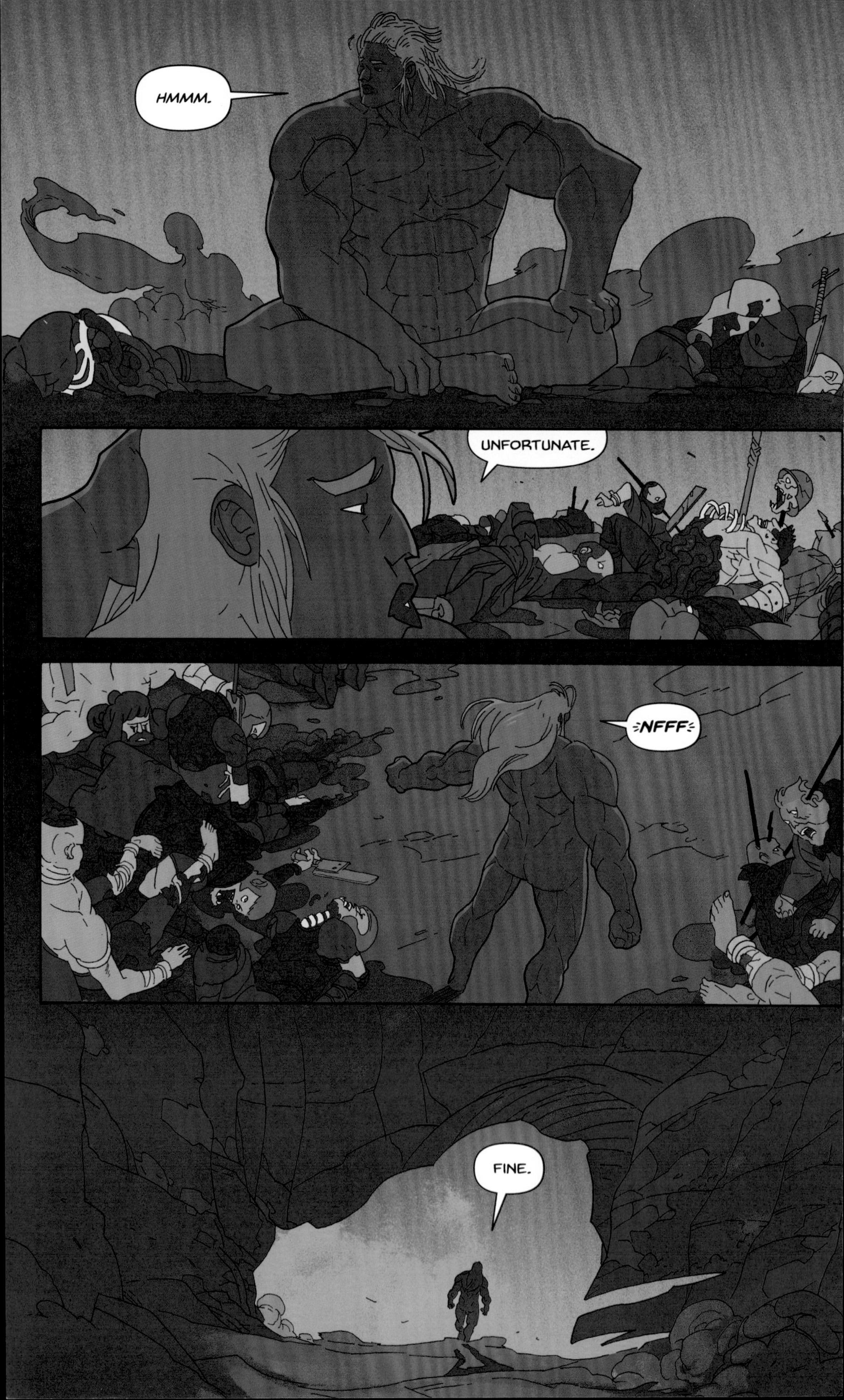
HMMM.
UNFORTUNATE.
NFFF
FINE.

"THE TRUCK DOESN'T DRIVE WITHOUT ME."

I MEAN, LITERALLY. MY *PYRO* IS WHAT POWERS THE STEAM ENGINE. WITHOUT ME IT'S DECORATION. SO, YEAH, I GET TO ASK QUESTIONS.

SUCH AS, ARE WE HEADING THE RIGHT WAY?

I'D LIKE TO KNOW THAT MYSELF.

I'M NOT AS YOUNG AS I ONCE WAS--

YES, THAT'S HOW TIME WORKS...

--BUT I CAN FEEL ADAM. ALMOST SEE HIM. SHAPERS, EVEN POTENTIALS, DON'T FEEL LIKE ANYTHING ELSE. IT'S LIKE LOOKING AT THE SUN.

THEN HOW IS IT YOU *JUST NOW* KNEW ABOUT HIM?

THAT'S A VERY GOOD QUESTION. BUT I CAN TELL YOU--

AND WILL.

I WOULD, AT SOME POINT, LIKE TO *FINISH* A STATEMENT. WHAT I WAS GOING TO SAY IS NOW THAT I CAN FEEL HIM, I WON'T BE THE ONLY ONE.

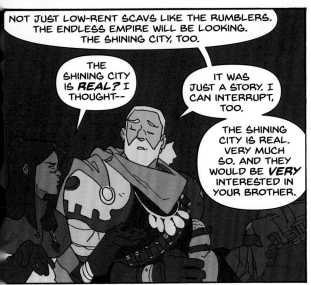

NOT JUST LOW-RENT SCAVS LIKE THE RUMBLERS. THE ENDLESS EMPIRE WILL BE LOOKING. THE SHINING CITY, TOO.

THE SHINING CITY IS *REAL?* I THOUGHT--

IT WAS JUST A STORY. I CAN INTERRUPT, TOO.

THE SHINING CITY IS REAL. VERY MUCH SO. AND THEY WOULD BE *VERY* INTERESTED IN YOUR BROTHER.

I DON'T KNOW HOW CLOSE WE ARE TO THE RUMBLERS...

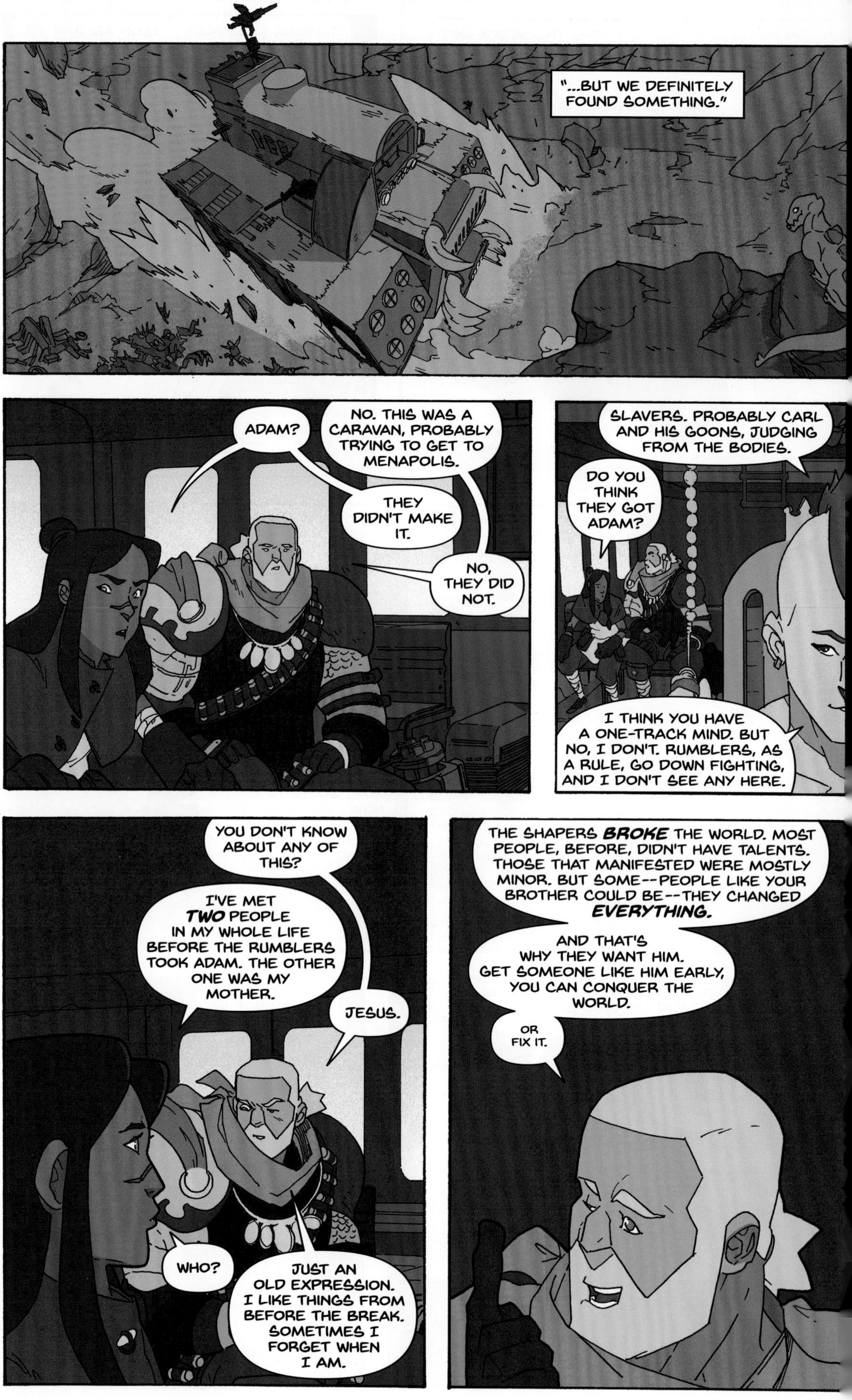
"...BUT WE DEFINITELY FOUND SOMETHING."
ADAM?
NO. THIS WAS A CARAVAN, PROBABLY TRYING TO GET TO MENAPOLIS.
THEY DIDN'T MAKE IT.
NO, THEY DID NOT.
SLAVERS. PROBABLY CARL AND HIS GOONS, JUDGING FROM THE BODIES.
DO YOU THINK THEY GOT ADAM?
I THINK YOU HAVE A ONE-TRACK MIND. BUT NO, I DON'T. RUMBLERS, AS A RULE, GO DOWN FIGHTING, AND I DON'T SEE ANY HERE.
YOU DON'T KNOW ABOUT ANY OF THIS?
I'VE MET **TWO** PEOPLE IN MY WHOLE LIFE BEFORE THE RUMBLERS TOOK ADAM. THE OTHER ONE WAS MY MOTHER.
JESUS.
WHO?
JUST AN OLD EXPRESSION. I LIKE THINGS FROM BEFORE THE BREAK. SOMETIMES I FORGET WHEN I AM.
THE SHAPERS **BROKE** THE WORLD. MOST PEOPLE, BEFORE, DIDN'T HAVE TALENTS. THOSE THAT MANIFESTED WERE MOSTLY MINOR. BUT SOME--PEOPLE LIKE YOUR BROTHER COULD BE--THEY CHANGED **EVERYTHING.**
AND THAT'S WHY THEY WANT HIM. GET SOMEONE LIKE HIM EARLY, YOU CAN CONQUER THE WORLD.
OR FIX IT.

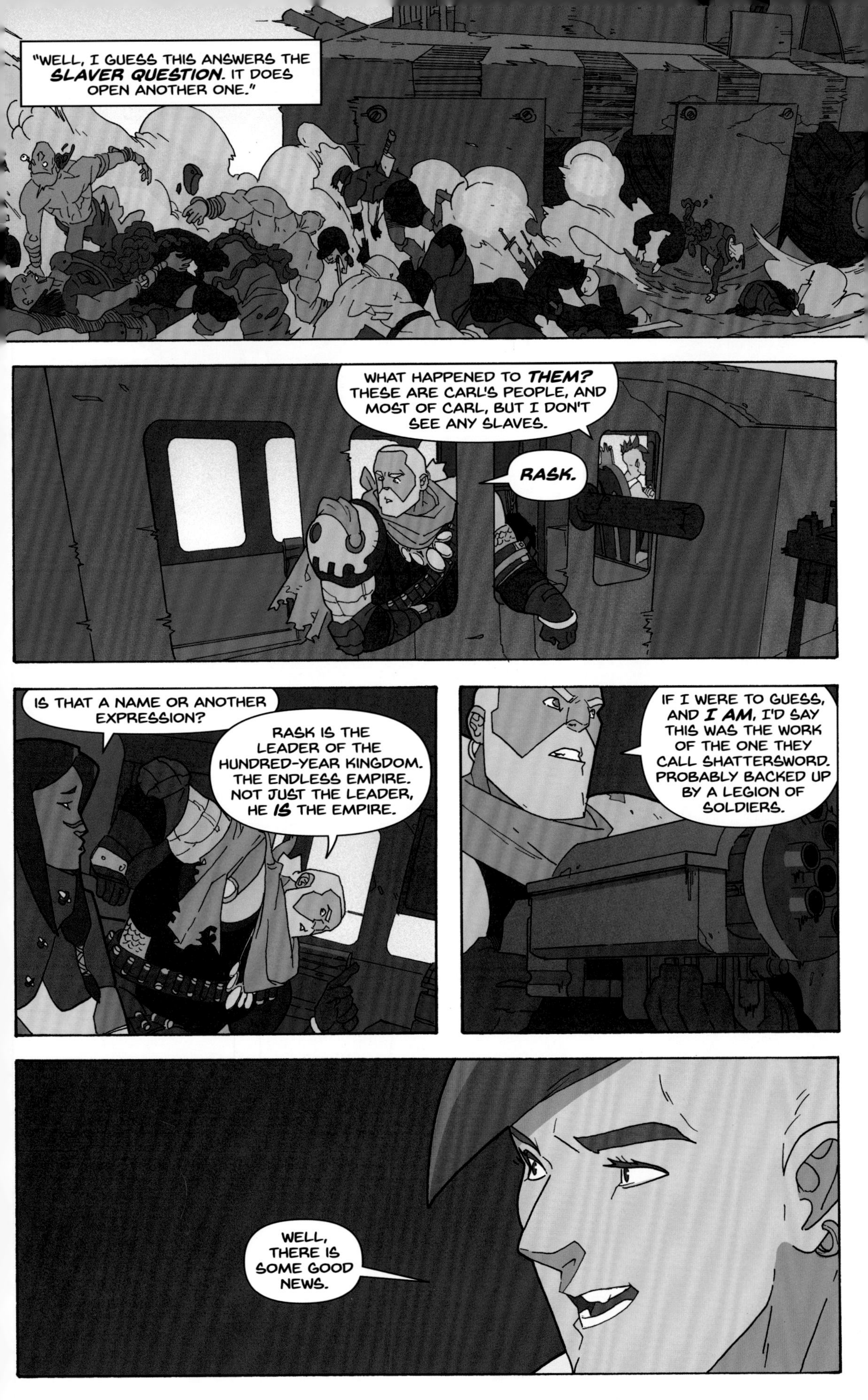

"WELL, I GUESS THIS ANSWERS THE SLAVER QUESTION. IT DOES OPEN ANOTHER ONE."
WHAT HAPPENED TO THEM? THESE ARE CARL'S PEOPLE, AND MOST OF CARL, BUT I DON'T SEE ANY SLAVES.
RASK.
IS THAT A NAME OR ANOTHER EXPRESSION?
RASK IS THE LEADER OF THE HUNDRED-YEAR KINGDOM. THE ENDLESS EMPIRE. NOT JUST THE LEADER, HE IS THE EMPIRE.
IF I WERE TO GUESS, AND I AM, I'D SAY THIS WAS THE WORK OF THE ONE THEY CALL SHATTERSWORD. PROBABLY BACKED UP BY A LEGION OF SOLDIERS.
WELL, THERE IS SOME GOOD NEWS.

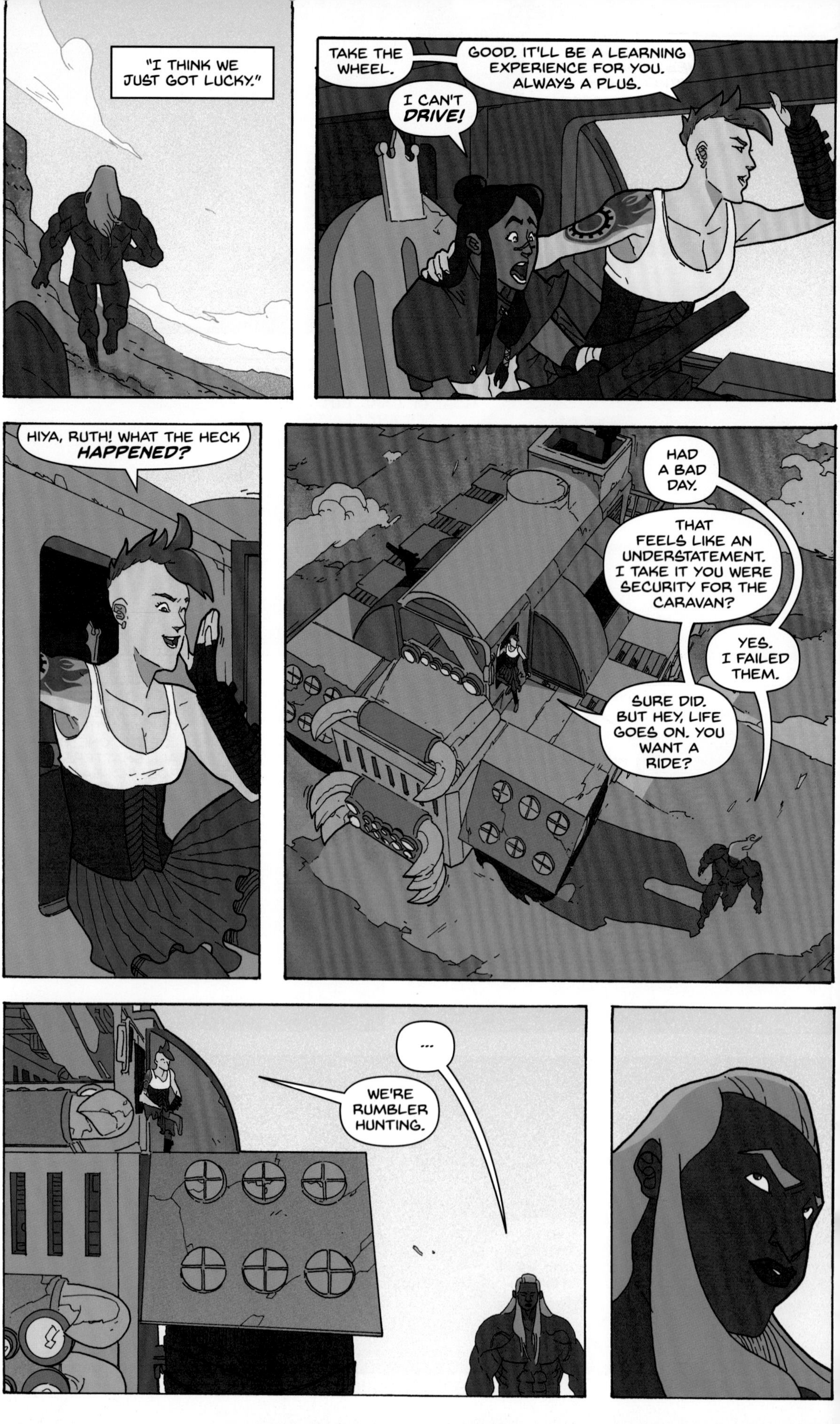
"I THINK WE JUST GOT LUCKY."
TAKE THE WHEEL.
GOOD. IT'LL BE A LEARNING EXPERIENCE FOR YOU. ALWAYS A PLUS.
I CAN'T DRIVE!
HIYA, RUTH! WHAT THE HECK HAPPENED?
HAD A BAD DAY.
THAT FEELS LIKE AN UNDERSTATEMENT. I TAKE IT YOU WERE SECURITY FOR THE CARAVAN?
YES. I FAILED THEM.
SURE DID. BUT HEY, LIFE GOES ON. YOU WANT A RIDE?
...
WE'RE RUMBLER HUNTING.

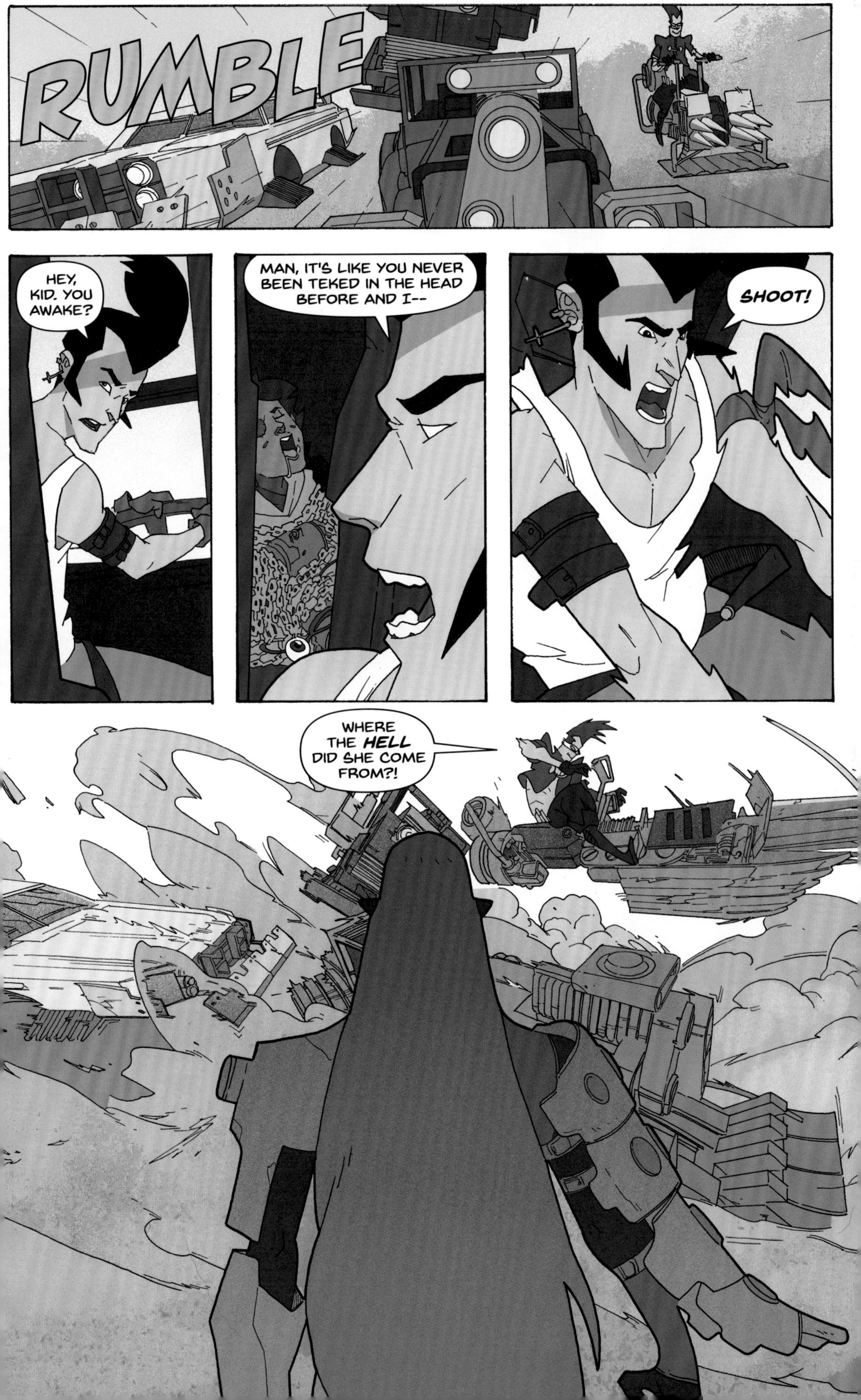
RUMBLE
HEY, KID. YOU AWAKE?
MAN, IT'S LIKE YOU NEVER BEEN TEKED IN THE HEAD BEFORE AND I--
SHOOT!
WHERE THE HELL DID SHE COME FROM?!

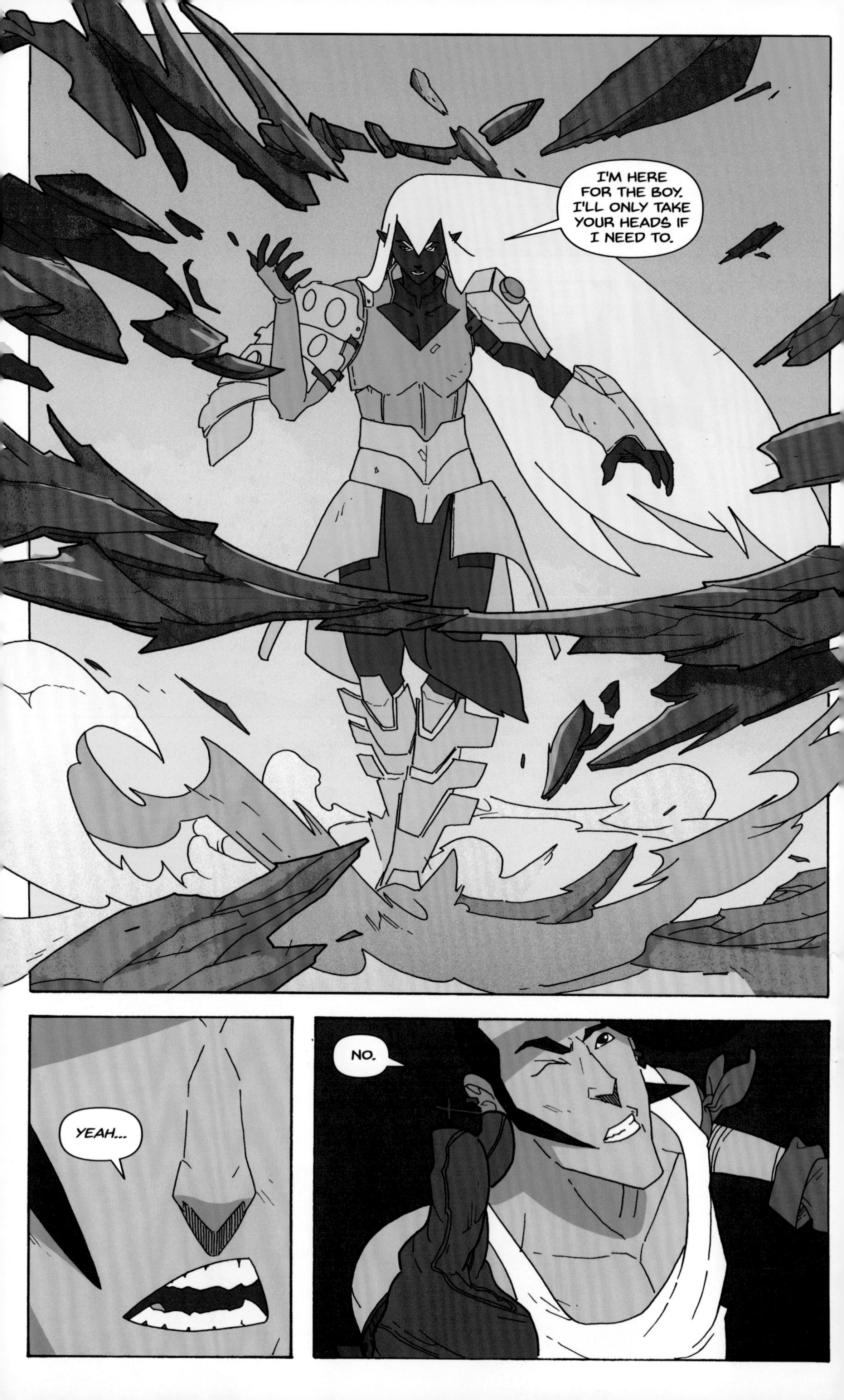
I'M HERE FOR THE BOY. I'LL ONLY TAKE YOUR HEADS IF I NEED TO.
YEAH...
NO.

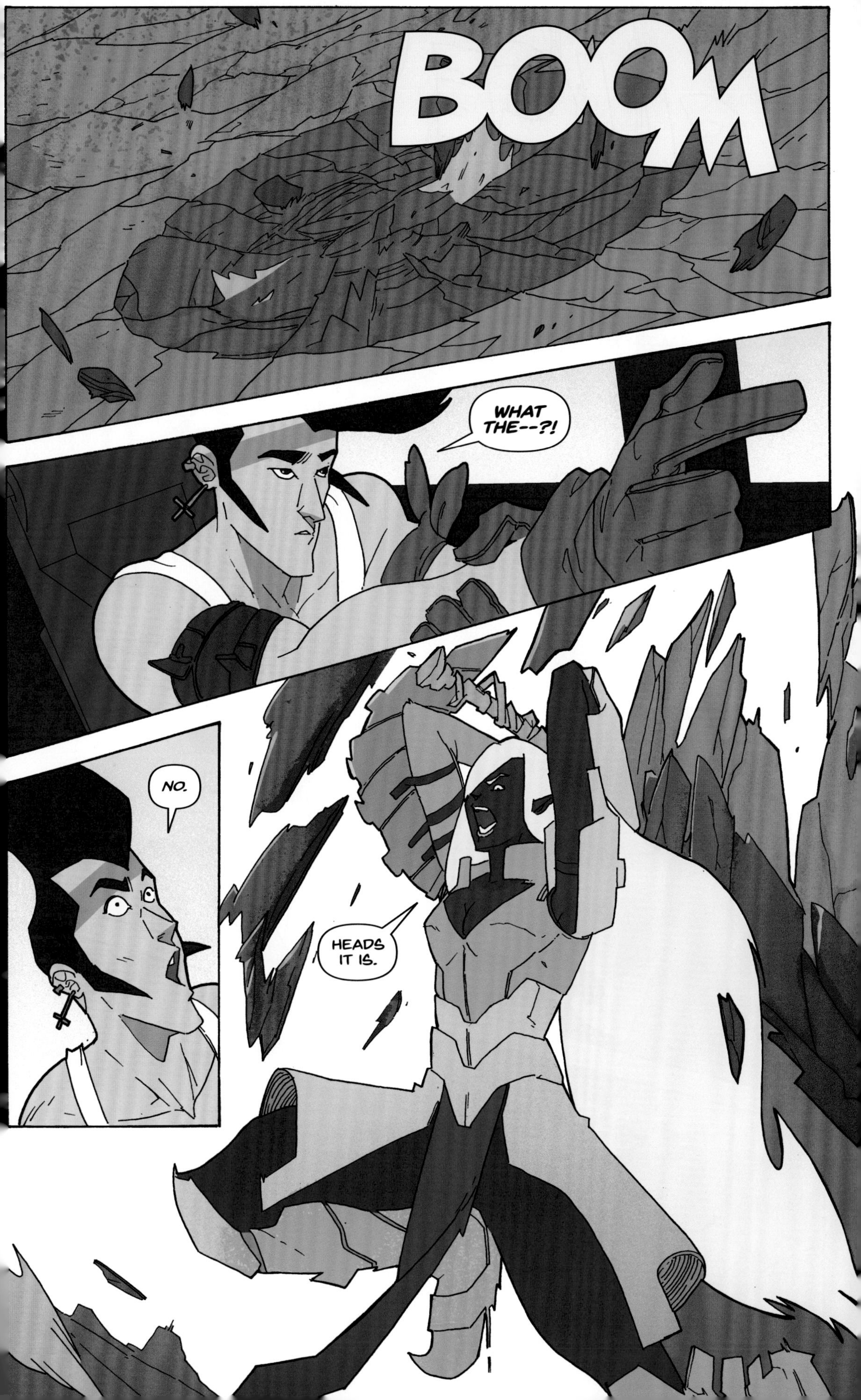
BOOM
WHAT THE--?!
NO.
HEADS IT IS.

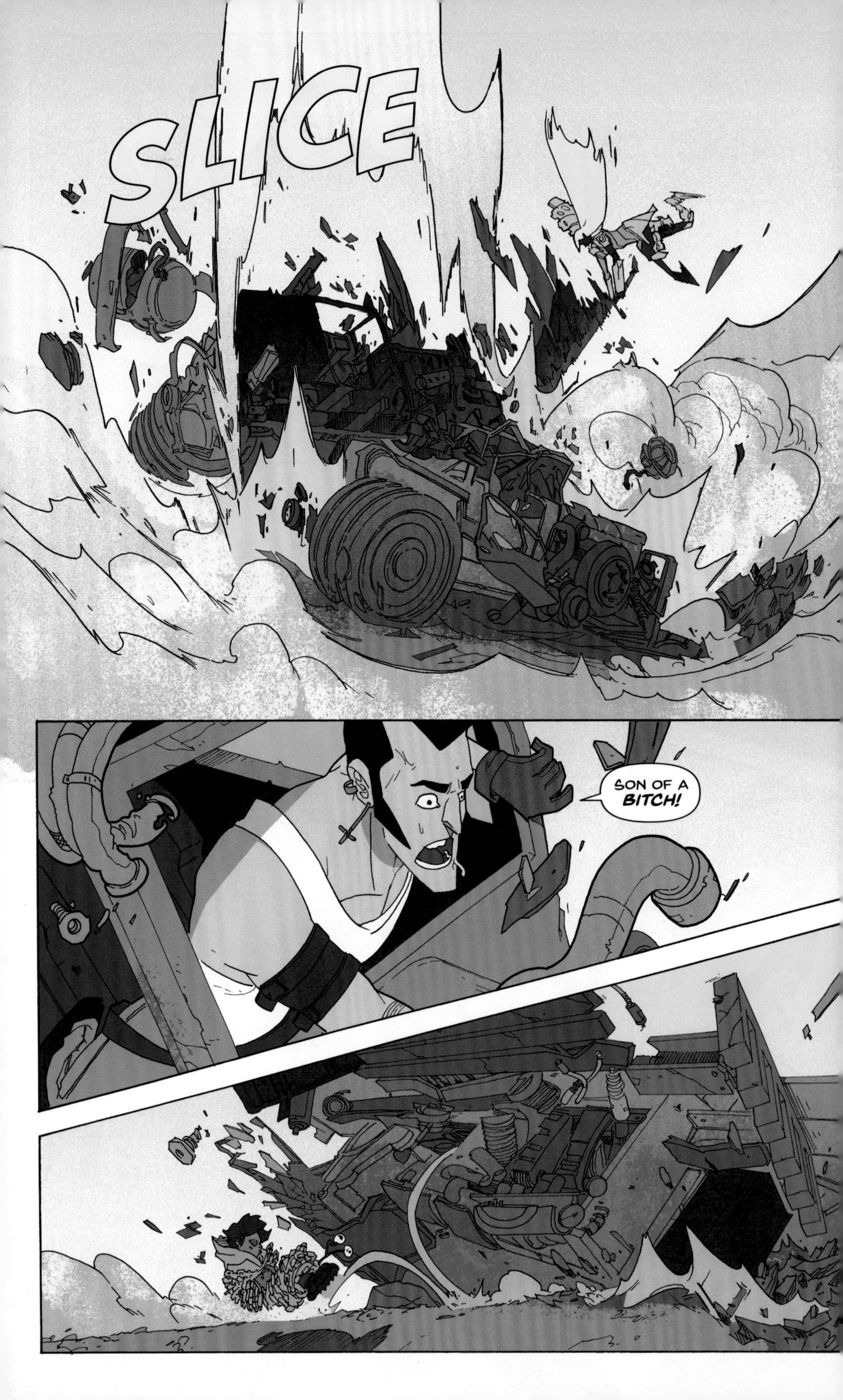
SLICE
SON OF A BITCH!

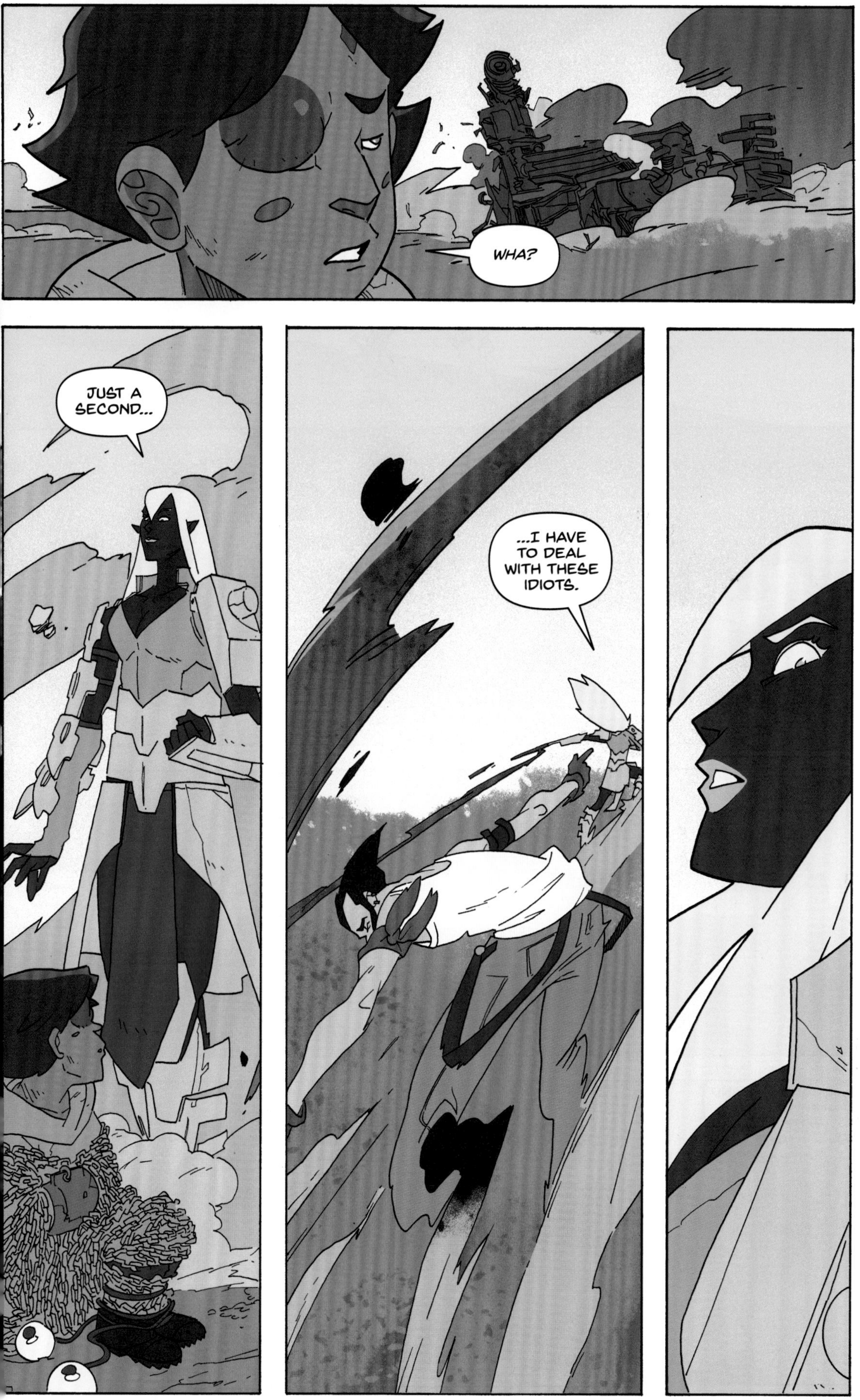
WHA?
JUST A SECOND...
...I HAVE TO DEAL WITH THESE IDIOTS.

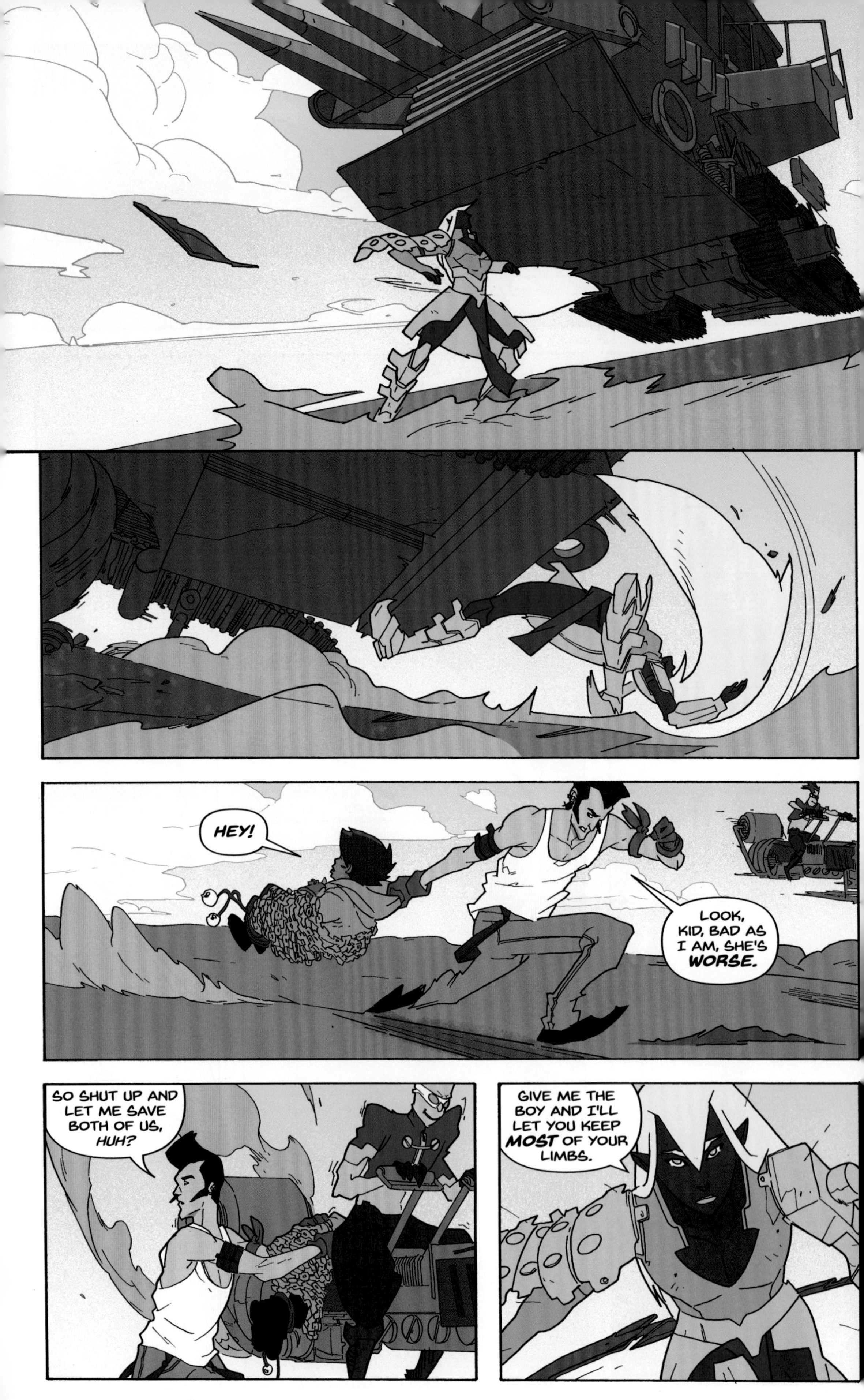
HEY!
LOOK, KID, BAD AS I AM, SHE'S **WORSE.**
SO SHUT UP AND LET ME SAVE BOTH OF US, *HUH?*
GIVE ME THE BOY AND I'LL LET YOU KEEP **MOST** OF YOUR LIMBS.

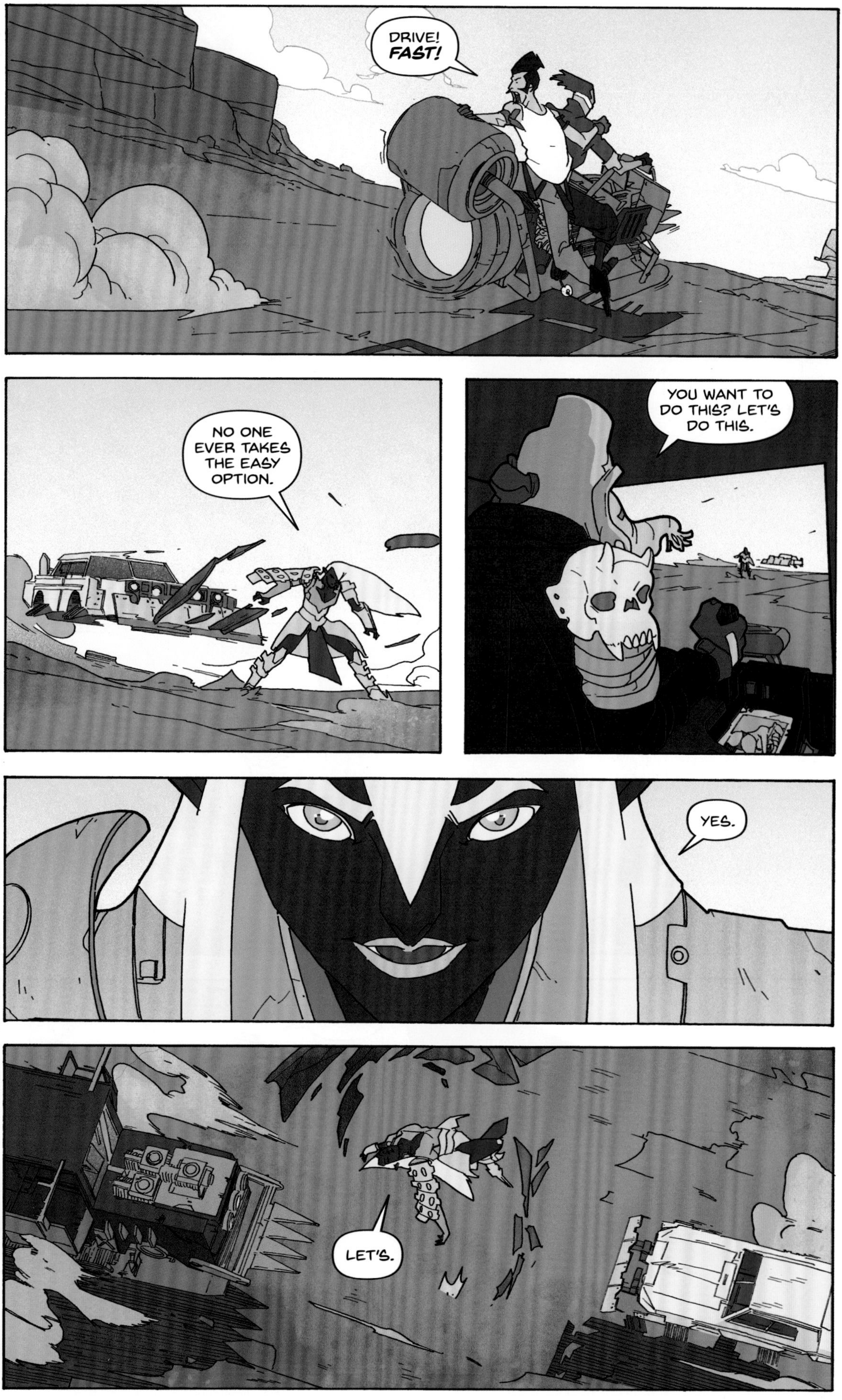
DRIVE! FAST!
NO ONE EVER TAKES THE EASY OPTION.
YOU WANT TO DO THIS? LET'S DO THIS.
YES.
LET'S.

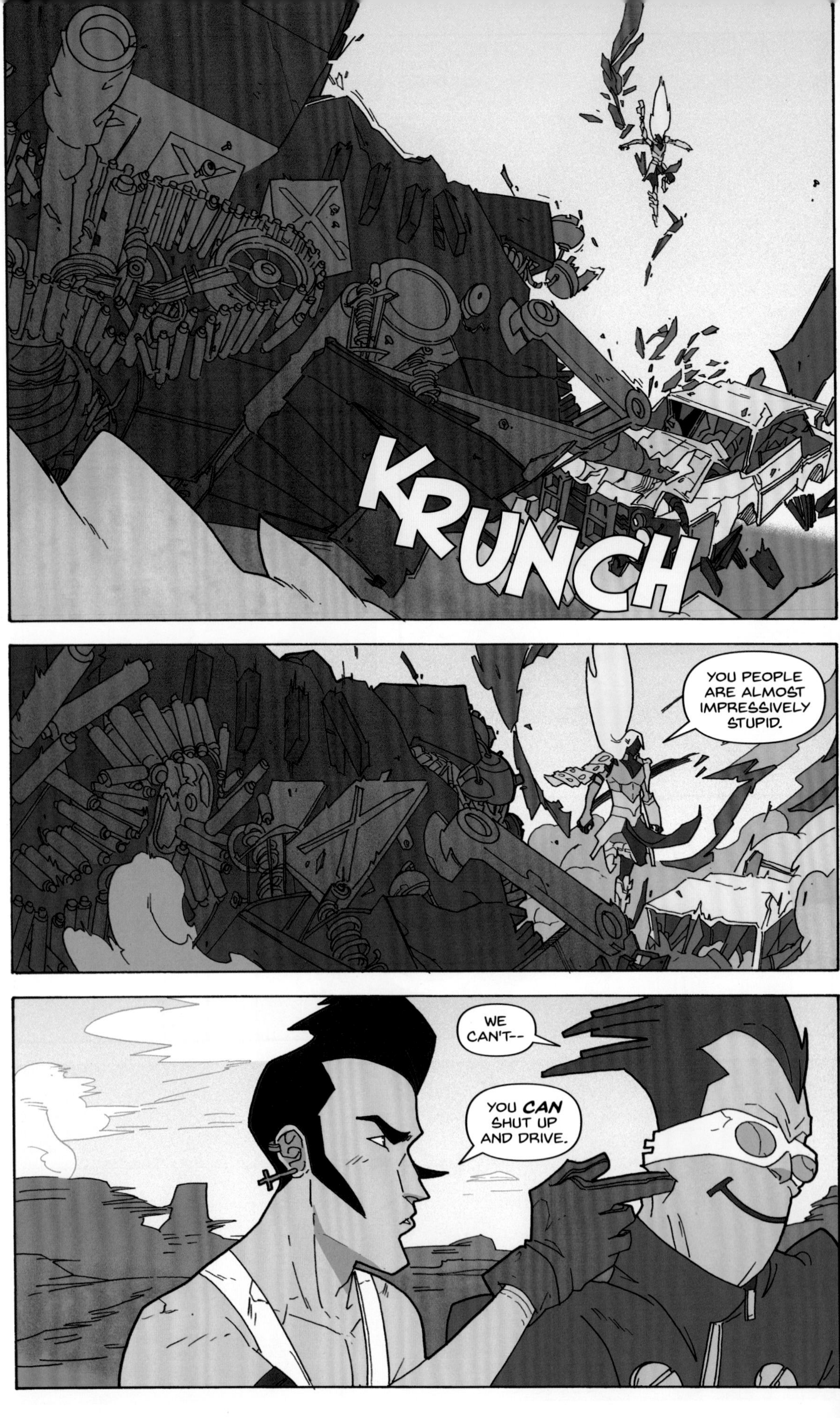
KRUNCH
YOU PEOPLE ARE ALMOST IMPRESSIVELY STUPID.
WE CAN'T--
YOU **CAN** SHUT UP AND DRIVE.

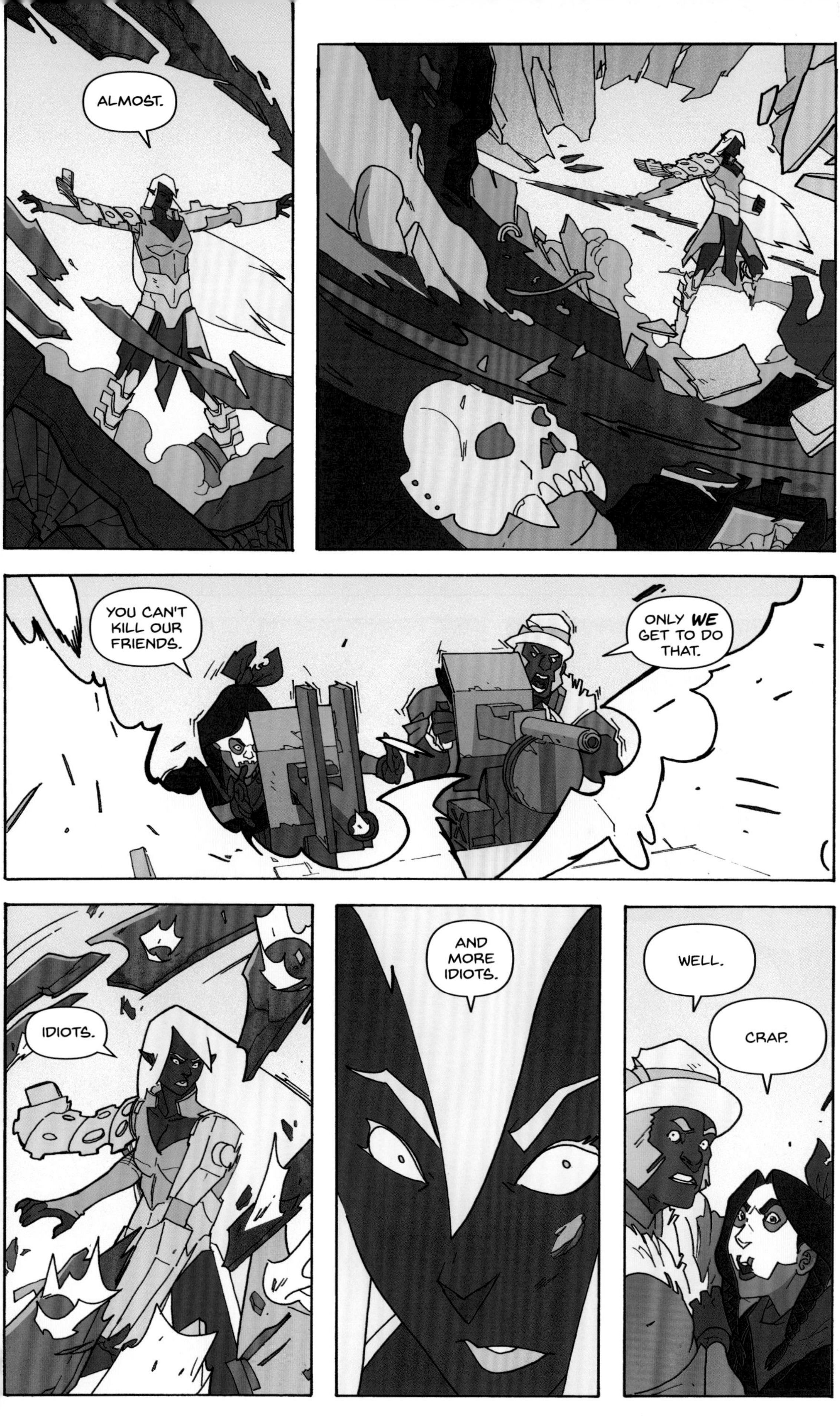
ALMOST.
YOU CAN'T KILL OUR FRIENDS.
ONLY WE GET TO DO THAT.
IDIOTS.
AND MORE IDIOTS.
WELL.
CRAP.

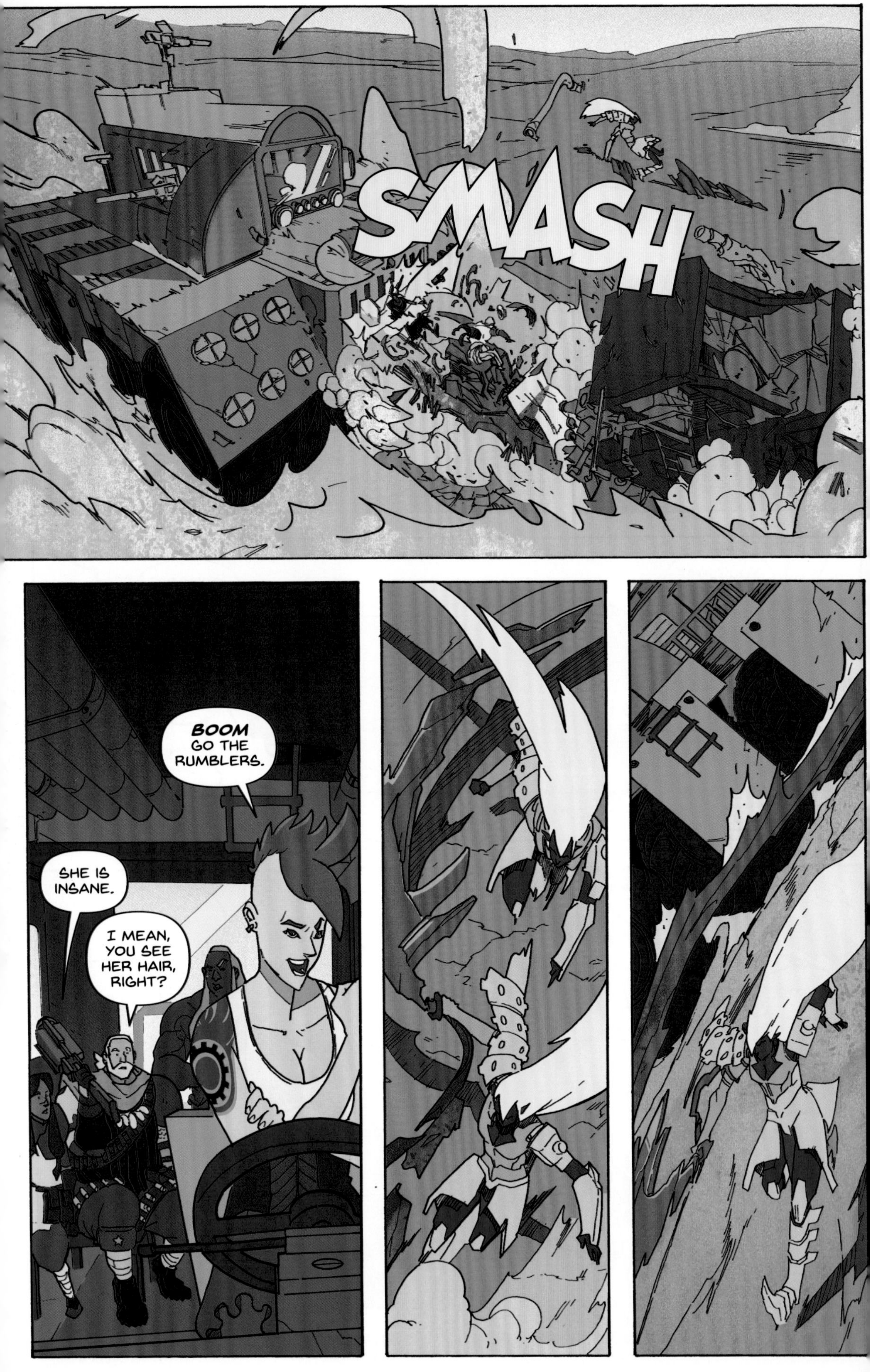
SMASH
BOOM GO THE RUMBLERS.
SHE IS INSANE.
I MEAN, YOU SEE HER HAIR, RIGHT?

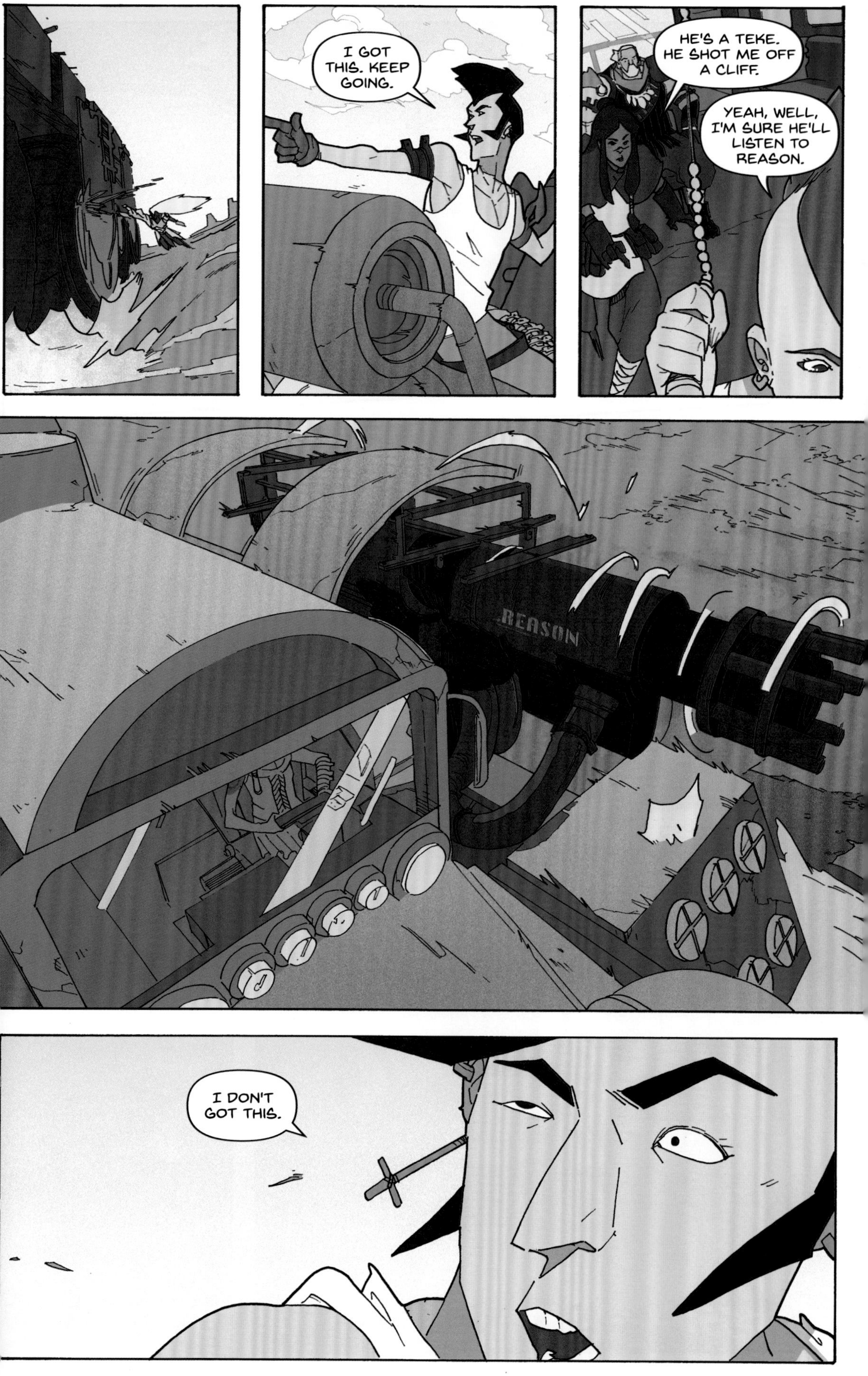
I GOT THIS. KEEP GOING.
HE'S A TEKE. HE SHOT ME OFF A CLIFF.
YEAH, WELL, I'M SURE HE'LL LISTEN TO REASON.
REASON
I DON'T GOT THIS.

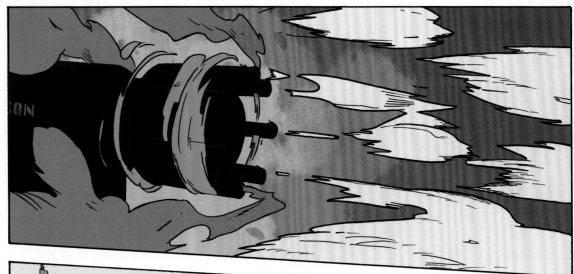

I CAN'T GET A SHOT. GO FASTER.

THIS *IS* FASTER. THIS IS AS FASTER AS IT GETS.

YOU'LL *HIT* ADAM!

IF YOU KEEP JACKING UP MY AIM, I *DEFINITELY* WILL. I KNOW I MAKE THIS LOOK EASY, BUT IT AIN'T.

KRAKRAKRAK

SSSSSSSSSS

WHY DID YOU STOP?

SHE DID NOT. STOP.

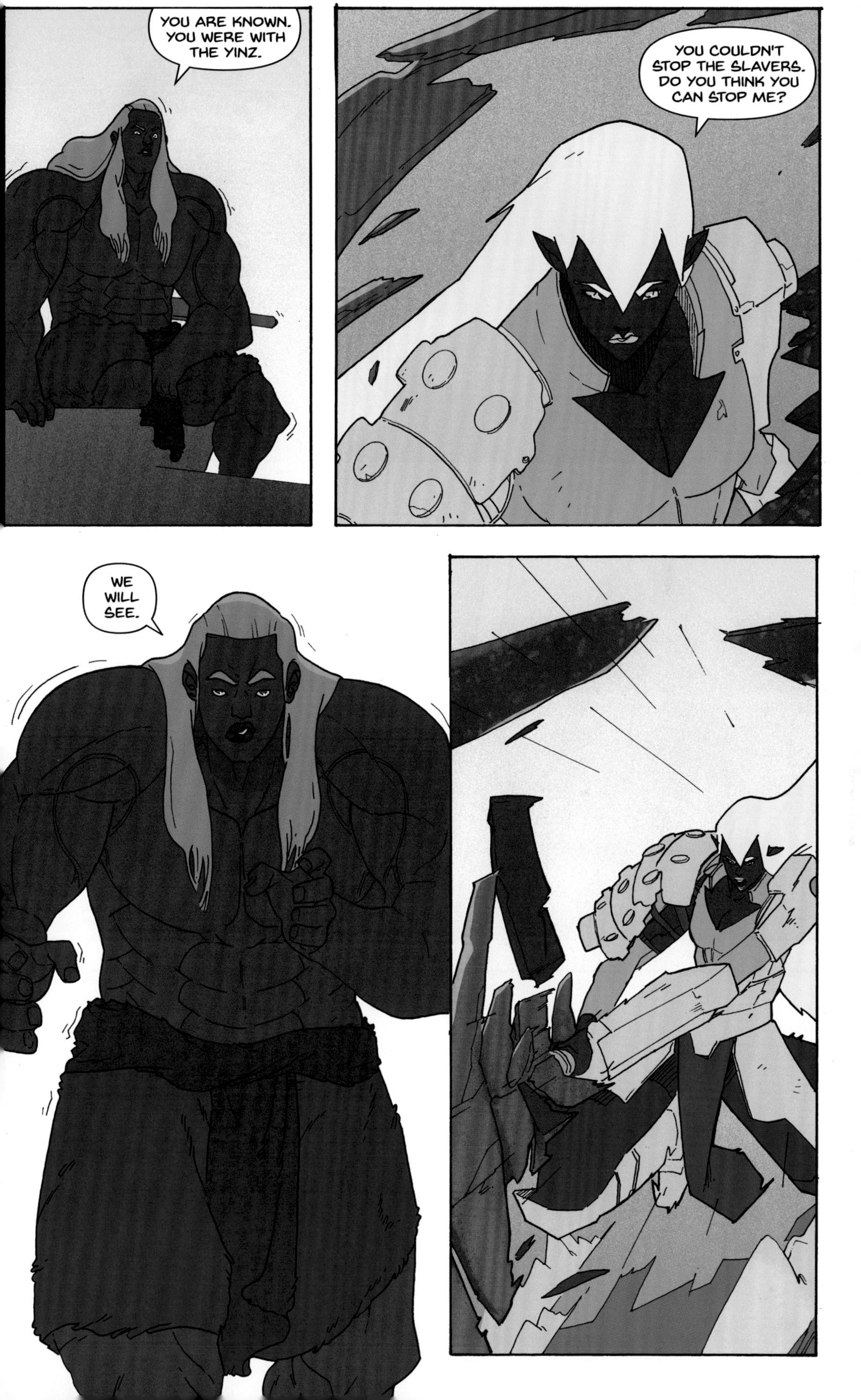
YOU ARE KNOWN. YOU WERE WITH THE YINZ.
YOU COULDN'T STOP THE SLAVERS. DO YOU THINK YOU CAN STOP ME?
WE WILL SEE.

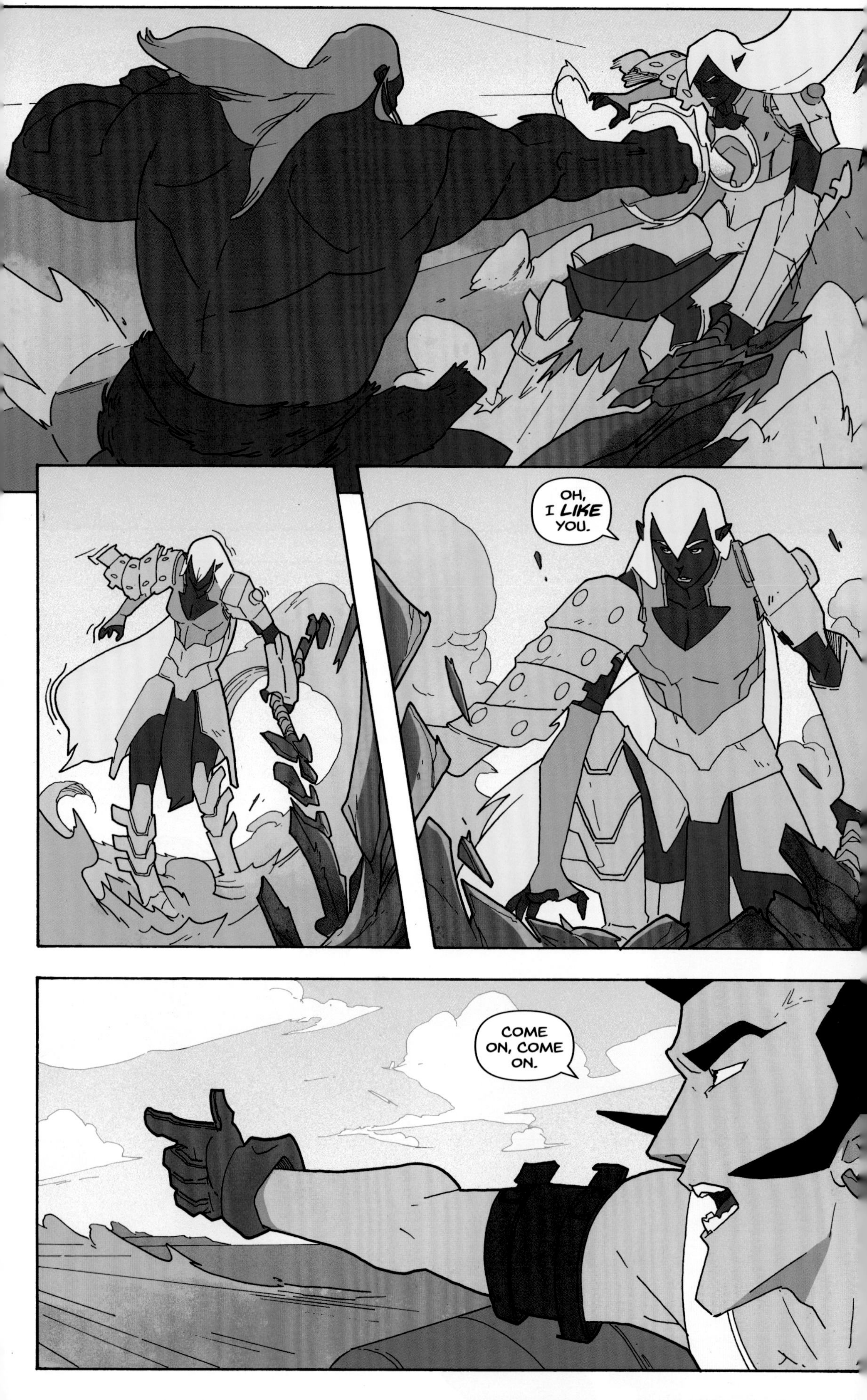
OH, I LIKE YOU.
COME ON, COME ON.

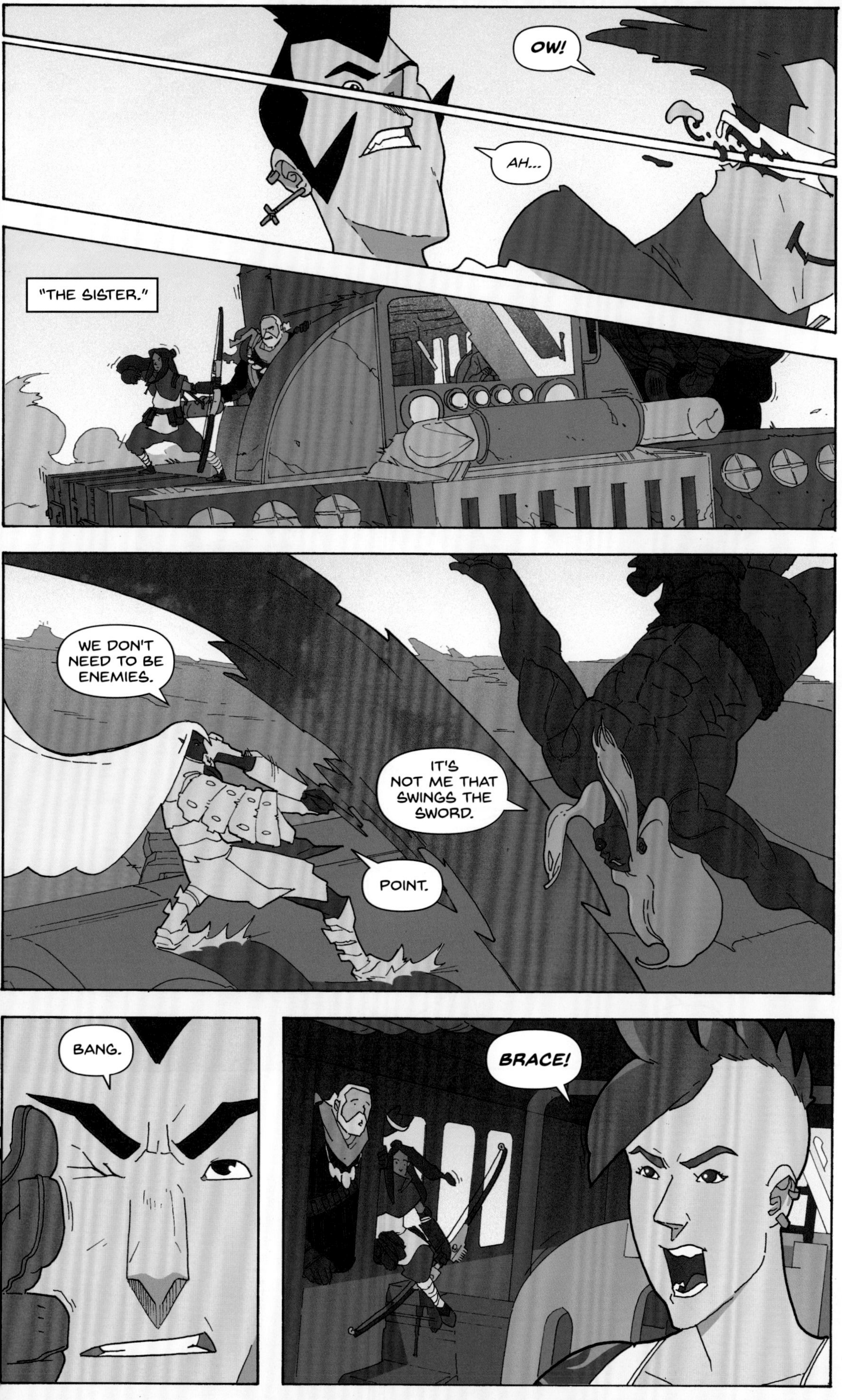
OW!
AH...
"THE SISTER."
WE DON'T NEED TO BE ENEMIES.
IT'S NOT ME THAT SWINGS THE SWORD.
POINT.
BANG.
BRACE!

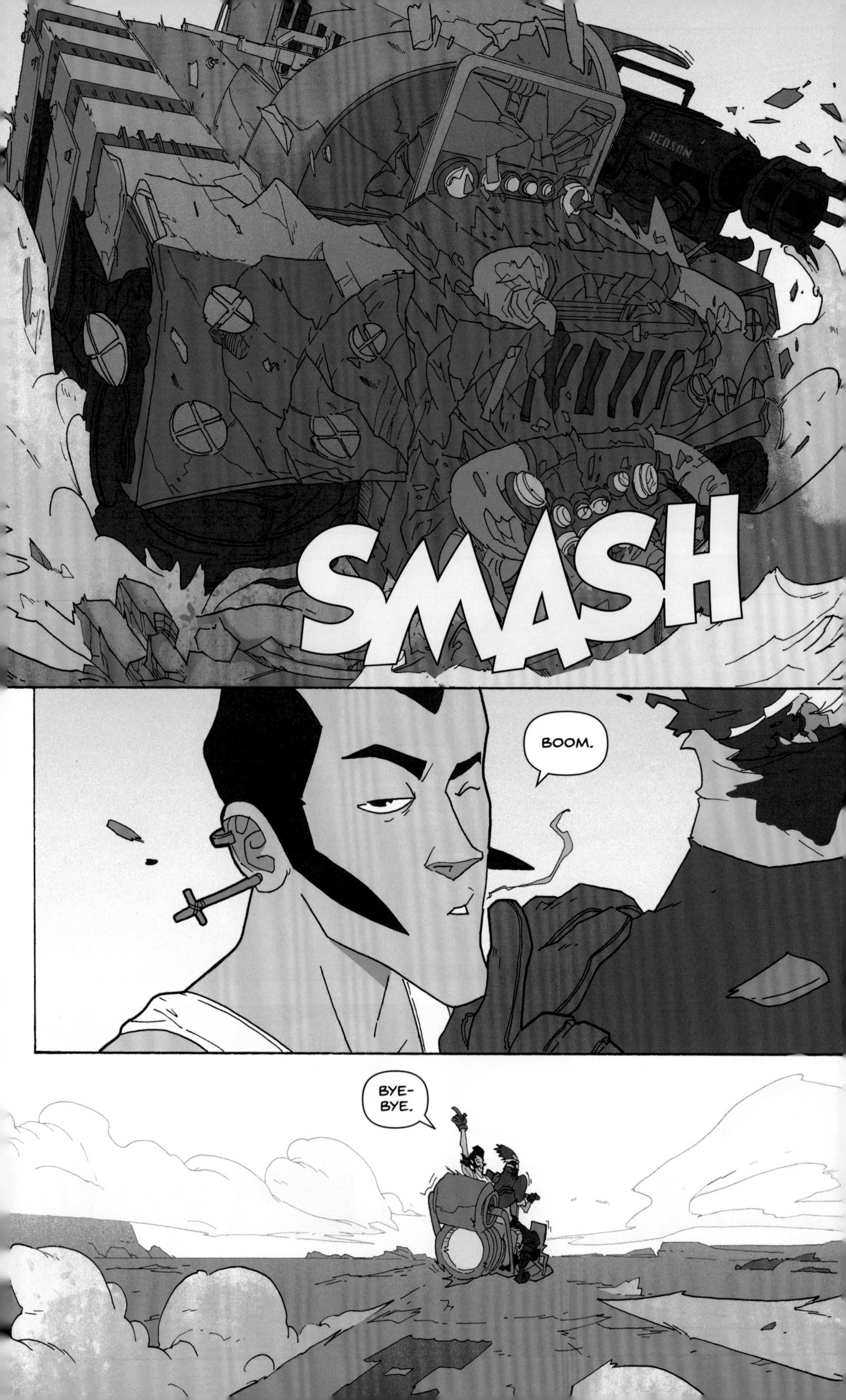
SMASH
BOOM.
BYE-BYE.

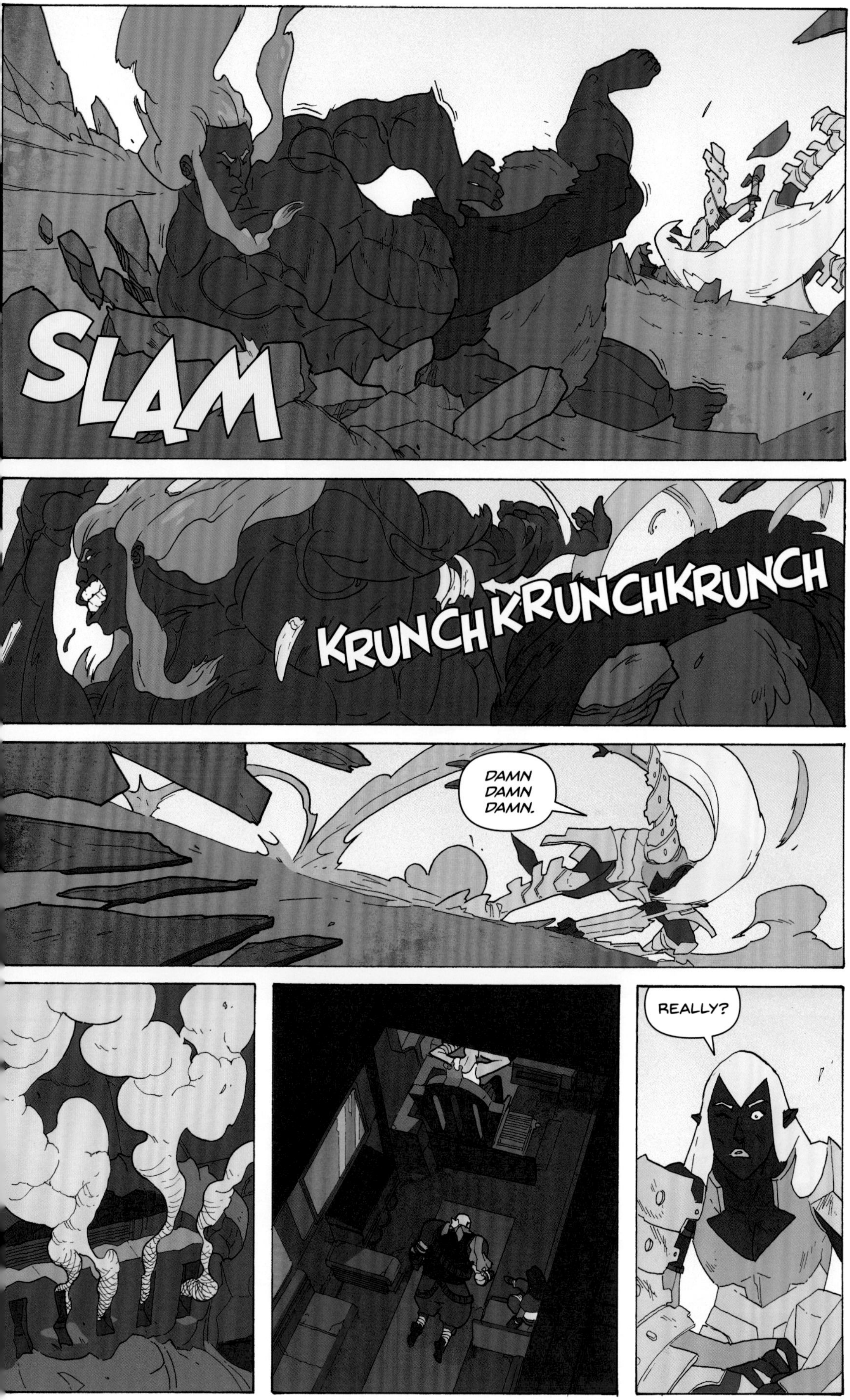
SLAM
KRUNCHKRUNCHKRUNCH
DAMN DAMN DAMN.
REALLY?

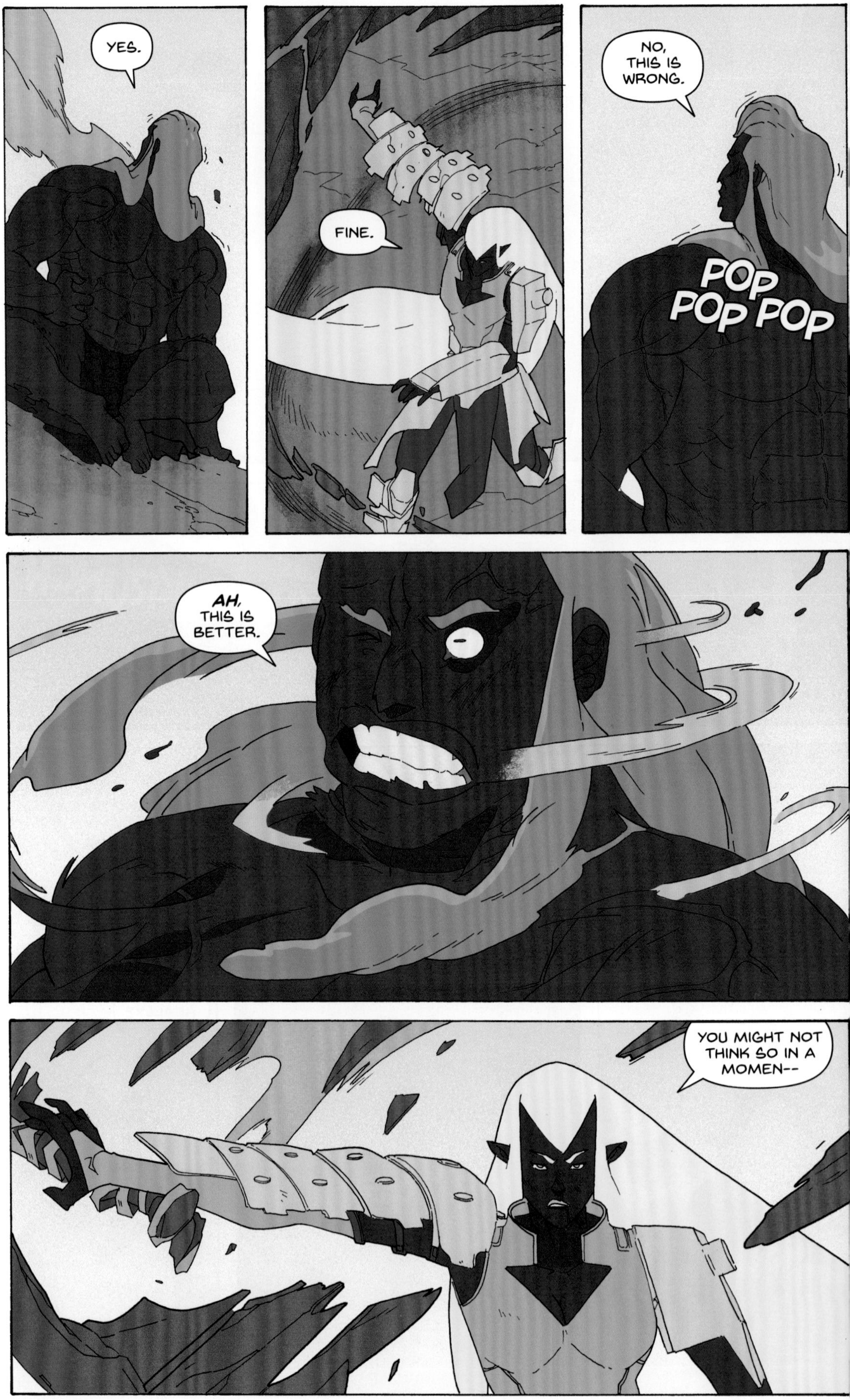
YES.
FINE.
NO, THIS IS WRONG.
POP POP POP
AH, THIS IS BETTER.
YOU MIGHT NOT THINK SO IN A MOMEN--

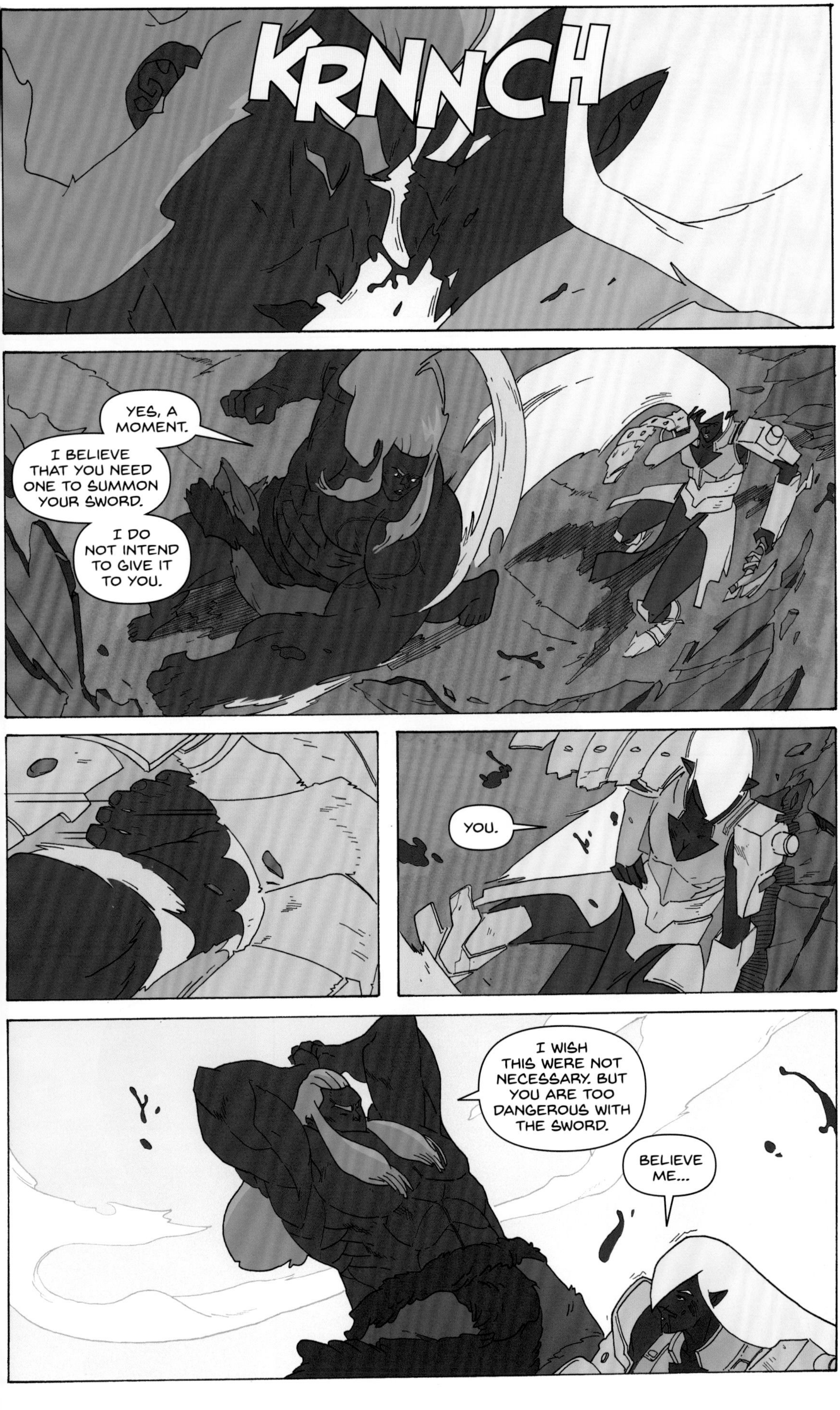
KRNNCH
YES, A MOMENT.
I BELIEVE THAT YOU NEED ONE TO SUMMON YOUR SWORD.
I DO NOT INTEND TO GIVE IT TO YOU.
YOU.
I WISH THIS WERE NOT NECESSARY. BUT YOU ARE TOO DANGEROUS WITH THE SWORD.
BELIEVE ME...

I'M PLENTY DANGEROUS WITHOUT IT.

MMF!

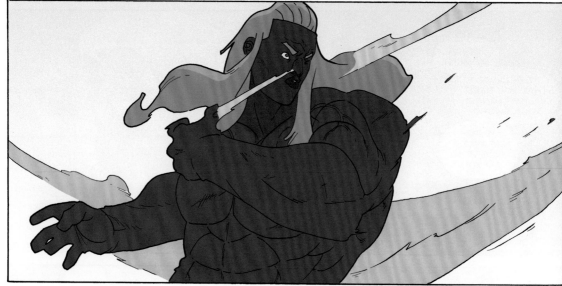

HMM...

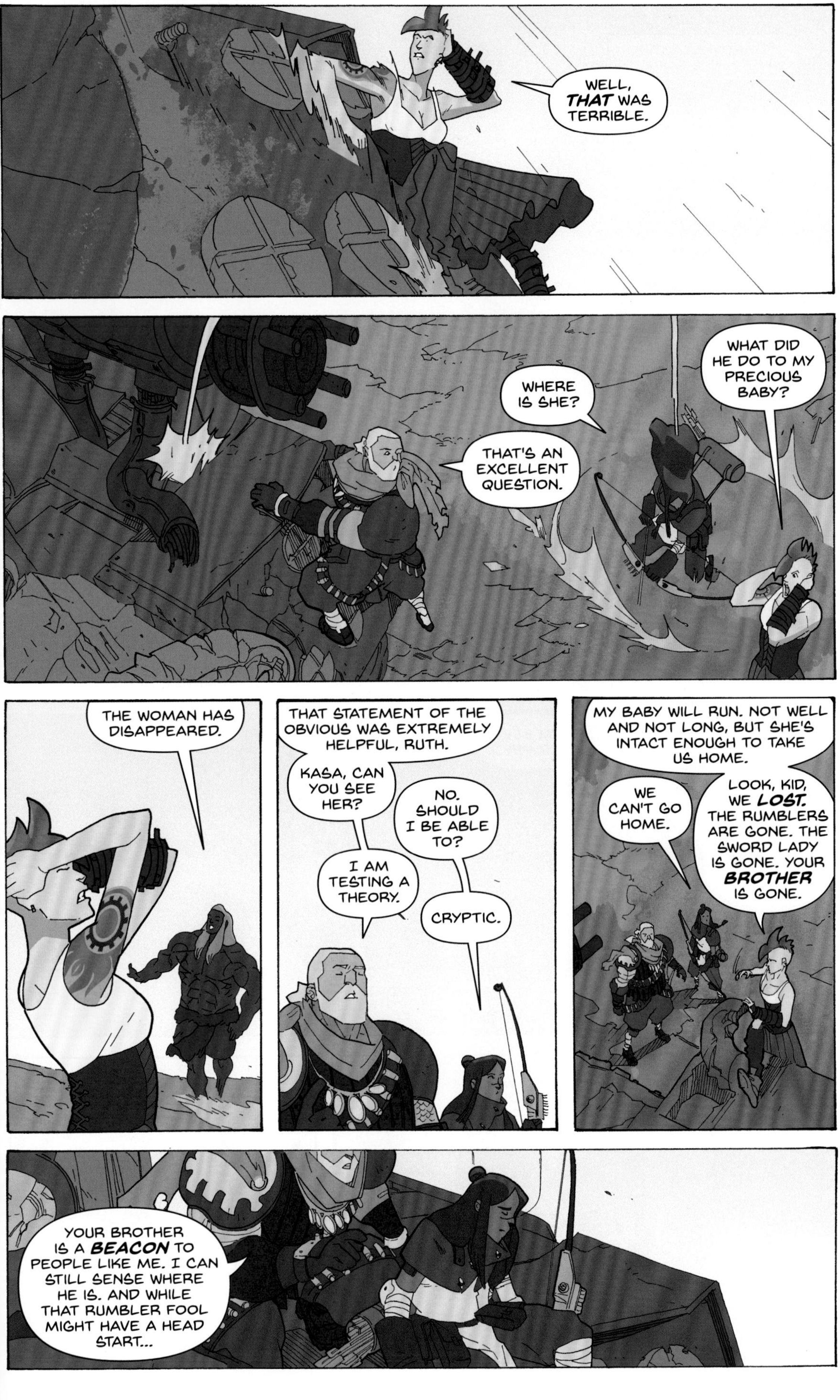
WELL, *THAT* WAS TERRIBLE.
WHERE IS SHE?
THAT'S AN EXCELLENT QUESTION.
WHAT DID HE DO TO MY PRECIOUS BABY?
THE WOMAN HAS DISAPPEARED.
THAT STATEMENT OF THE OBVIOUS WAS EXTREMELY HELPFUL, RUTH.
KASA, CAN YOU SEE HER?
NO. SHOULD I BE ABLE TO?
I AM TESTING A THEORY.
CRYPTIC.
MY BABY WILL RUN. NOT WELL AND NOT LONG, BUT SHE'S INTACT ENOUGH TO TAKE US HOME.
WE CAN'T GO HOME.
LOOK, KID, WE *LOST.* THE RUMBLERS ARE GONE. THE SWORD LADY IS GONE. YOUR *BROTHER* IS GONE.
YOUR BROTHER IS A *BEACON* TO PEOPLE LIKE ME. I CAN STILL SENSE WHERE HE IS. AND WHILE THAT RUMBLER FOOL MIGHT HAVE A HEAD START...

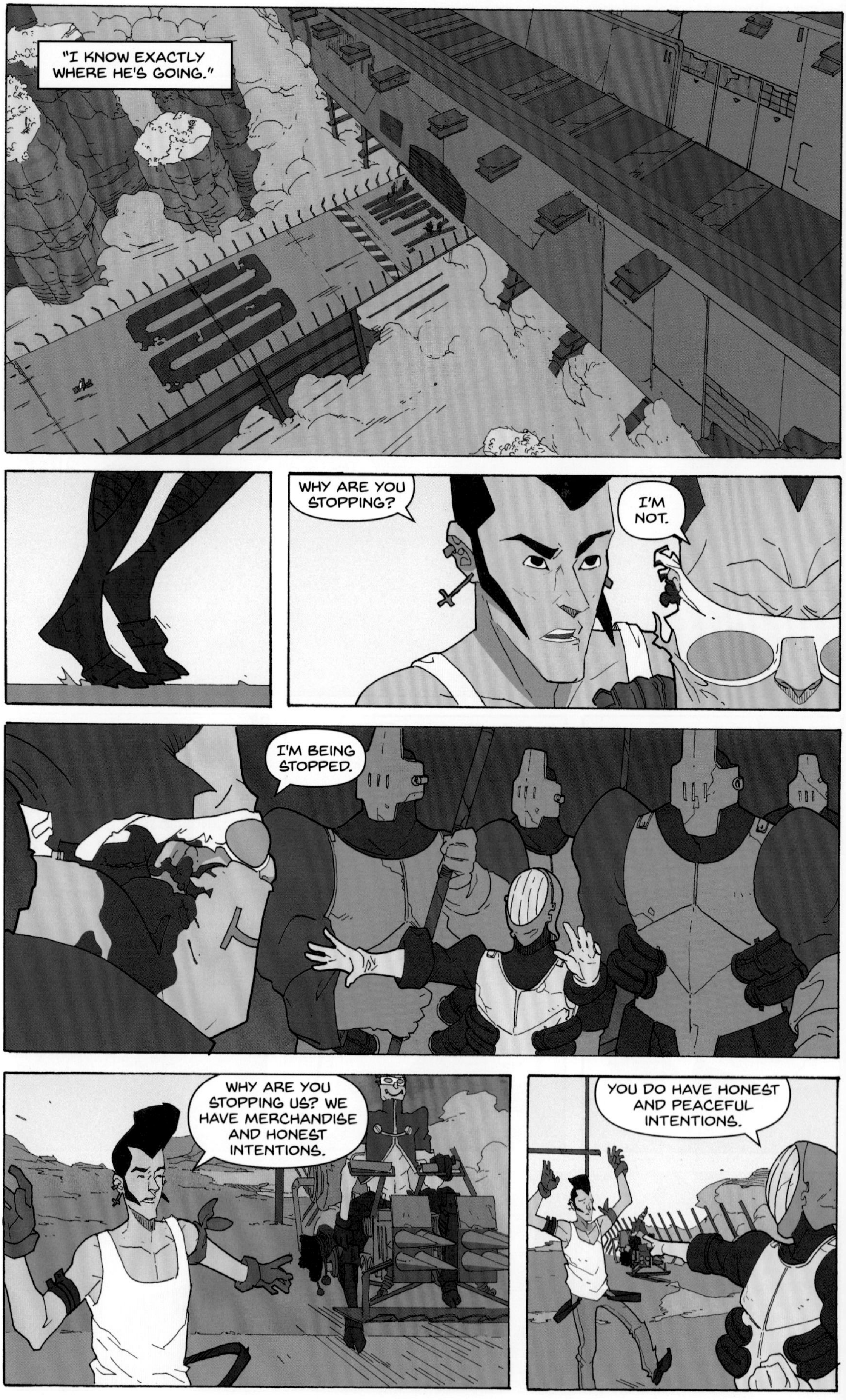
"I KNOW EXACTLY WHERE HE'S GOING."
WHY ARE YOU STOPPING?
I'M NOT.
I'M BEING STOPPED.
WHY ARE YOU STOPPING US? WE HAVE MERCHANDISE AND HONEST INTENTIONS.
YOU DO HAVE HONEST AND PEACEFUL INTENTIONS.

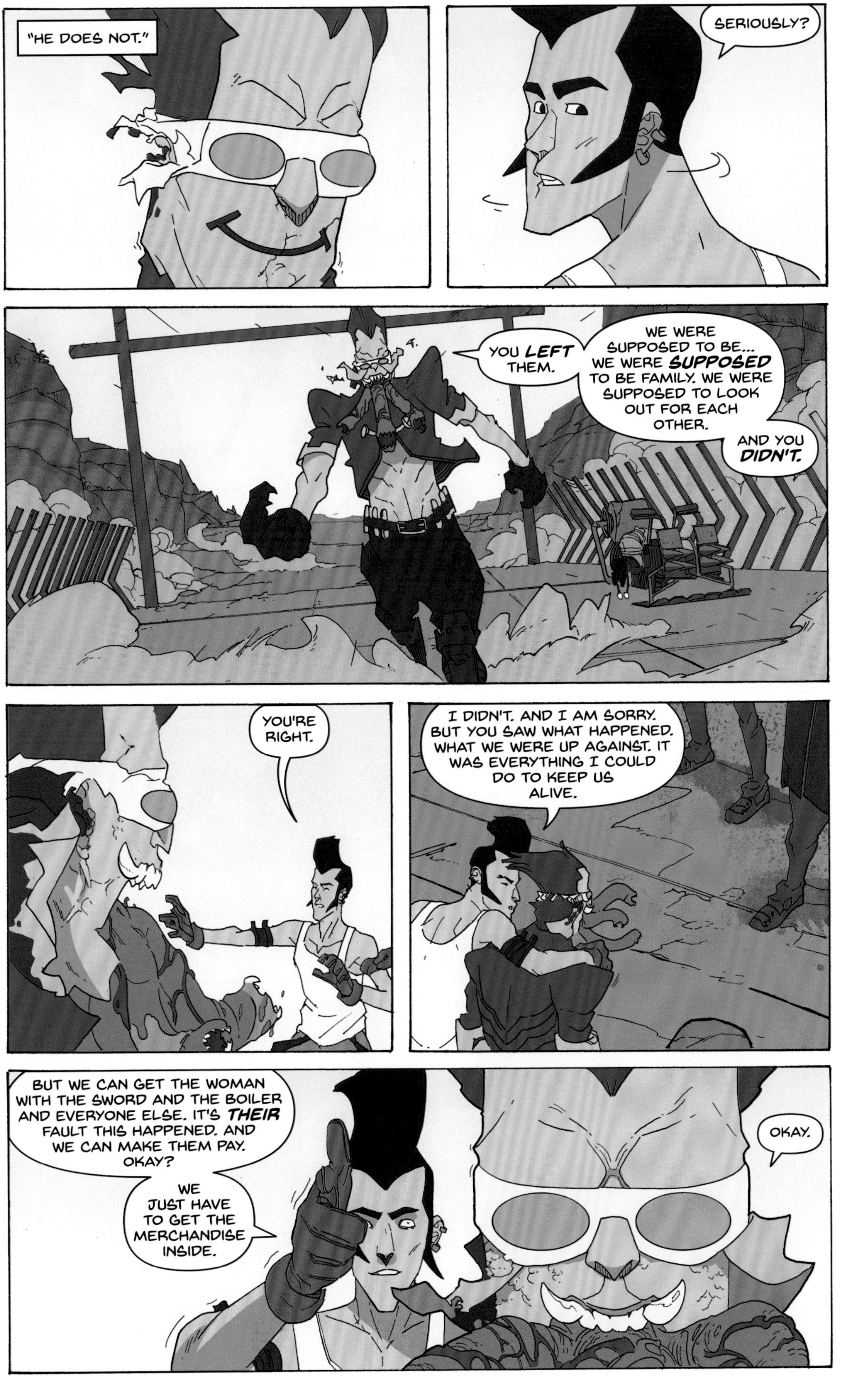
"HE DOES NOT."
SERIOUSLY?
YOU LEFT THEM.
WE WERE SUPPOSED TO BE... WE WERE SUPPOSED TO BE FAMILY. WE WERE SUPPOSED TO LOOK OUT FOR EACH OTHER.
AND YOU DIDN'T.
YOU'RE RIGHT.
I DIDN'T. AND I AM SORRY. BUT YOU SAW WHAT HAPPENED. WHAT WE WERE UP AGAINST. IT WAS EVERYTHING I COULD DO TO KEEP US ALIVE.
BUT WE CAN GET THE WOMAN WITH THE SWORD AND THE BOILER AND EVERYONE ELSE. IT'S THEIR FAULT THIS HAPPENED. AND WE CAN MAKE THEM PAY. OKAY?
WE JUST HAVE TO GET THE MERCHANDISE INSIDE.
OKAY.

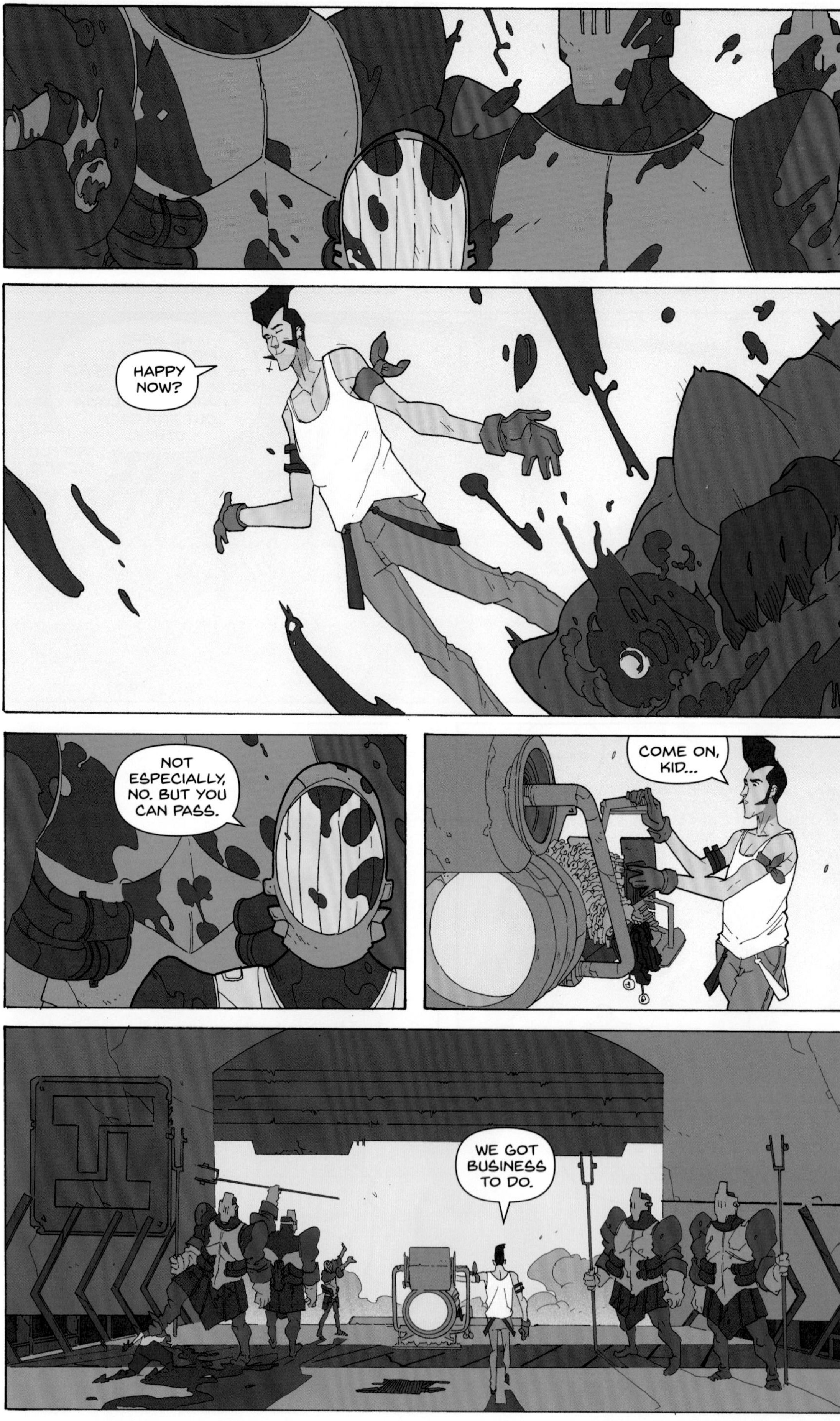
HAPPY NOW?
NOT ESPECIALLY, NO. BUT YOU CAN PASS.
COME ON, KID...
WE GOT BUSINESS TO DO.

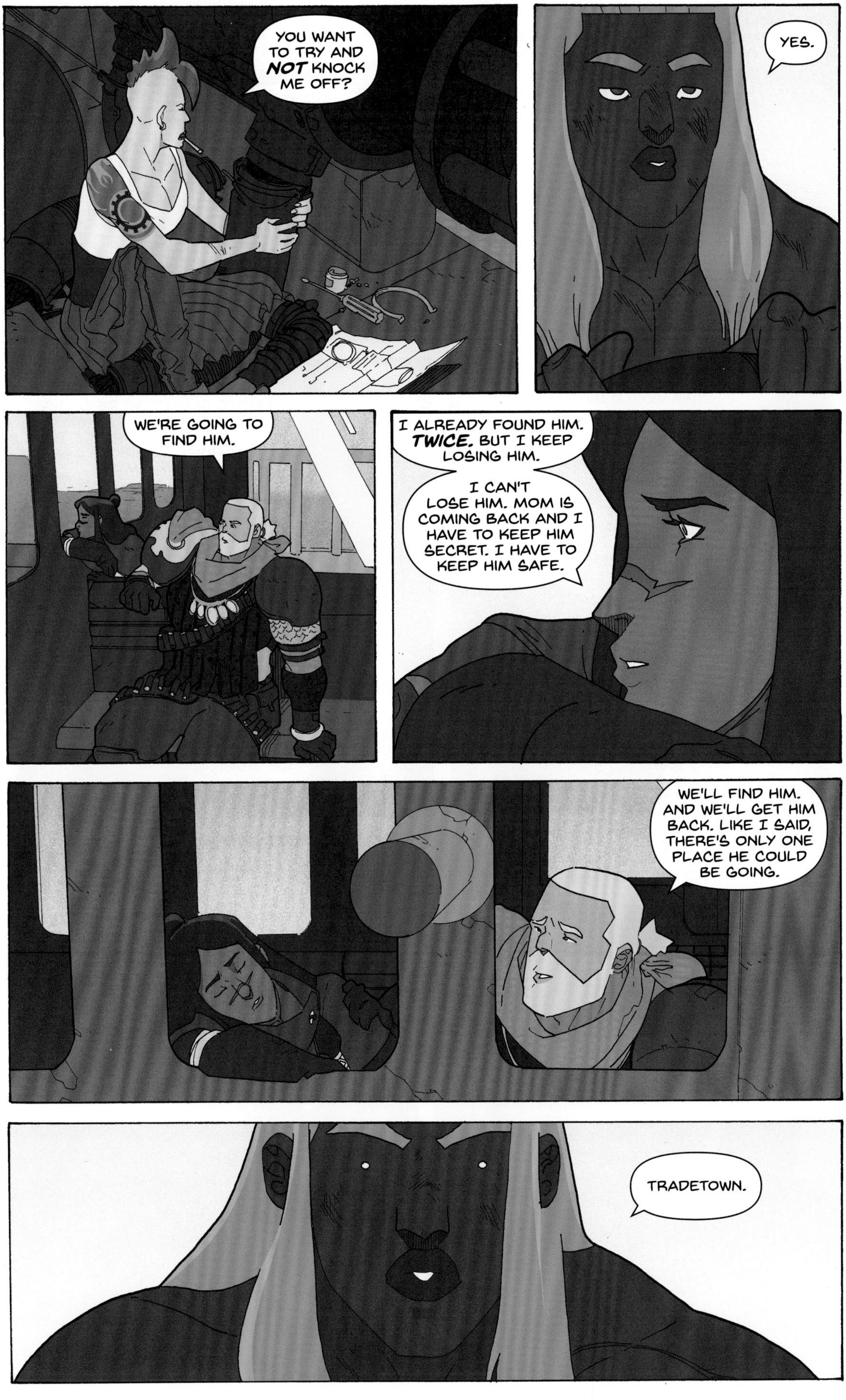
YOU WANT TO TRY AND NOT KNOCK ME OFF?
YES.
WE'RE GOING TO FIND HIM.
I ALREADY FOUND HIM. TWICE. BUT I KEEP LOSING HIM.
I CAN'T LOSE HIM. MOM IS COMING BACK AND I HAVE TO KEEP HIM SECRET. I HAVE TO KEEP HIM SAFE.
WE'LL FIND HIM. AND WE'LL GET HIM BACK. LIKE I SAID, THERE'S ONLY ONE PLACE HE COULD BE GOING.
TRADETOWN.

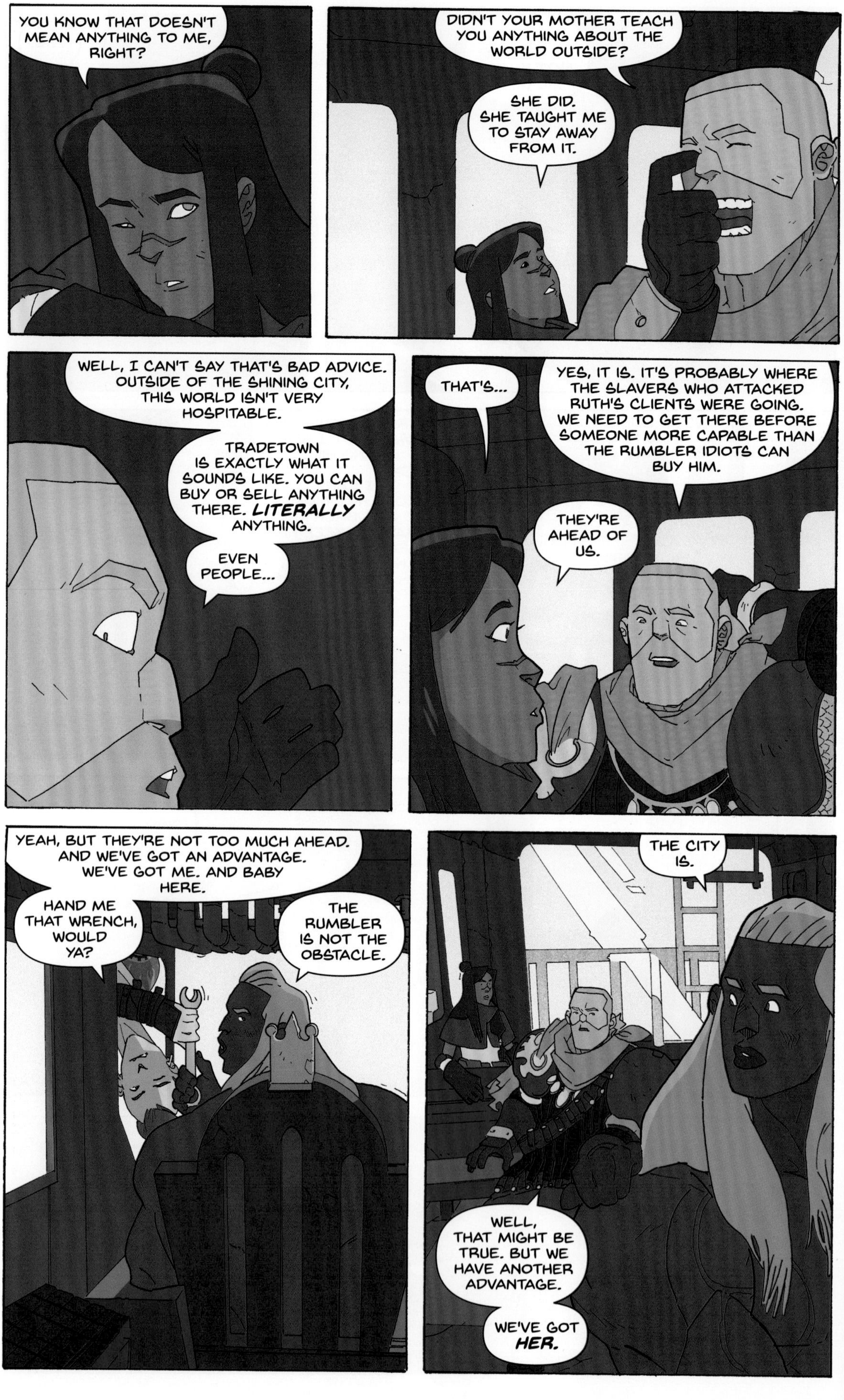
YOU KNOW THAT DOESN'T MEAN ANYTHING TO ME, RIGHT?
DIDN'T YOUR MOTHER TEACH YOU ANYTHING ABOUT THE WORLD OUTSIDE?
SHE DID. SHE TAUGHT ME TO STAY AWAY FROM IT.
WELL, I CAN'T SAY THAT'S BAD ADVICE. OUTSIDE OF THE SHINING CITY, THIS WORLD ISN'T VERY HOSPITABLE.
TRADETOWN IS EXACTLY WHAT IT SOUNDS LIKE. YOU CAN BUY OR SELL ANYTHING THERE. *LITERALLY* ANYTHING.
EVEN PEOPLE...
THAT'S...
YES, IT IS. IT'S PROBABLY WHERE THE SLAVERS WHO ATTACKED RUTH'S CLIENTS WERE GOING. WE NEED TO GET THERE BEFORE SOMEONE MORE CAPABLE THAN THE RUMBLER IDIOTS CAN BUY HIM.
THEY'RE AHEAD OF US.
YEAH, BUT THEY'RE NOT TOO MUCH AHEAD. AND WE'VE GOT AN ADVANTAGE. WE'VE GOT ME. AND BABY HERE.
HAND ME THAT WRENCH, WOULD YA?
THE RUMBLER IS NOT THE OBSTACLE.
THE CITY IS.
WELL, THAT MIGHT BE TRUE. BUT WE HAVE ANOTHER ADVANTAGE.
WE'VE GOT *HER.*

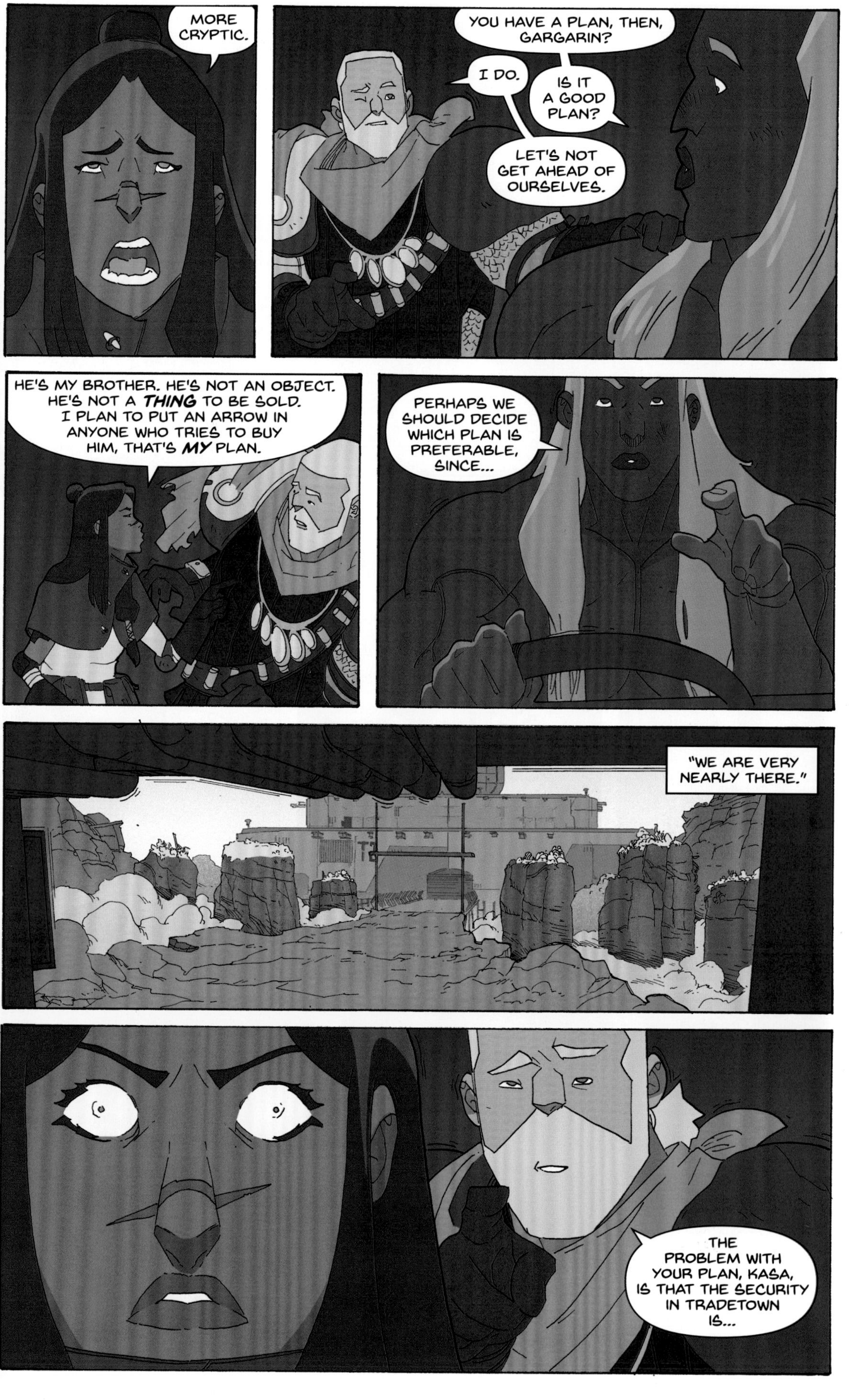
MORE CRYPTIC.
YOU HAVE A PLAN, THEN, GARGARIN?
I DO.
IS IT A GOOD PLAN?
LET'S NOT GET AHEAD OF OURSELVES.
HE'S MY BROTHER. HE'S NOT AN OBJECT. HE'S NOT A THING TO BE SOLD. I PLAN TO PUT AN ARROW IN ANYONE WHO TRIES TO BUY HIM, THAT'S MY PLAN.
PERHAPS WE SHOULD DECIDE WHICH PLAN IS PREFERABLE, SINCE...
"WE ARE VERY NEARLY THERE."
THE PROBLEM WITH YOUR PLAN, KASA, IS THAT THE SECURITY IN TRADETOWN IS...

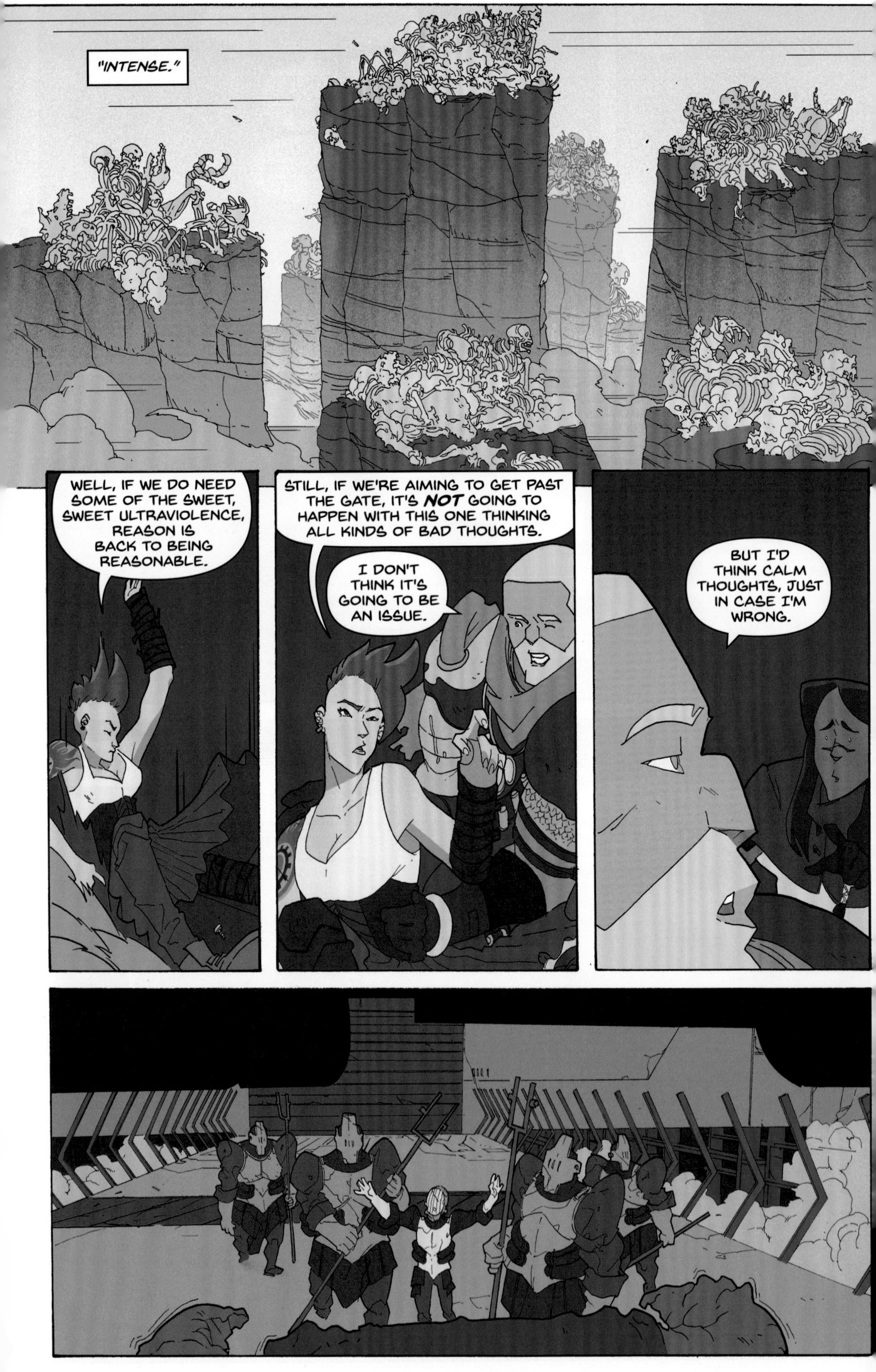
"INTENSE."
WELL, IF WE DO NEED SOME OF THE SWEET, SWEET ULTRAVIOLENCE, REASON IS BACK TO BEING REASONABLE.
STILL, IF WE'RE AIMING TO GET PAST THE GATE, IT'S NOT GOING TO HAPPEN WITH THIS ONE THINKING ALL KINDS OF BAD THOUGHTS.
I DON'T THINK IT'S GOING TO BE AN ISSUE.
BUT I'D THINK CALM THOUGHTS, JUST IN CASE I'M WRONG.

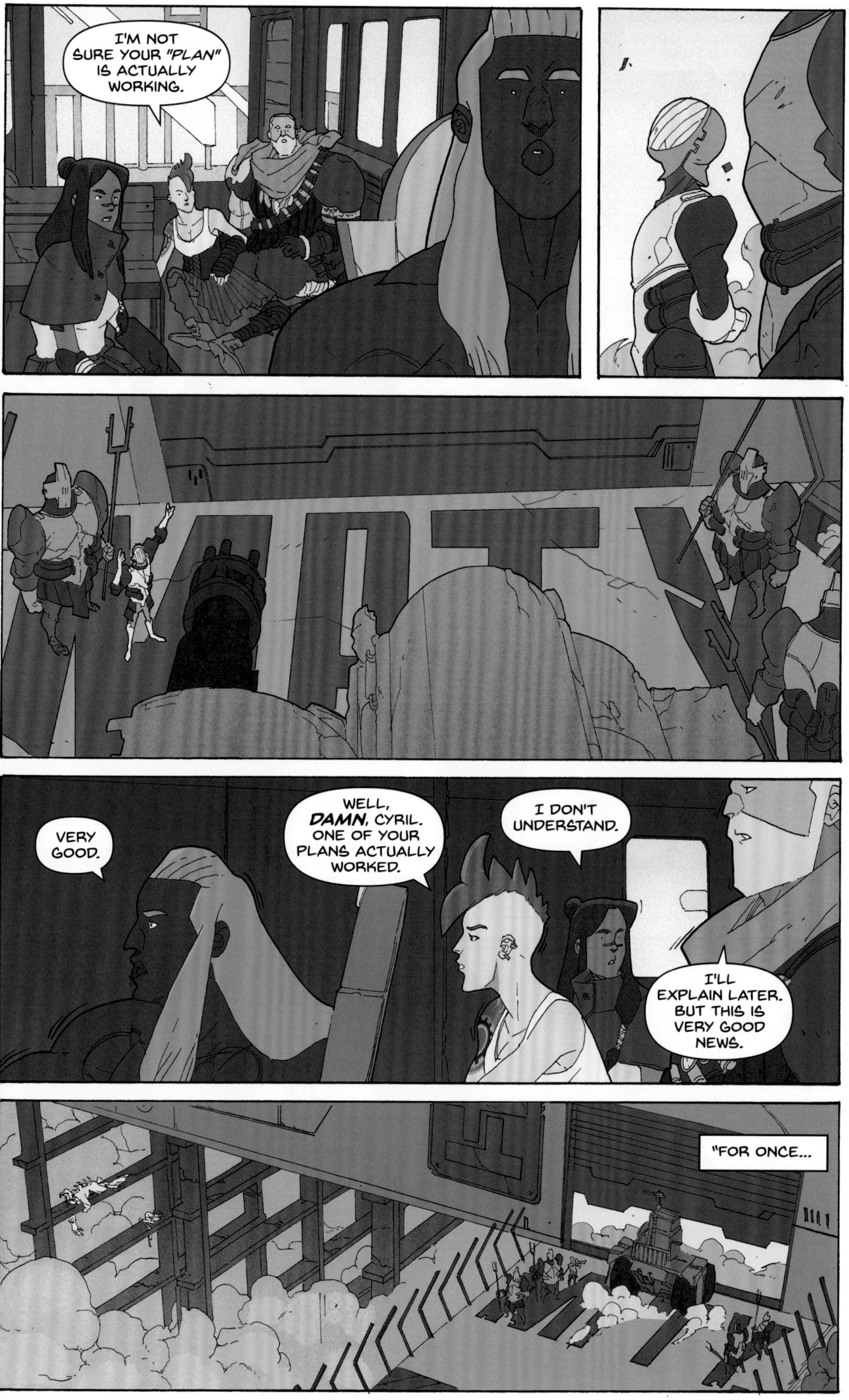
I'M NOT SURE YOUR "PLAN" IS ACTUALLY WORKING.
VERY GOOD.
WELL, DAMN, CYRIL. ONE OF YOUR PLANS ACTUALLY WORKED.
I DON'T UNDERSTAND.
I'LL EXPLAIN LATER. BUT THIS IS VERY GOOD NEWS.
"FOR ONCE...

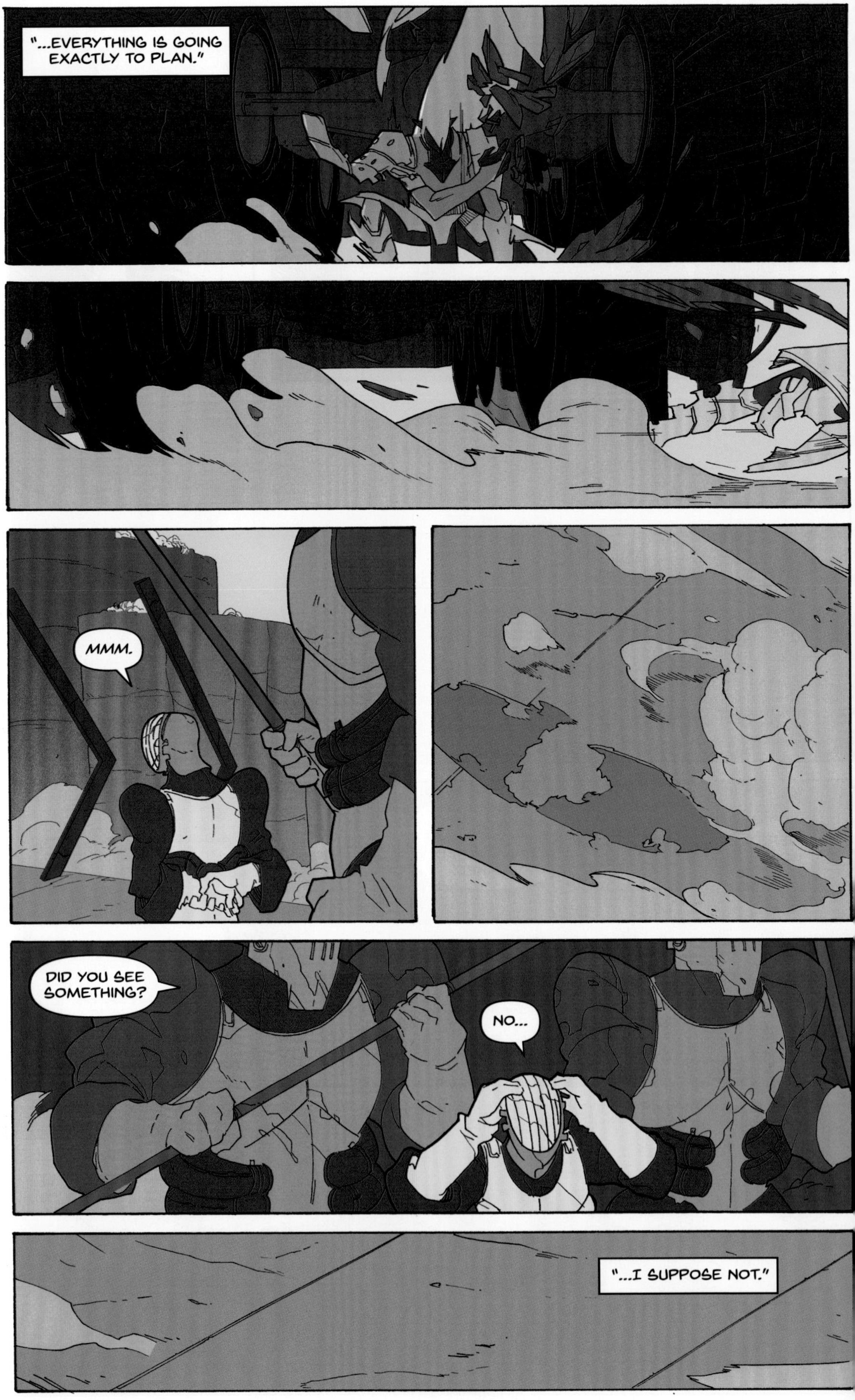
"...EVERYTHING IS GOING EXACTLY TO PLAN."
MMM.
DID YOU SEE SOMETHING?
NO...
"...I SUPPOSE NOT."

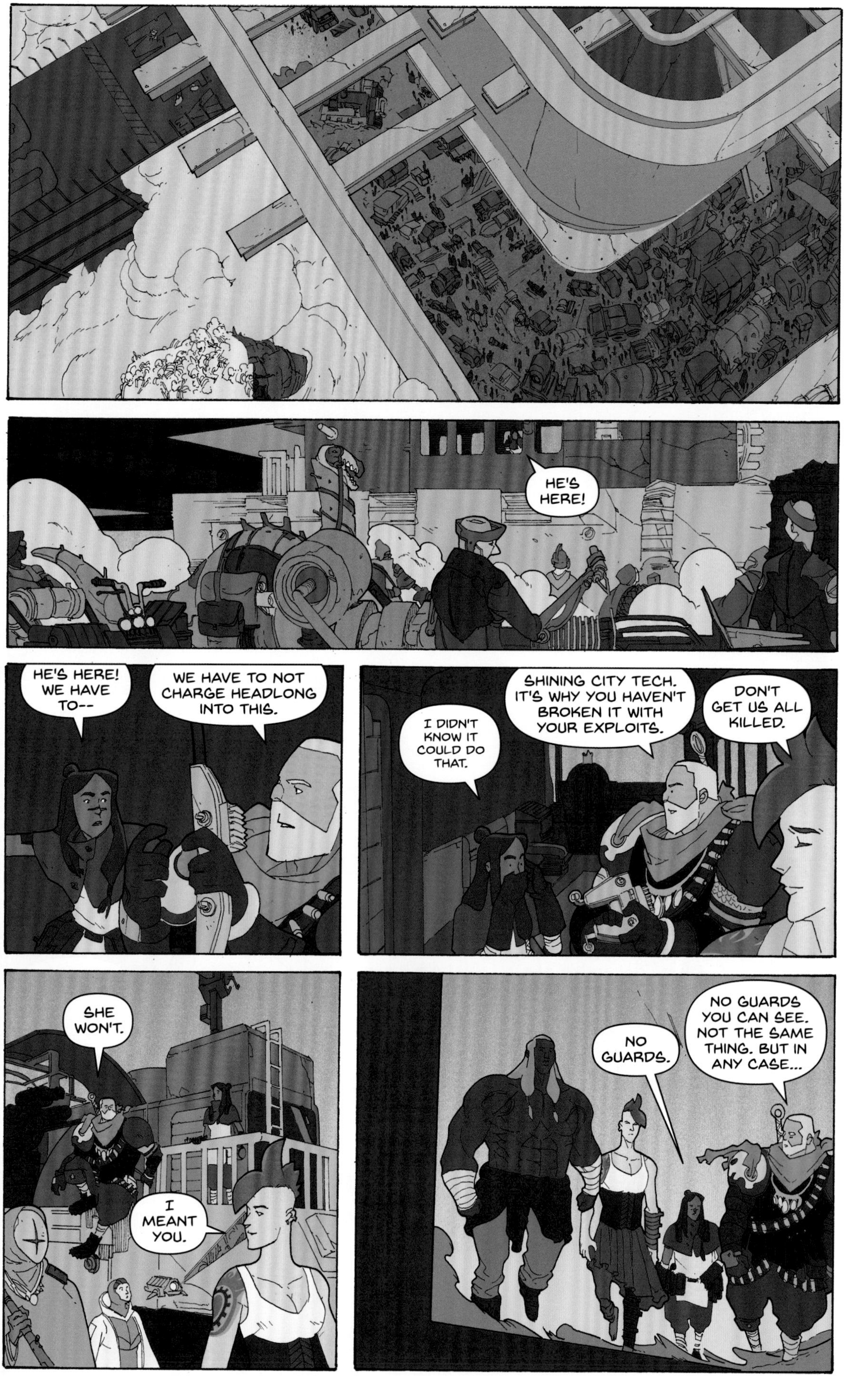
HE'S HERE!
HE'S HERE! WE HAVE TO--
WE HAVE TO NOT CHARGE HEADLONG INTO THIS.
I DIDN'T KNOW IT COULD DO THAT.
SHINING CITY TECH. IT'S WHY YOU HAVEN'T BROKEN IT WITH YOUR EXPLOITS.
DON'T GET US ALL KILLED.
SHE WON'T.
I MEANT YOU.
NO GUARDS.
NO GUARDS YOU CAN SEE. NOT THE SAME THING. BUT IN ANY CASE...

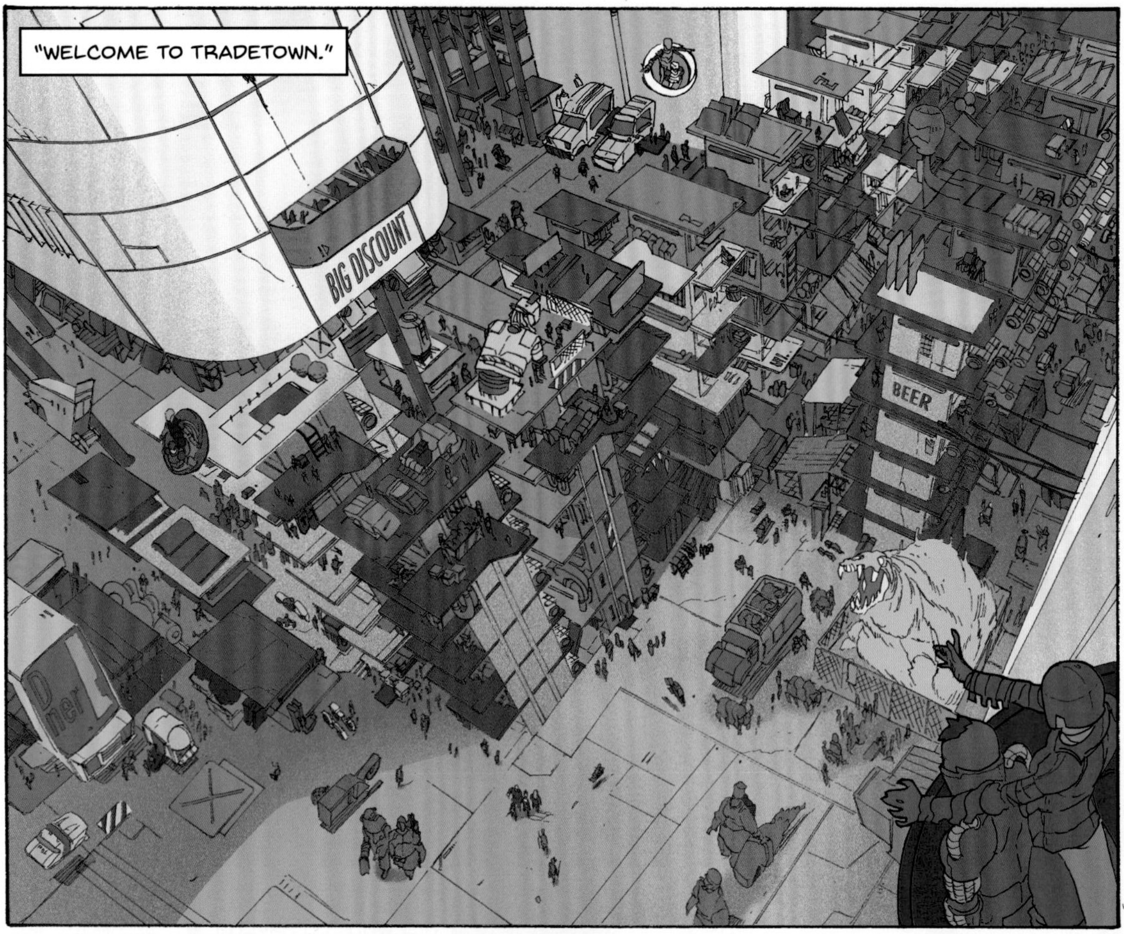
"WELCOME TO TRADETOWN."
BIG DISCOUNT
BEER

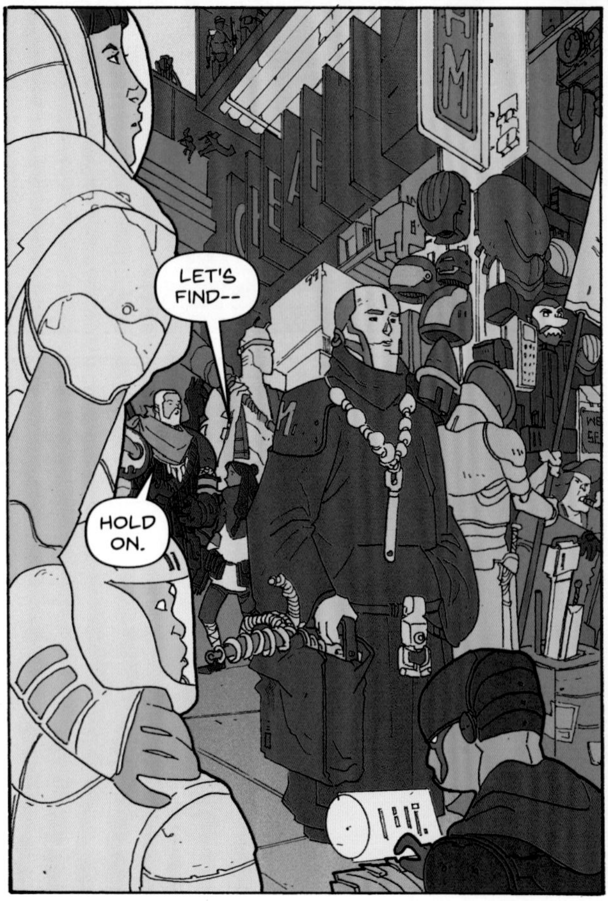
LET'S FIND--
HOLD ON.

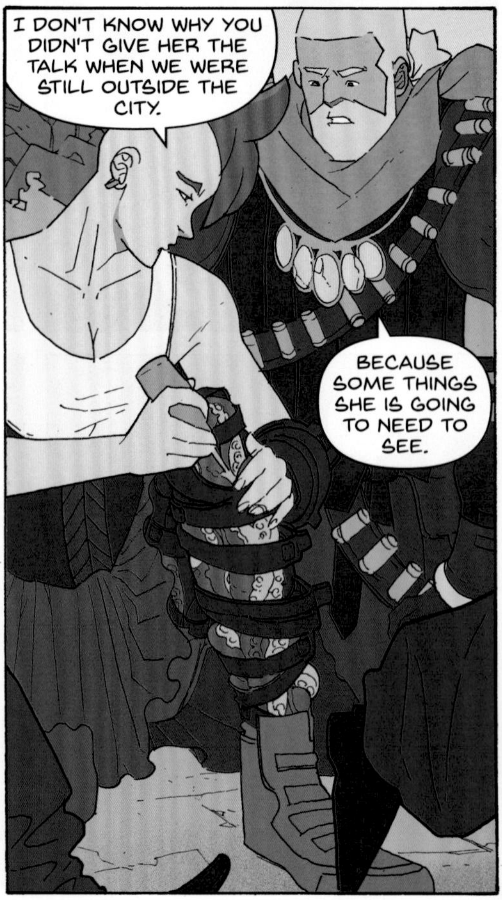
I DON'T KNOW WHY YOU DIDN'T GIVE HER THE TALK WHEN WE WERE STILL OUTSIDE THE CITY.
BECAUSE SOME THINGS SHE IS GOING TO NEED TO SEE.

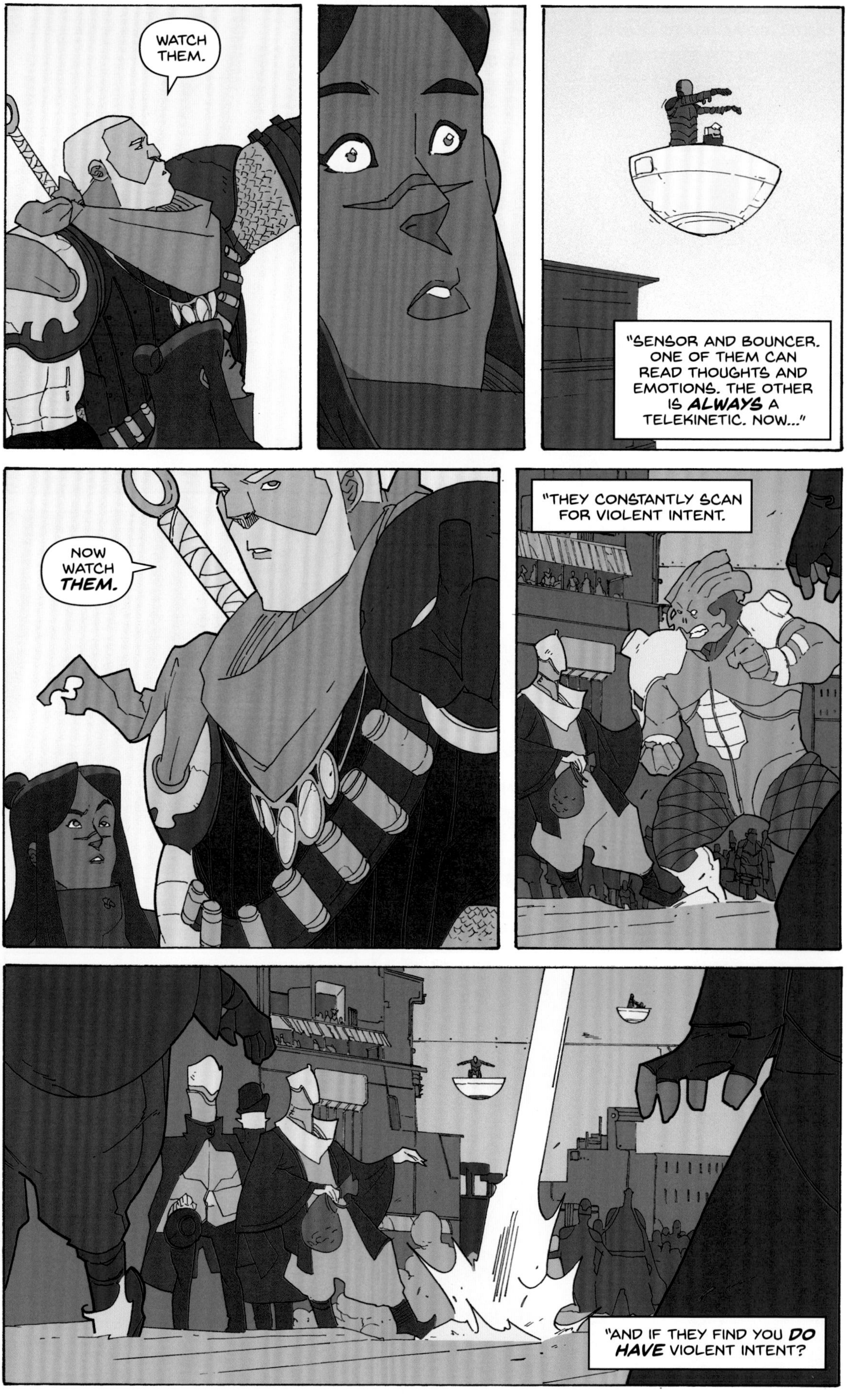
WATCH THEM.
"SENSOR AND BOUNCER. ONE OF THEM CAN READ THOUGHTS AND EMOTIONS. THE OTHER IS *ALWAYS* A TELEKINETIC. NOW..."
NOW WATCH *THEM.*
"THEY CONSTANTLY SCAN FOR VIOLENT INTENT.
"AND IF THEY FIND YOU *DO HAVE* VIOLENT INTENT?

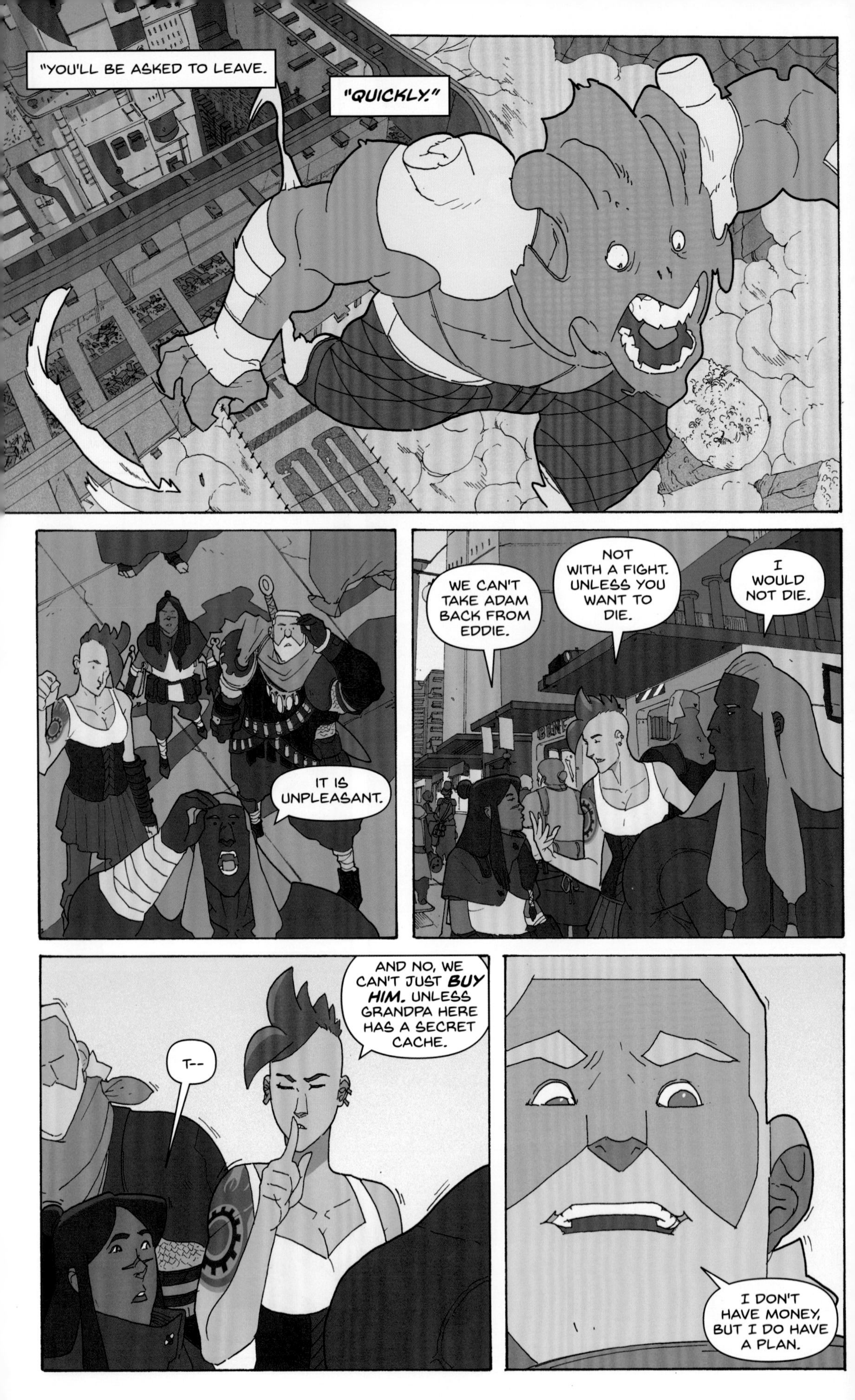
"YOU'LL BE ASKED TO LEAVE.
"QUICKLY."
IT IS UNPLEASANT.
WE CAN'T TAKE ADAM BACK FROM EDDIE.
NOT WITH A FIGHT. UNLESS YOU WANT TO DIE.
I WOULD NOT DIE.
T--
AND NO, WE CAN'T JUST BUY HIM. UNLESS GRANDPA HERE HAS A SECRET CACHE.
I DON'T HAVE MONEY, BUT I DO HAVE A PLAN.

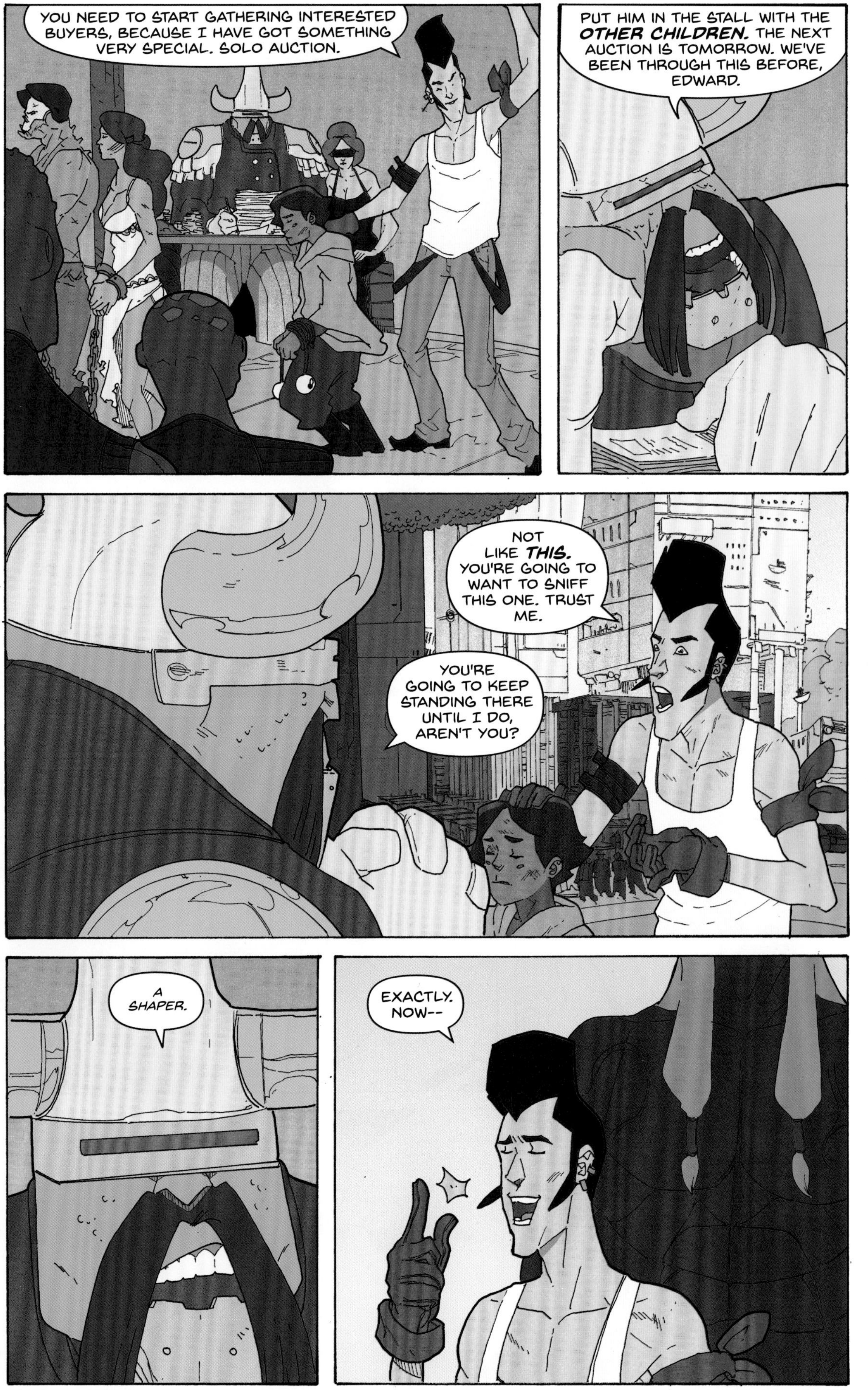
YOU NEED TO START GATHERING INTERESTED BUYERS, BECAUSE I HAVE GOT SOMETHING VERY SPECIAL. SOLO AUCTION.
PUT HIM IN THE STALL WITH THE OTHER CHILDREN. THE NEXT AUCTION IS TOMORROW. WE'VE BEEN THROUGH THIS BEFORE, EDWARD.
NOT LIKE THIS. YOU'RE GOING TO WANT TO SNIFF THIS ONE. TRUST ME.
YOU'RE GOING TO KEEP STANDING THERE UNTIL I DO, AREN'T YOU?
A SHAPER.
EXACTLY. NOW--

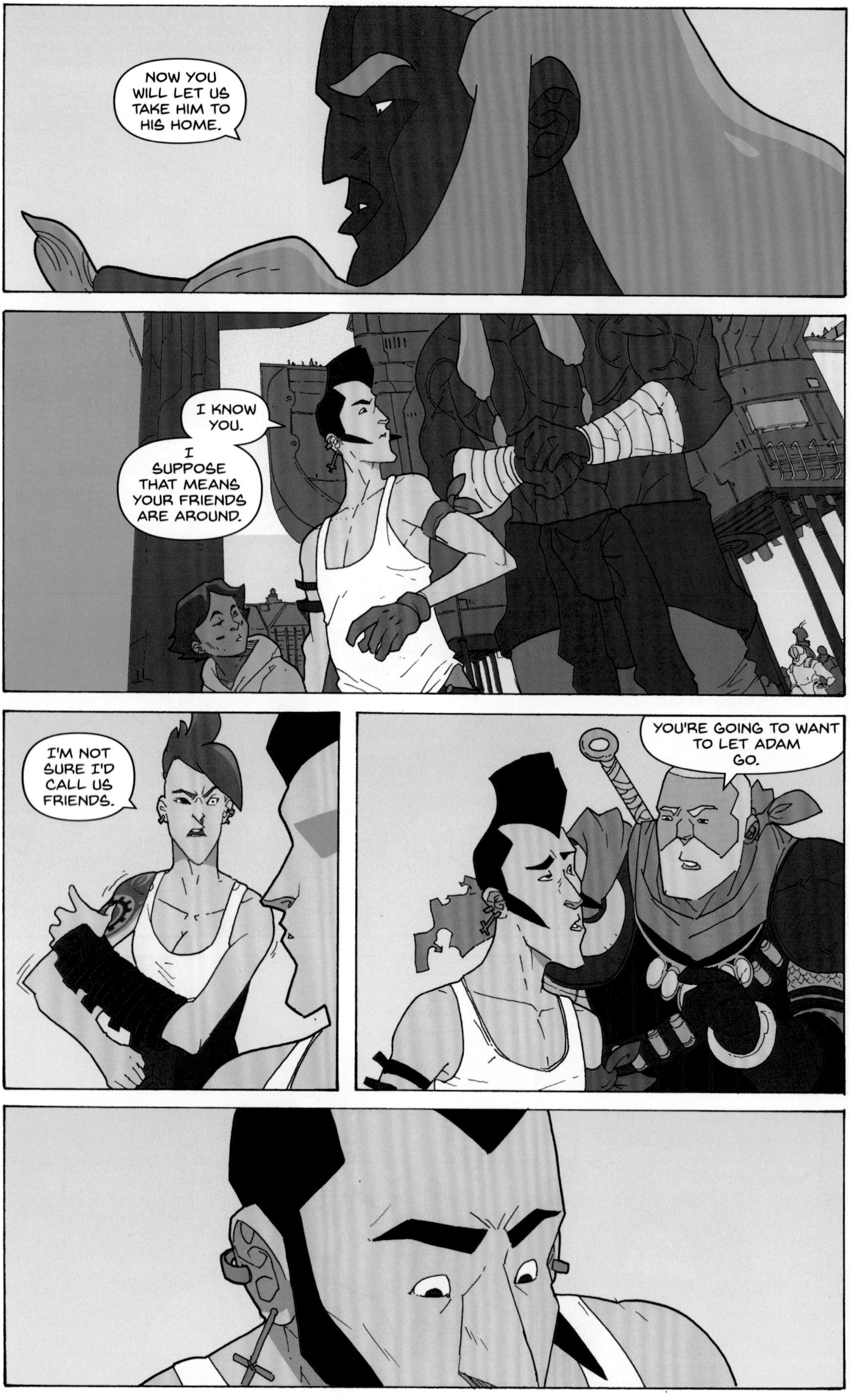
NOW YOU WILL LET US TAKE HIM TO HIS HOME.
I KNOW YOU.
I SUPPOSE THAT MEANS YOUR FRIENDS ARE AROUND.
I'M NOT SURE I'D CALL US FRIENDS.
YOU'RE GOING TO WANT TO LET ADAM GO.

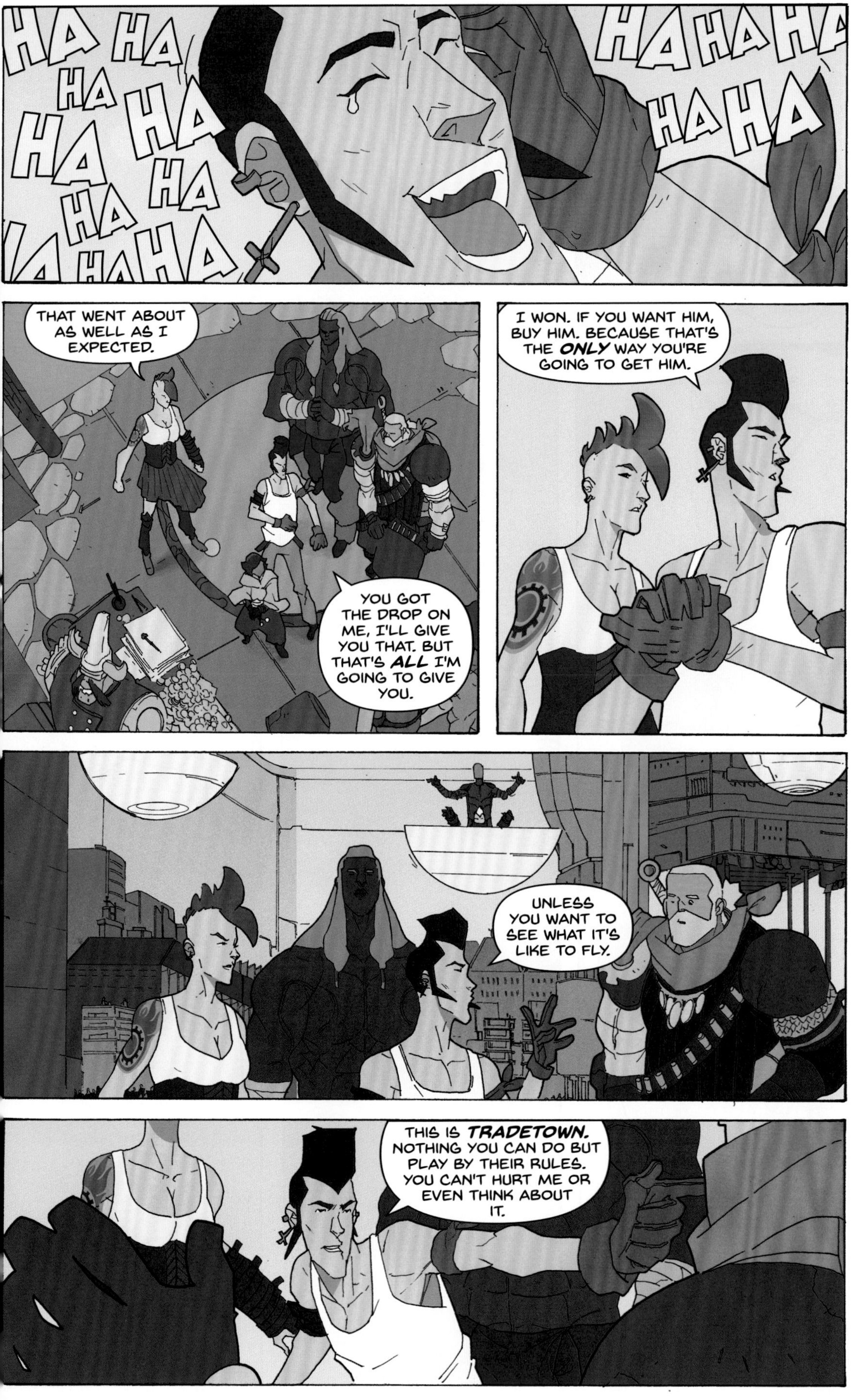
HA HA HA HA HA HA HA HA HAHA
HAHAHAHA HAHA
THAT WENT ABOUT AS WELL AS I EXPECTED.
YOU GOT THE DROP ON ME, I'LL GIVE YOU THAT. BUT THAT'S ALL I'M GOING TO GIVE YOU.
I WON. IF YOU WANT HIM, BUY HIM. BECAUSE THAT'S THE ONLY WAY YOU'RE GOING TO GET HIM.
UNLESS YOU WANT TO SEE WHAT IT'S LIKE TO FLY.
THIS IS TRADETOWN. NOTHING YOU CAN DO BUT PLAY BY THEIR RULES. YOU CAN'T HURT ME OR EVEN THINK ABOUT IT.

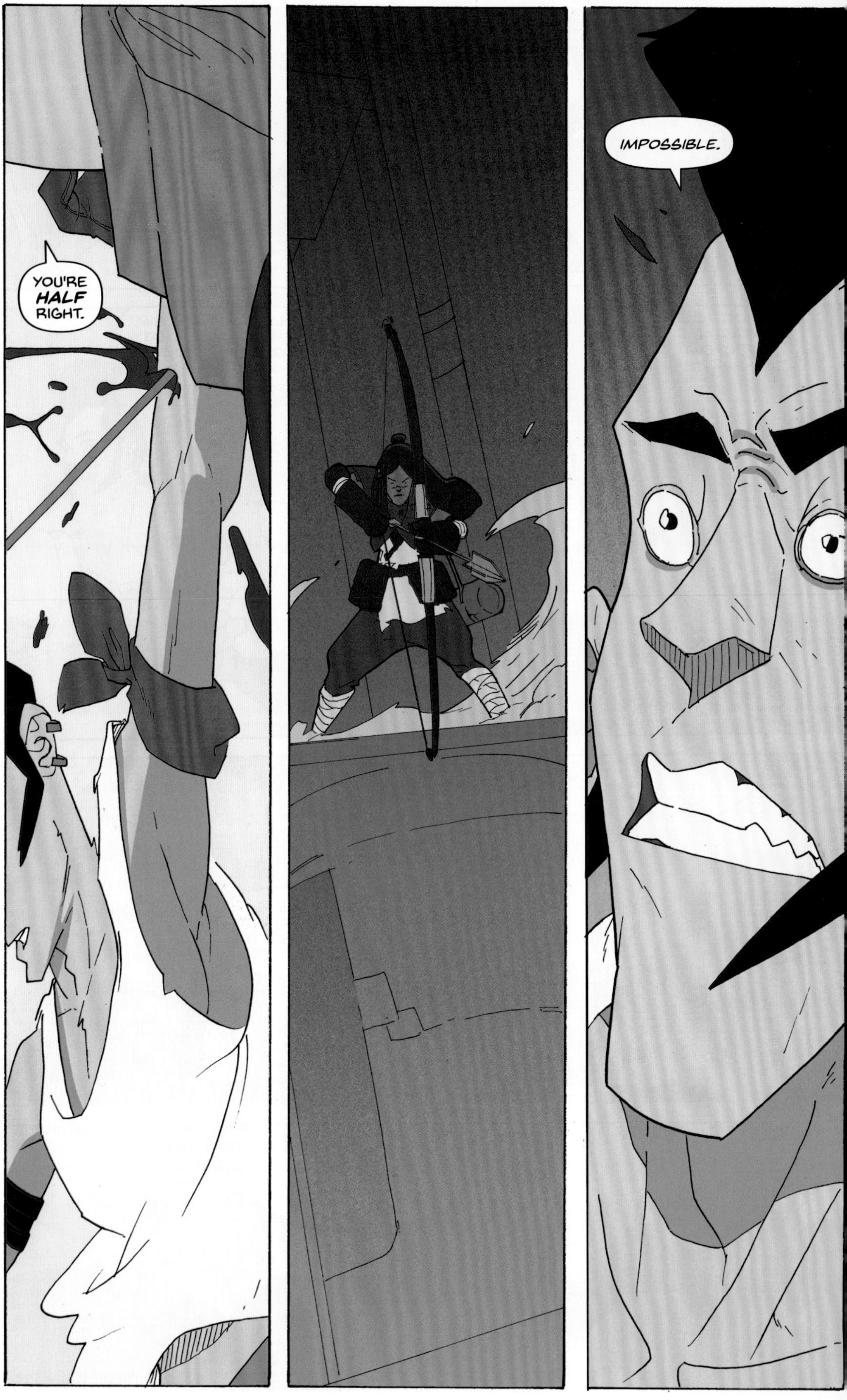
YOU'RE **HALF** RIGHT.
IMPOSSIBLE.

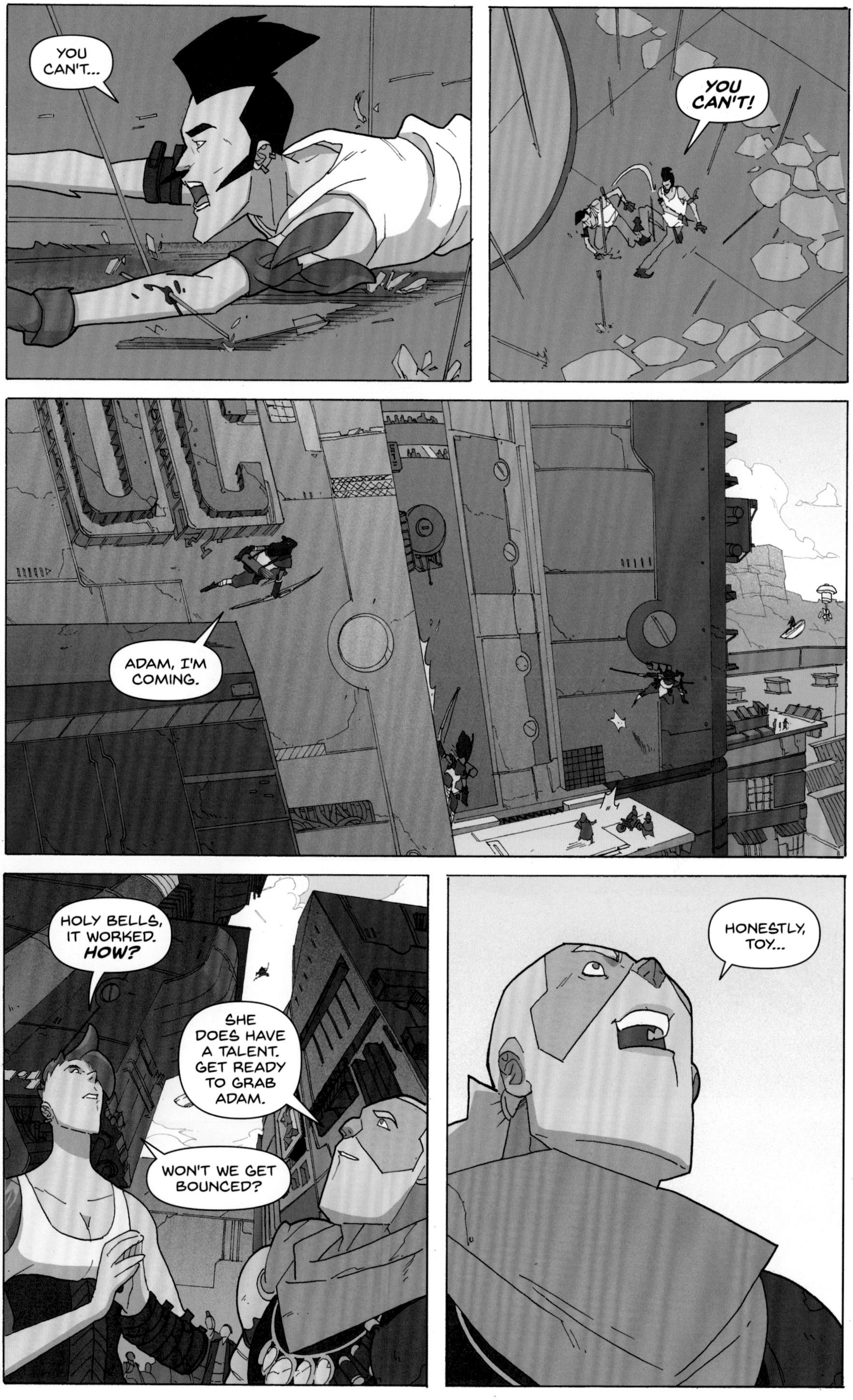
YOU CAN'T...
YOU CAN'T!
ADAM, I'M COMING.
HOLY BELLS, IT WORKED. HOW?
SHE DOES HAVE A TALENT. GET READY TO GRAB ADAM.
WON'T WE GET BOUNCED?
HONESTLY, TOY...

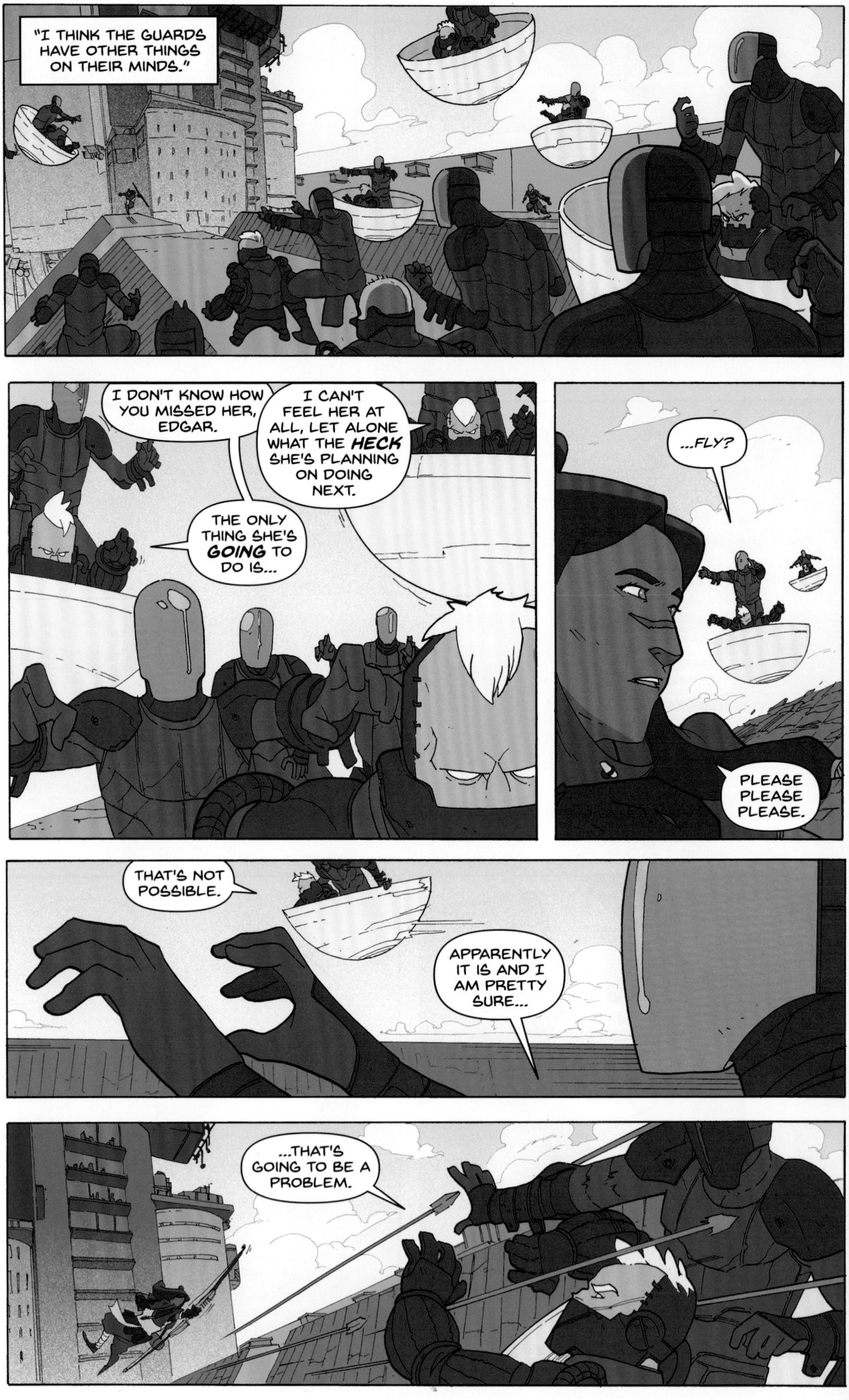
"I THINK THE GUARDS HAVE OTHER THINGS ON THEIR MINDS."
I DON'T KNOW HOW YOU MISSED HER, EDGAR.
I CAN'T FEEL HER AT ALL, LET ALONE WHAT THE HECK SHE'S PLANNING ON DOING NEXT.
THE ONLY THING SHE'S GOING TO DO IS...
...FLY?
PLEASE PLEASE PLEASE.
THAT'S NOT POSSIBLE.
APPARENTLY IT IS AND I AM PRETTY SURE...
...THAT'S GOING TO BE A PROBLEM.

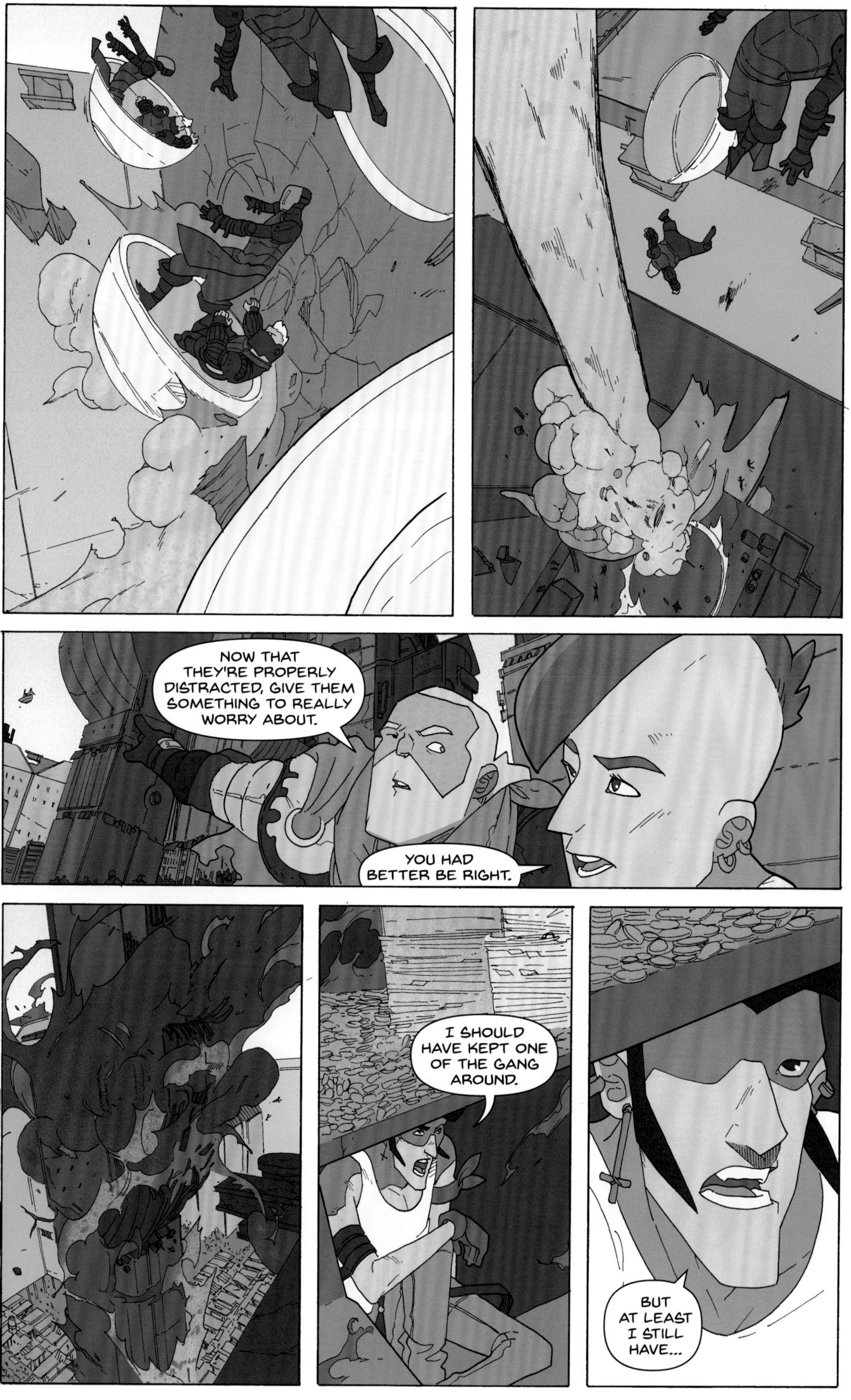
NOW THAT THEY'RE PROPERLY DISTRACTED, GIVE THEM SOMETHING TO REALLY WORRY ABOUT.
YOU HAD BETTER BE RIGHT.
I SHOULD HAVE KEPT ONE OF THE GANG AROUND.
BUT AT LEAST I STILL HAVE...

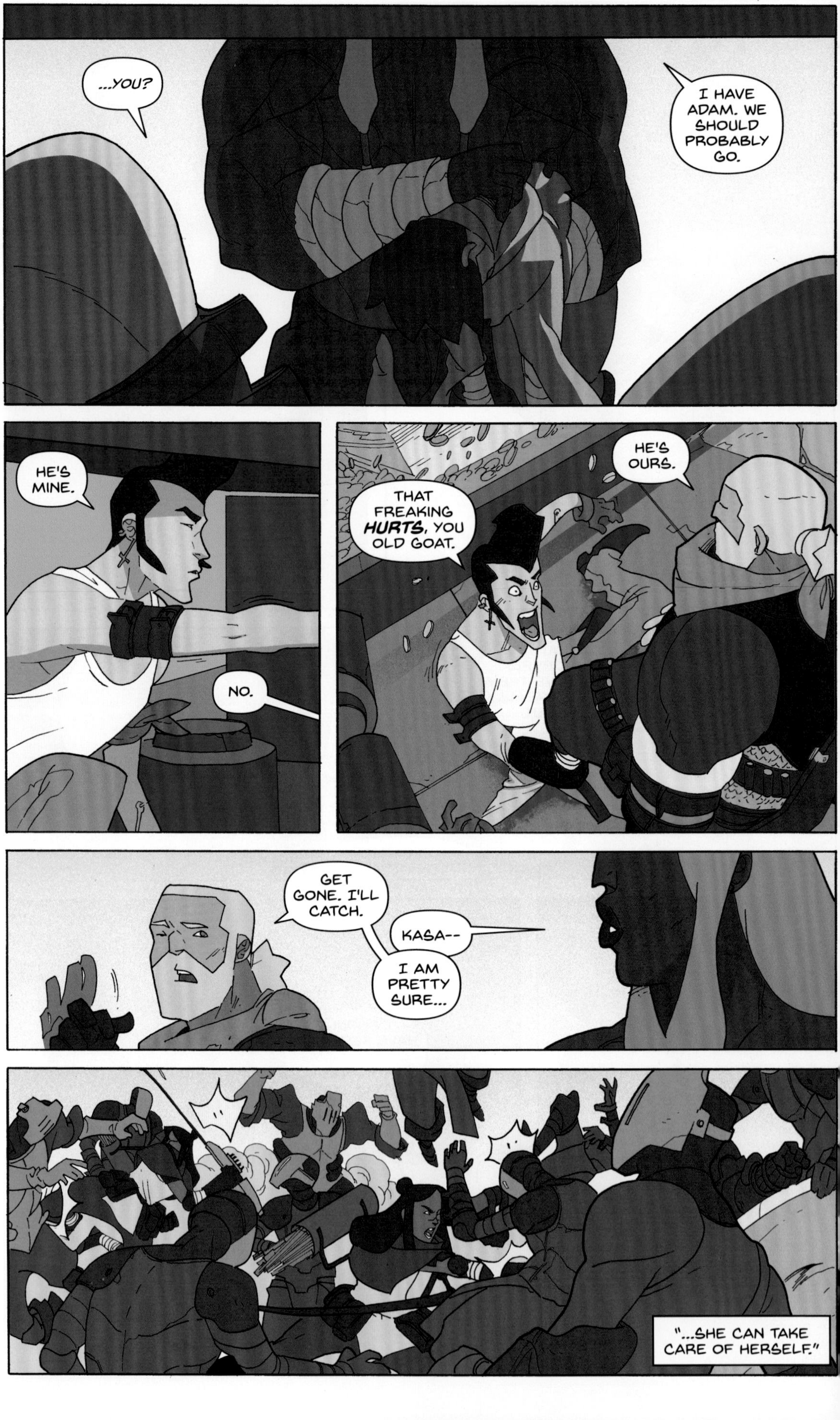
...YOU?
I HAVE ADAM. WE SHOULD PROBABLY GO.
HE'S MINE.
NO.
HE'S OURS.
THAT FREAKING HURTS, YOU OLD GOAT.
GET GONE. I'LL CATCH.
KASA--
I AM PRETTY SURE...
"...SHE CAN TAKE CARE OF HERSELF."

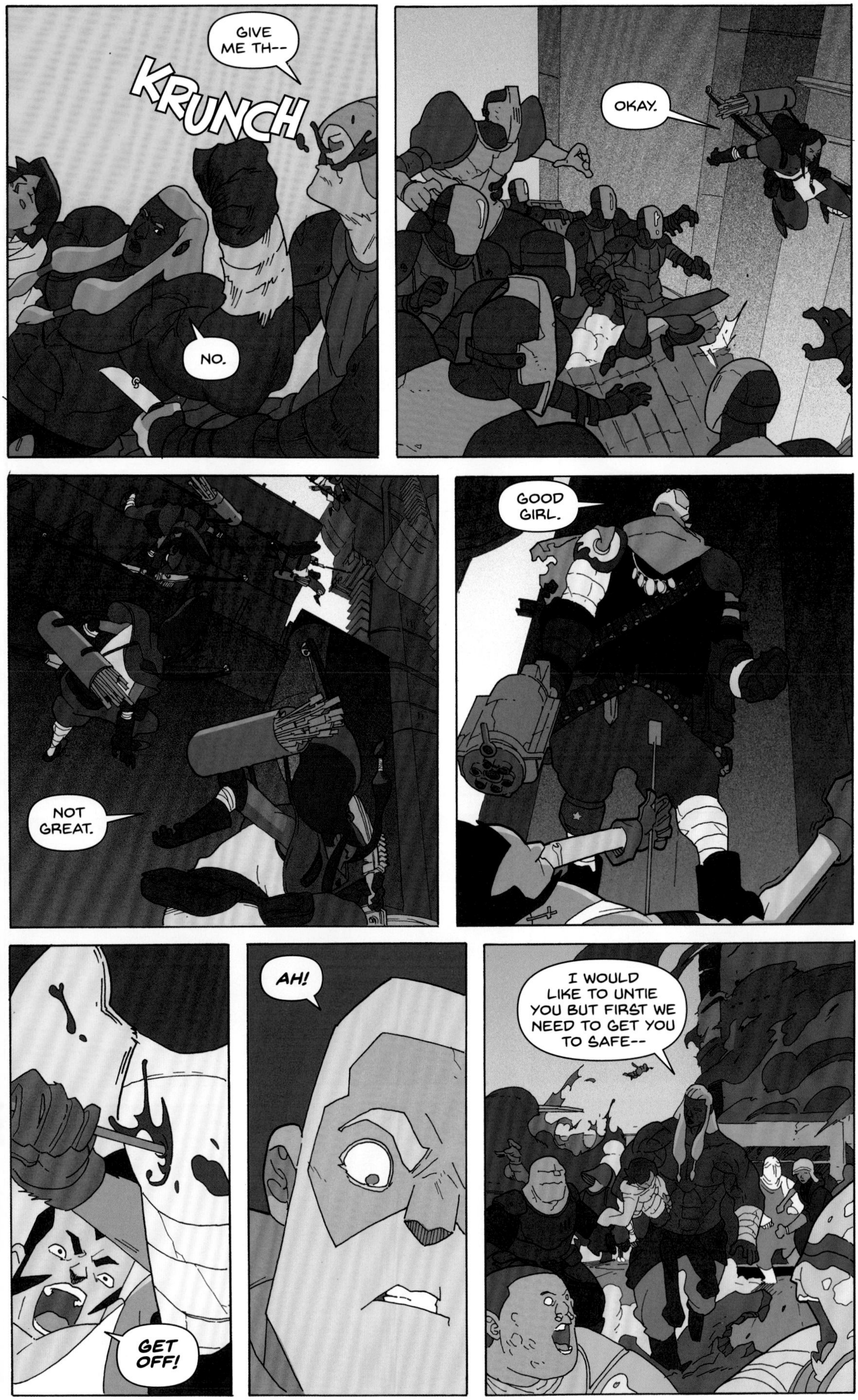
GIVE ME TH--
KRUNCH
NO.
OKAY.
NOT GREAT.
GOOD GIRL.
GET OFF!
AH!
I WOULD LIKE TO UNTIE YOU BUT FIRST WE NEED TO GET YOU TO SAFE--

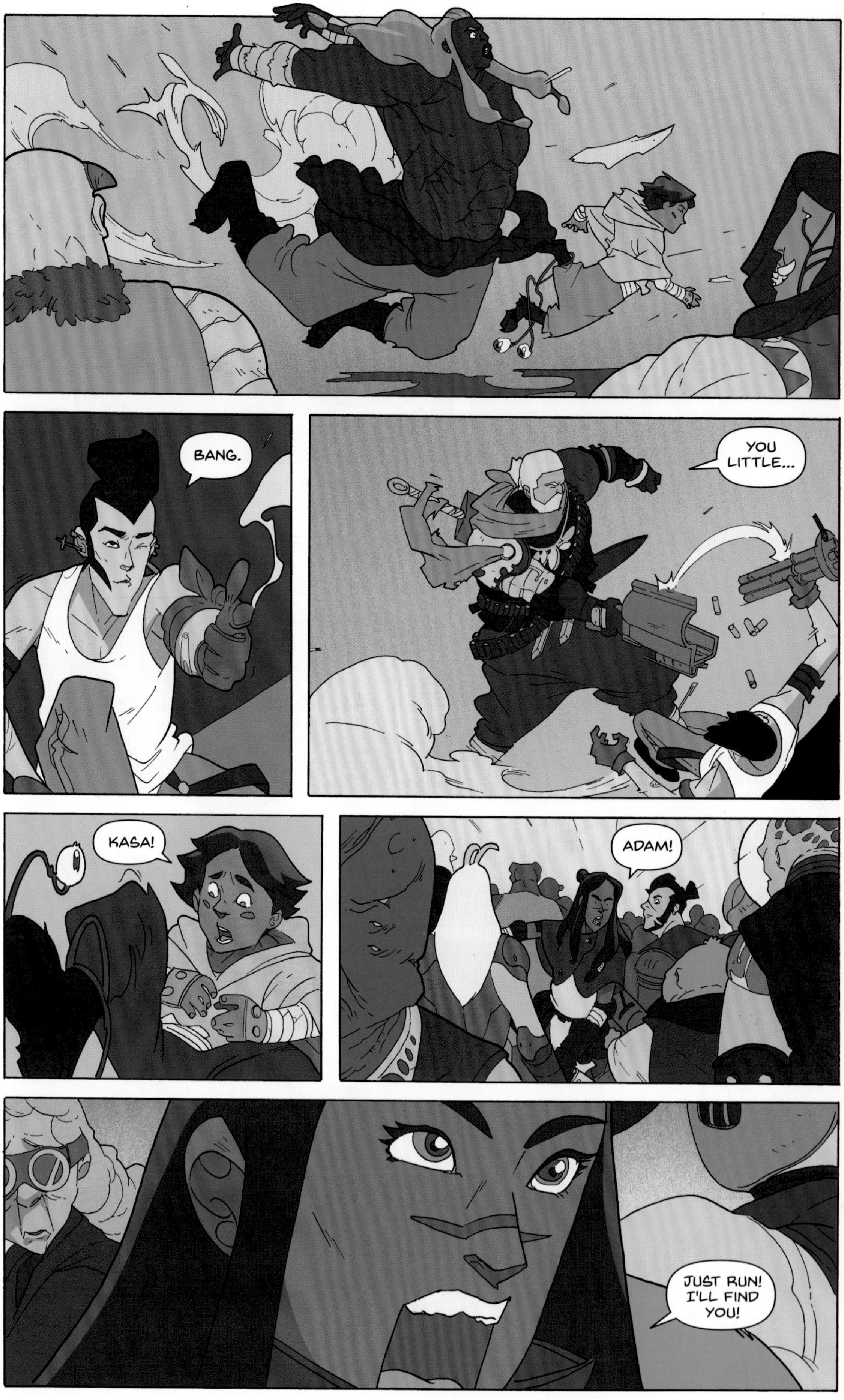
BANG.
YOU LITTLE...
KASA!
ADAM!
JUST RUN! I'LL FIND YOU!

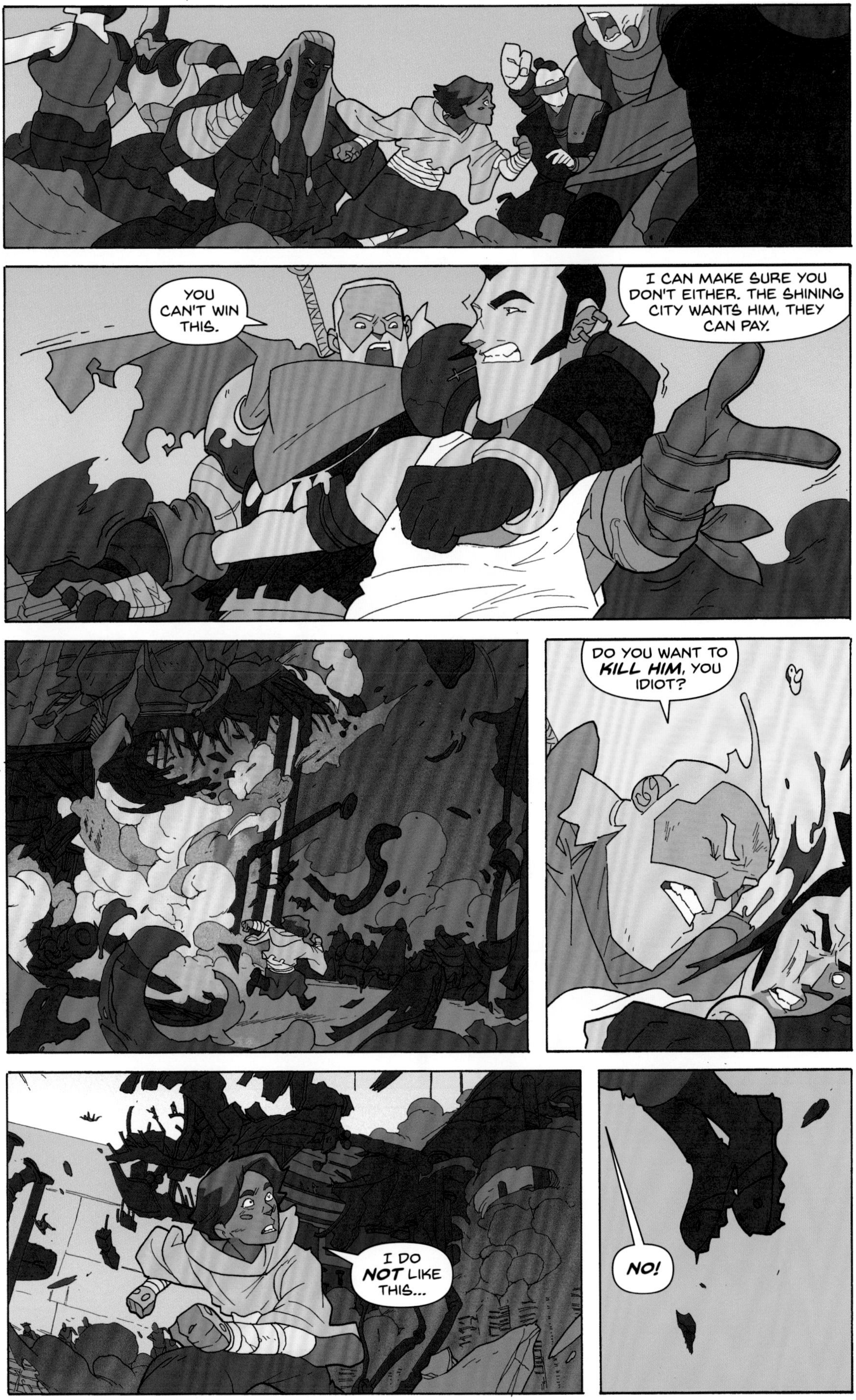
YOU CAN'T WIN THIS.
I CAN MAKE SURE YOU DON'T EITHER. THE SHINING CITY WANTS HIM, THEY CAN PAY.
DO YOU WANT TO KILL HIM, YOU IDIOT?
I DO NOT LIKE THIS...
NO!

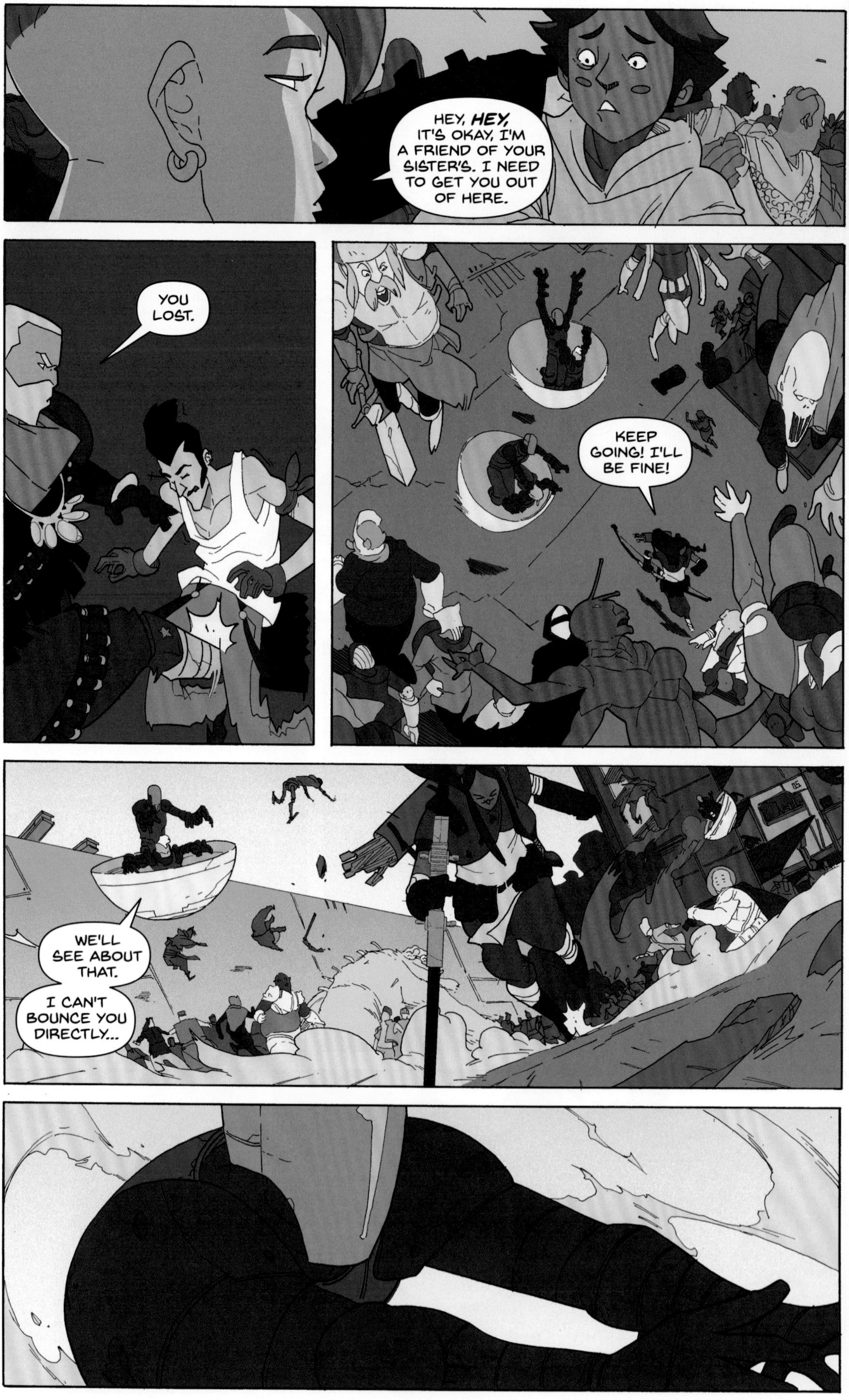
HEY, *HEY,* IT'S OKAY, I'M A FRIEND OF YOUR SISTER'S. I NEED TO GET YOU OUT OF HERE.
YOU LOST.
KEEP GOING! I'LL BE FINE!
WE'LL SEE ABOUT THAT.
I CAN'T BOUNCE YOU DIRECTLY...

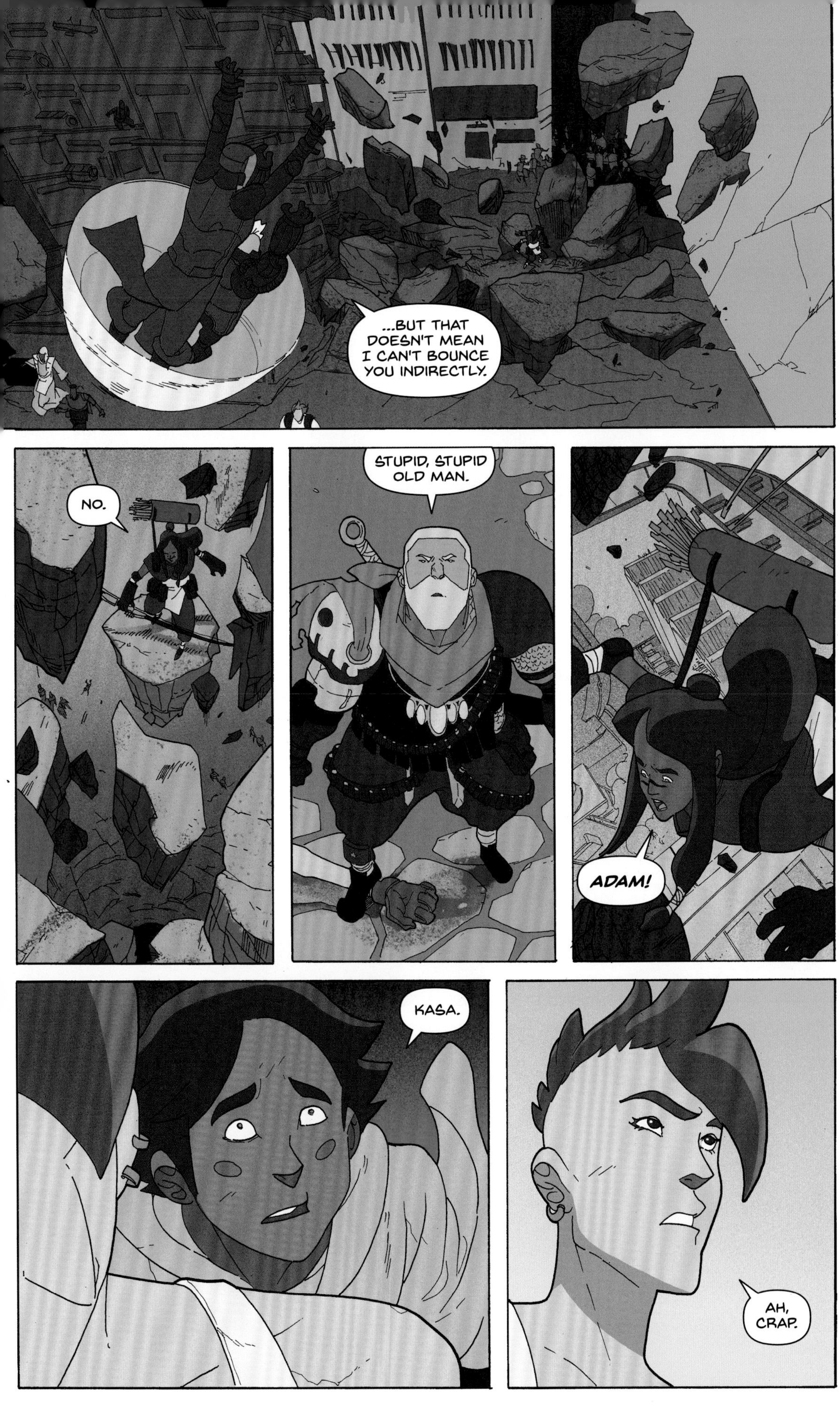
...BUT THAT DOESN'T MEAN I CAN'T BOUNCE YOU INDIRECTLY.
NO.
STUPID, STUPID OLD MAN.
ADAM!
KASA.
AH, CRAP.

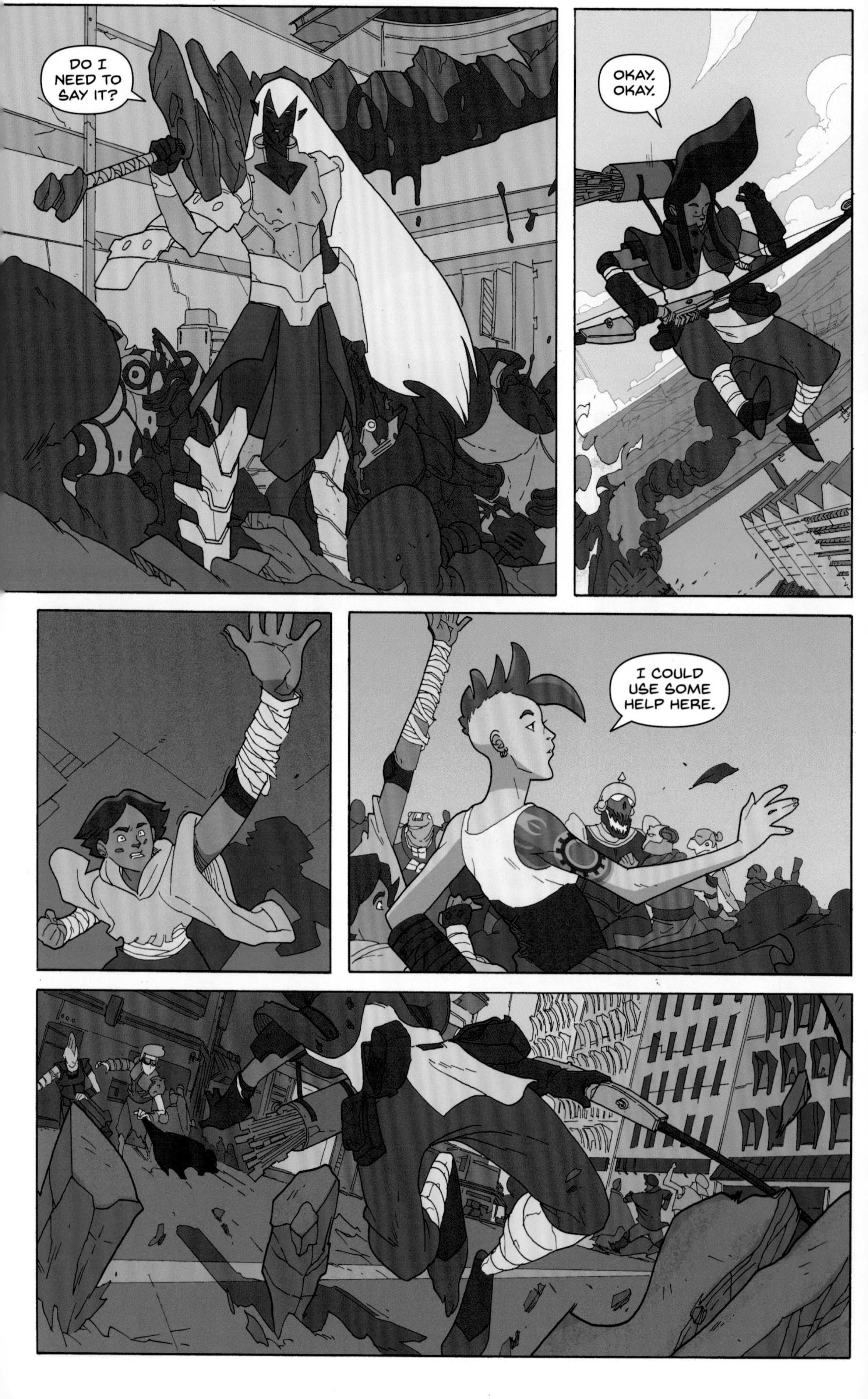
DO I NEED TO SAY IT?
OKAY. OKAY.
I COULD USE SOME HELP HERE.

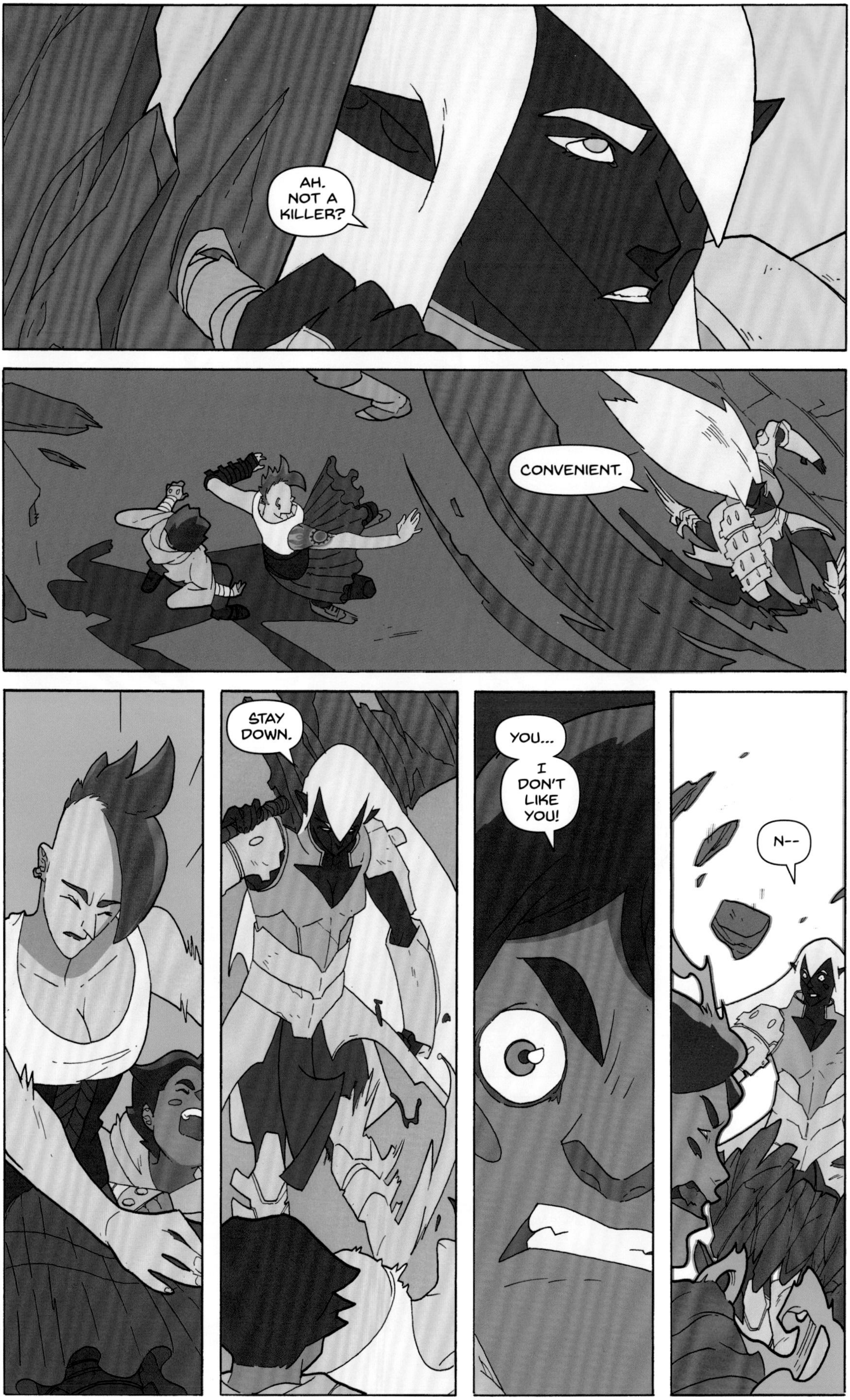
AH. NOT A KILLER?
CONVENIENT.
STAY DOWN.
YOU...
I DON'T LIKE YOU!
N--

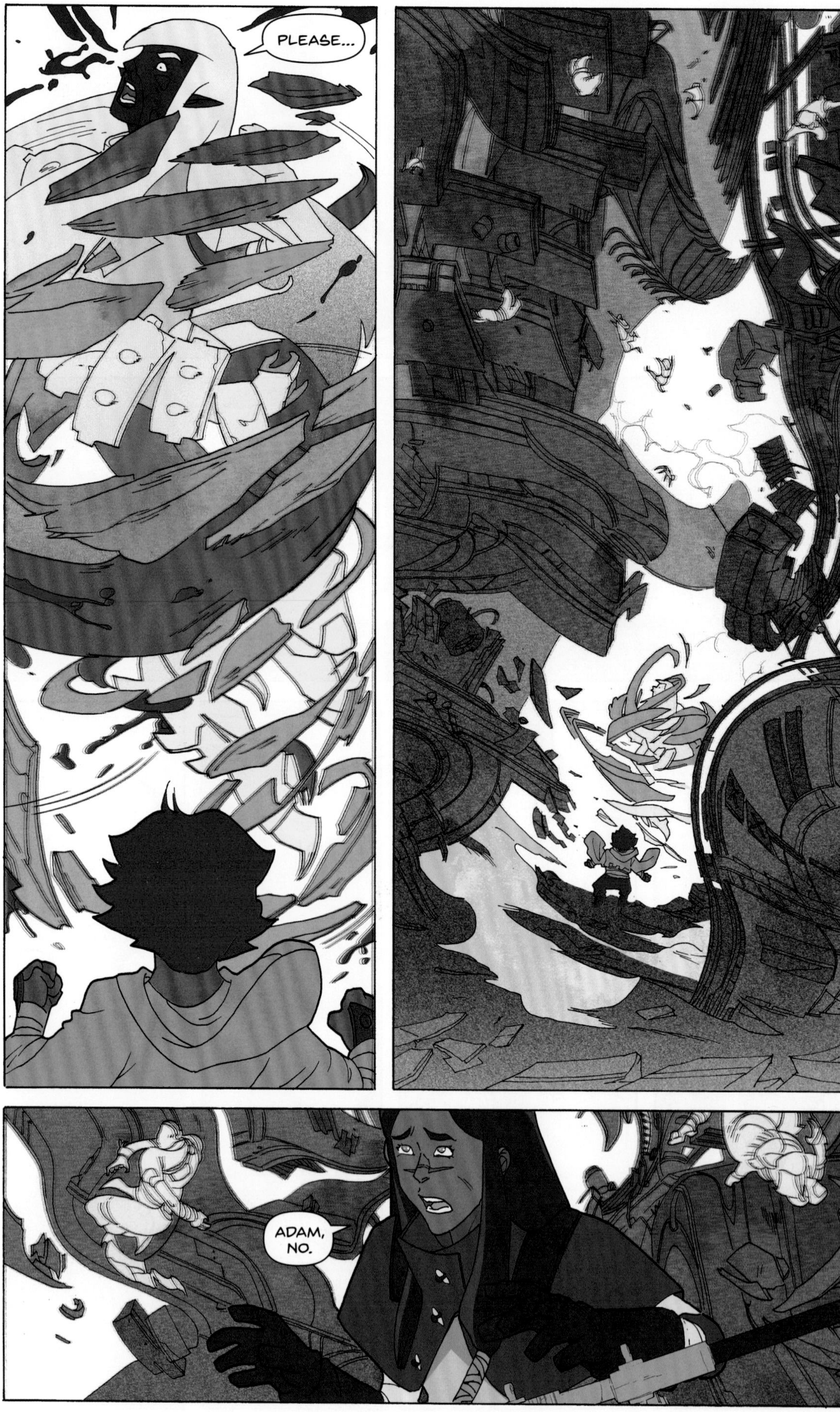
PLEASE...
ADAM, NO.

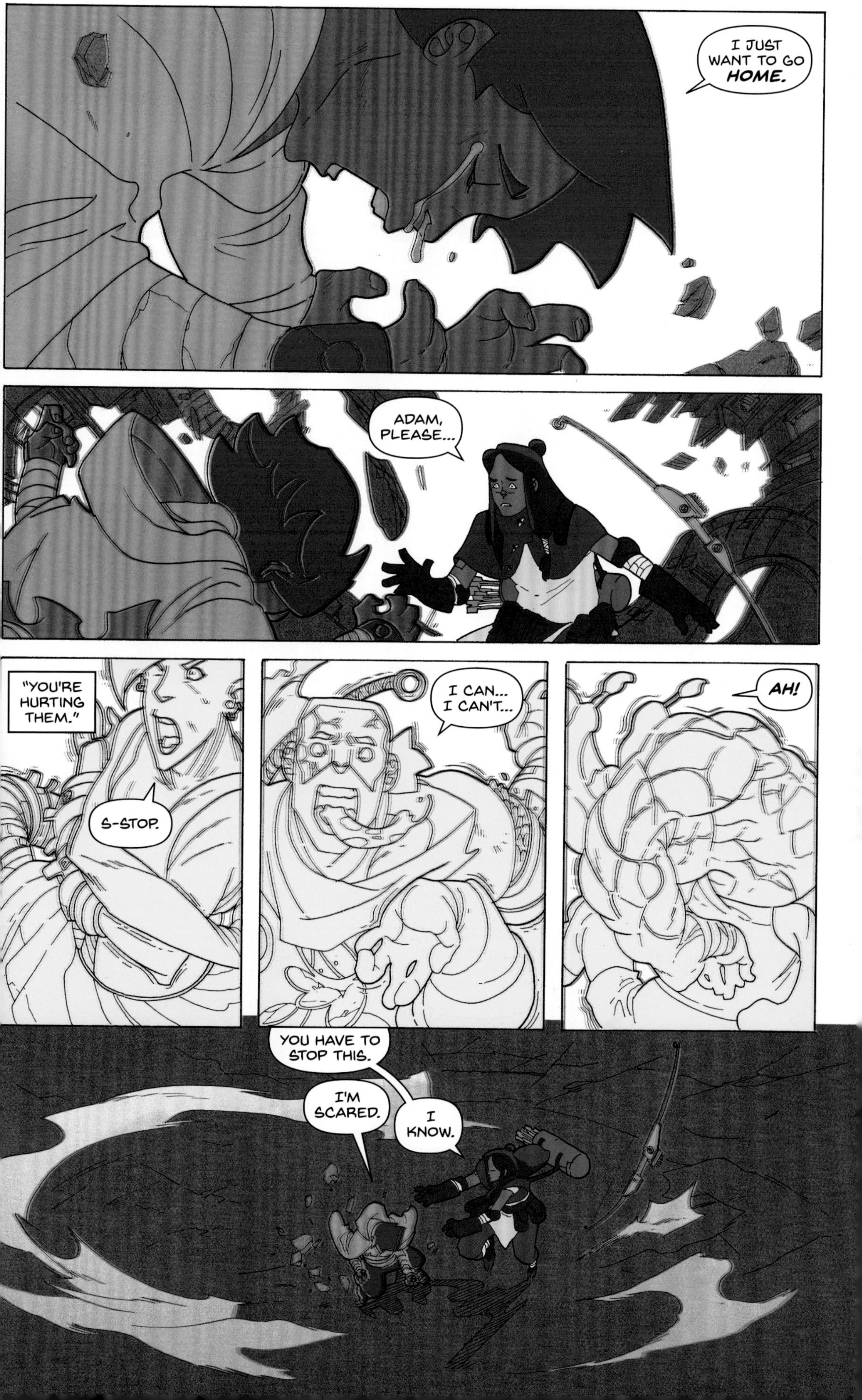
I JUST WANT TO GO HOME.
ADAM, PLEASE...
"YOU'RE HURTING THEM."
S-STOP.
I CAN... I CAN'T...
AH!
YOU HAVE TO STOP THIS.
I'M SCARED.
I KNOW.

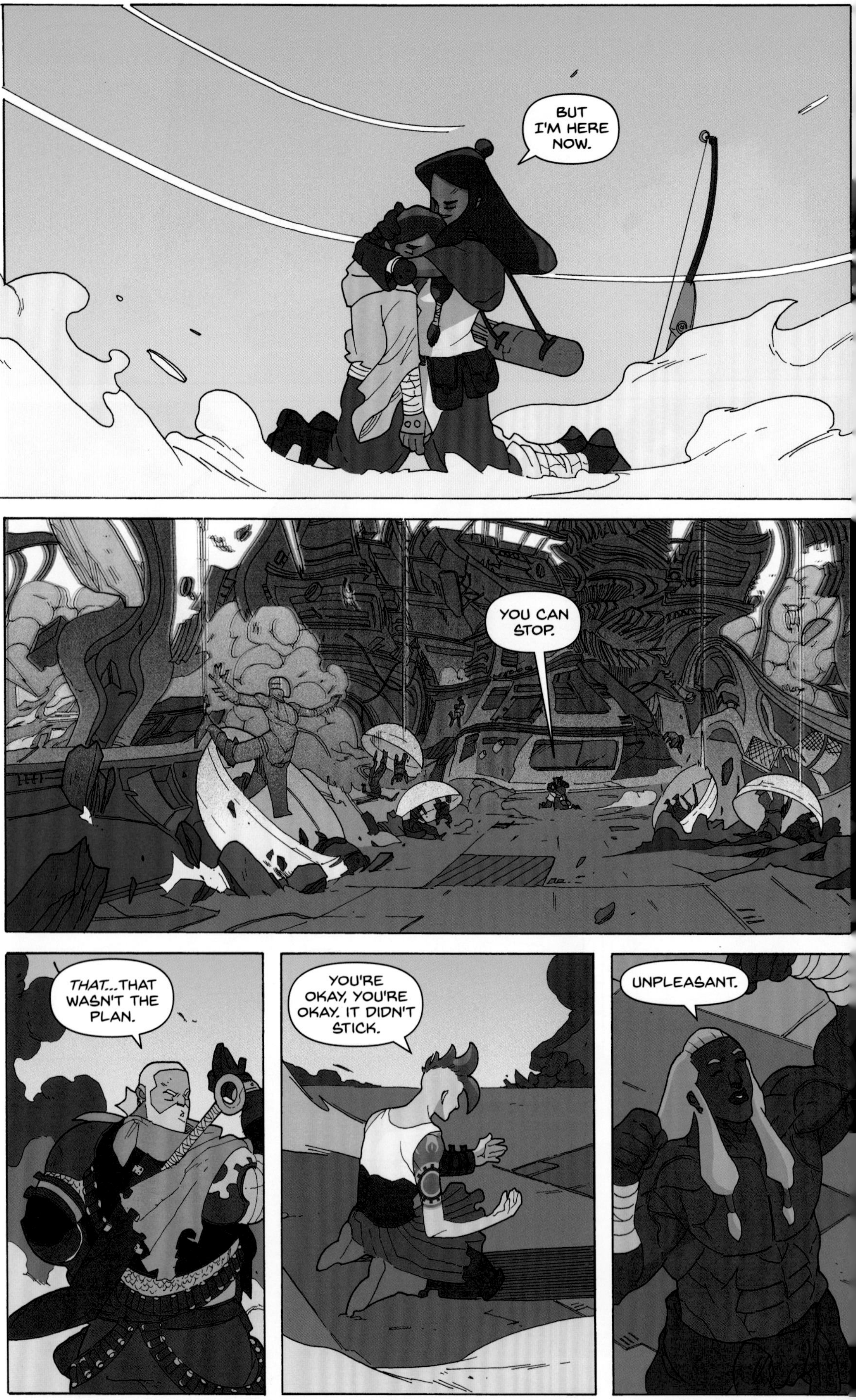
BUT I'M HERE NOW.
YOU CAN STOP.
THAT...THAT WASN'T THE PLAN.
YOU'RE OKAY, YOU'RE OKAY. IT DIDN'T STICK.
UNPLEASANT.

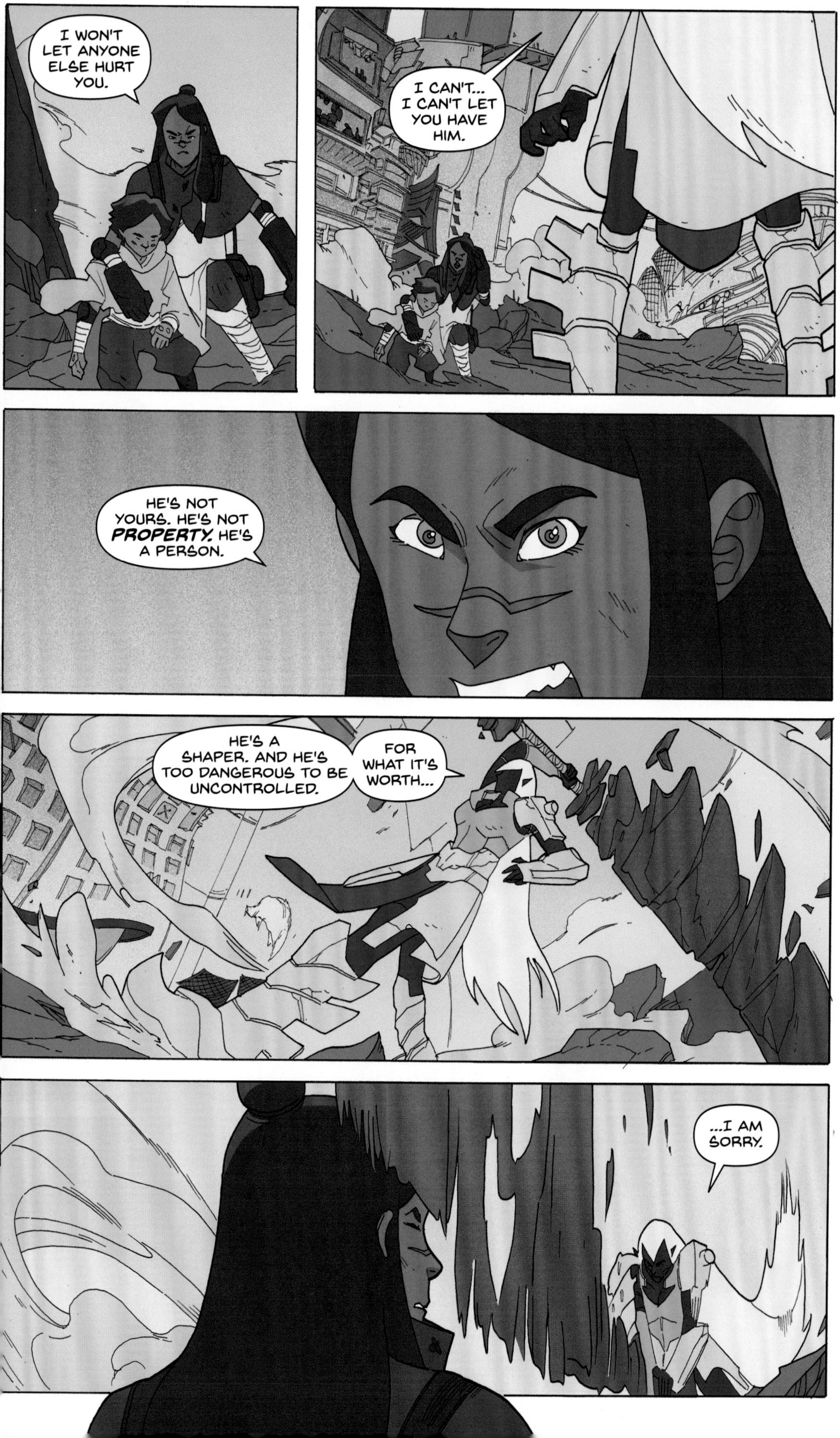
I WON'T LET ANYONE ELSE HURT YOU.
I CAN'T... I CAN'T LET YOU HAVE HIM.
HE'S NOT YOURS. HE'S NOT ***PROPERTY.*** HE'S A PERSON.
HE'S A SHAPER. AND HE'S TOO DANGEROUS TO BE UNCONTROLLED.
FOR WHAT IT'S WORTH...
...I AM SORRY.

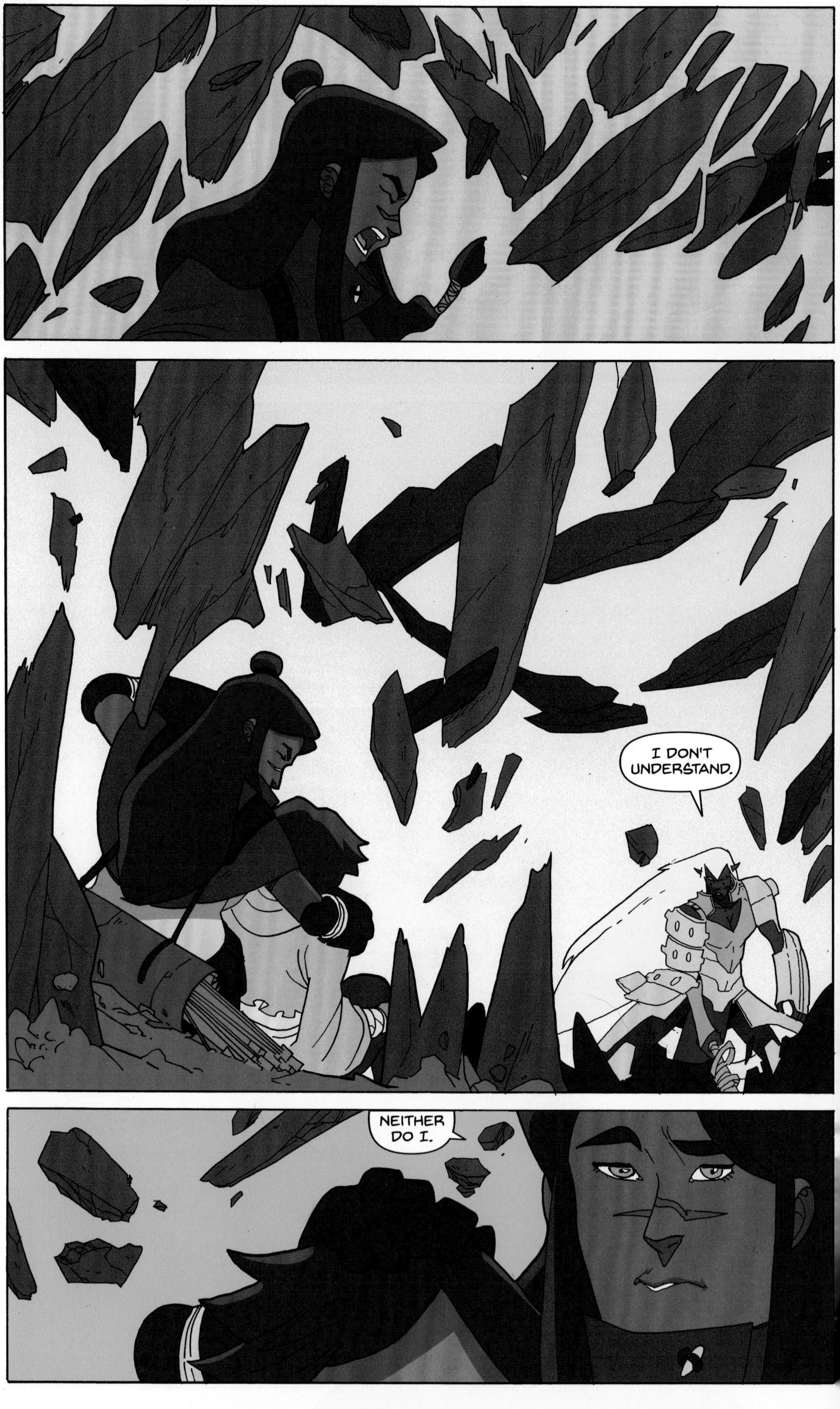
I DON'T UNDERSTAND.
NEITHER DO I.

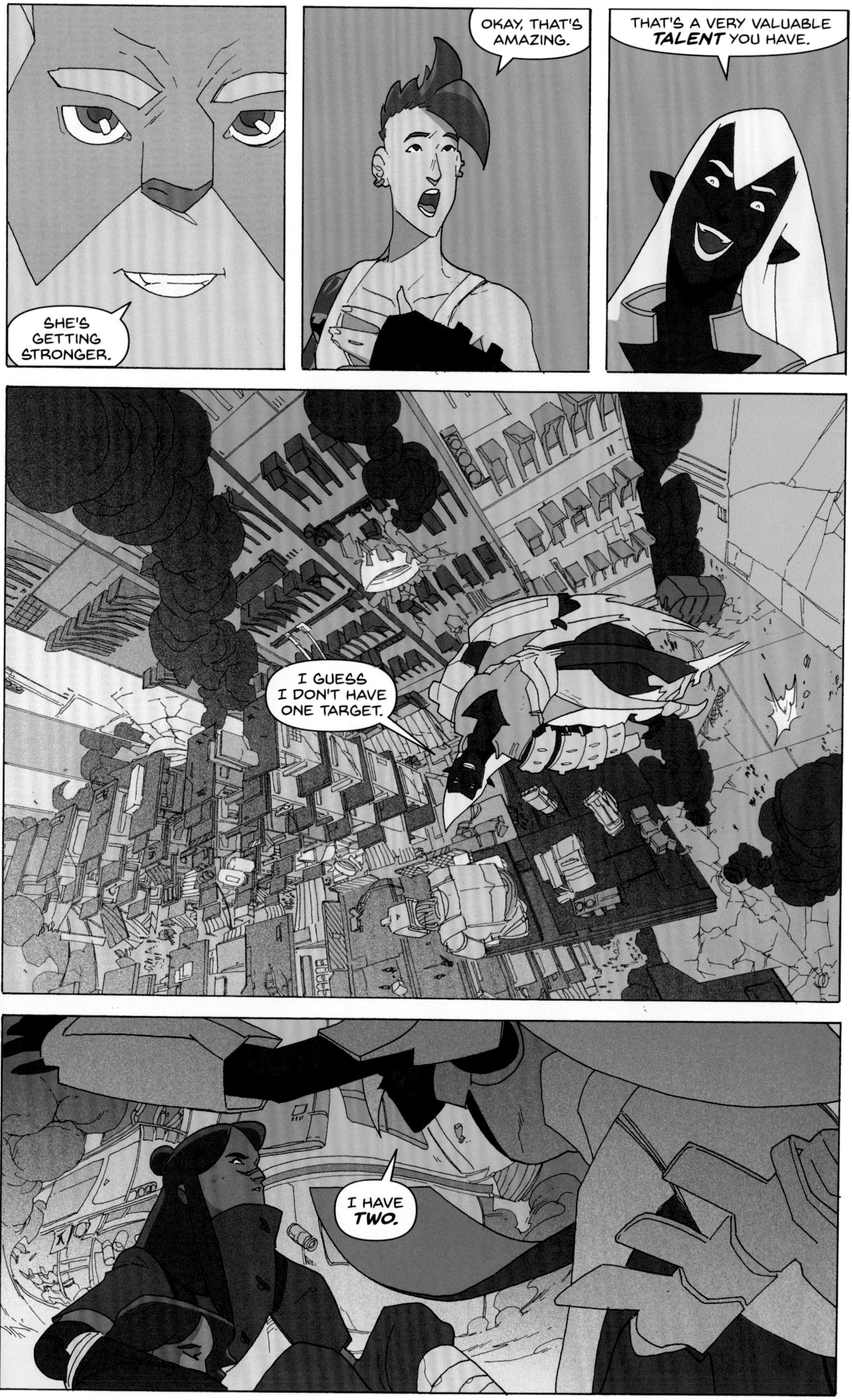
SHE'S GETTING STRONGER.
OKAY, THAT'S AMAZING.
THAT'S A VERY VALUABLE TALENT YOU HAVE.
I GUESS I DON'T HAVE ONE TARGET.
I HAVE TWO.

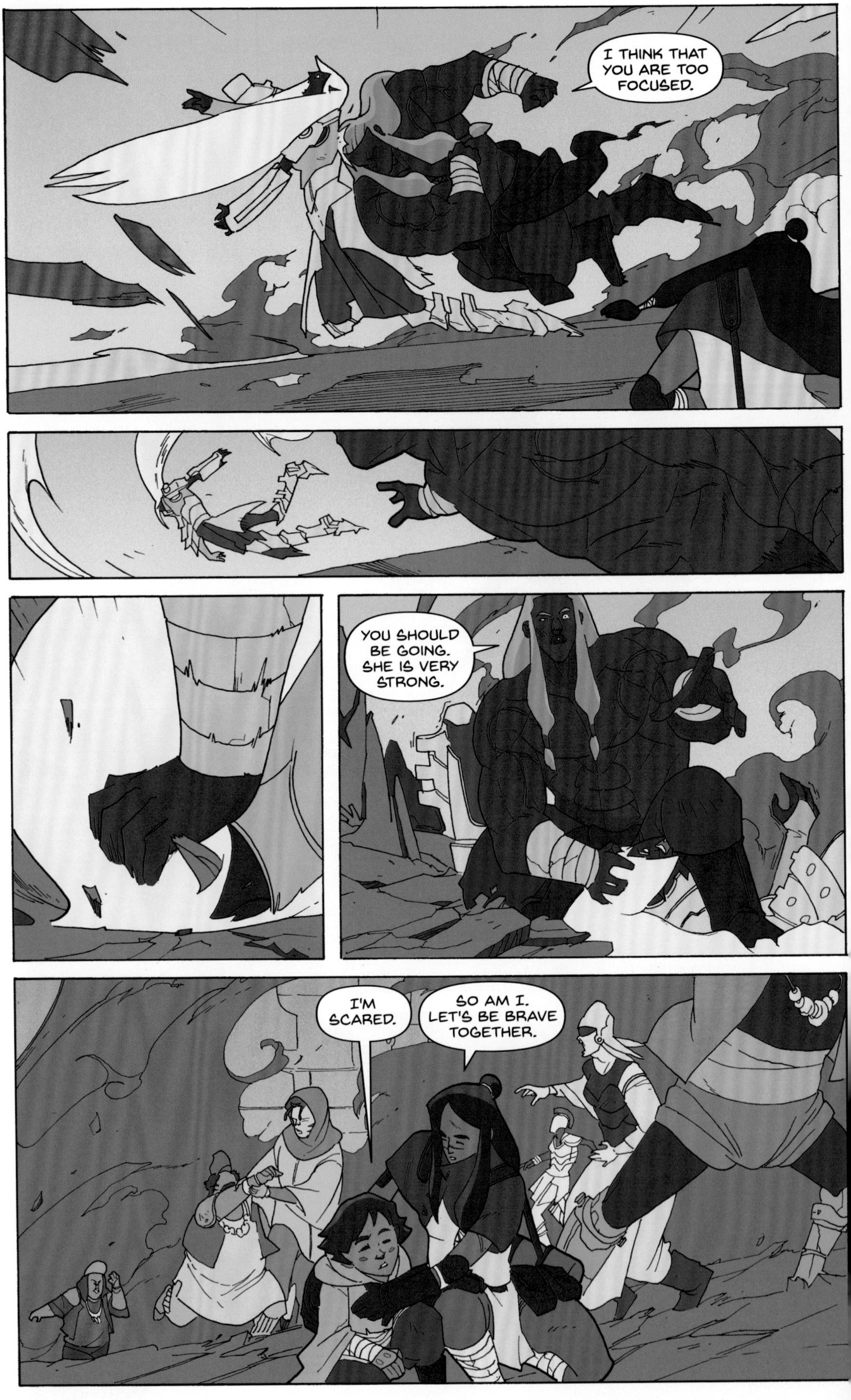
I THINK THAT YOU ARE TOO FOCUSED.
YOU SHOULD BE GOING. SHE IS VERY STRONG.
I'M SCARED.
SO AM I. LET'S BE BRAVE TOGETHER.

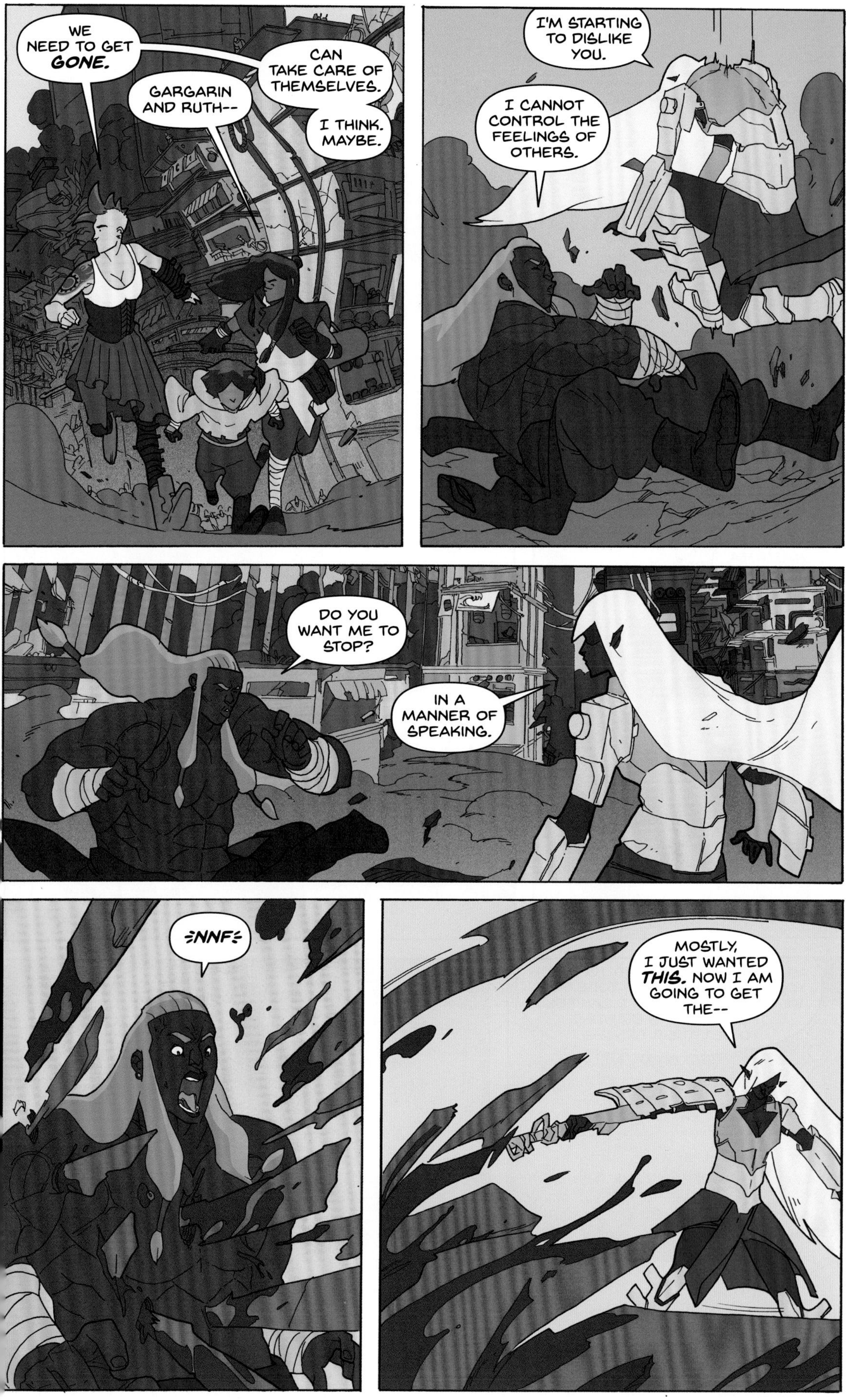
WE NEED TO GET GONE.
GARGARIN AND RUTH--
CAN TAKE CARE OF THEMSELVES.
I THINK. MAYBE.
I'M STARTING TO DISLIKE YOU.
I CANNOT CONTROL THE FEELINGS OF OTHERS.
DO YOU WANT ME TO STOP?
IN A MANNER OF SPEAKING.
NNF
MOSTLY, I JUST WANTED THIS. NOW I AM GOING TO GET THE--

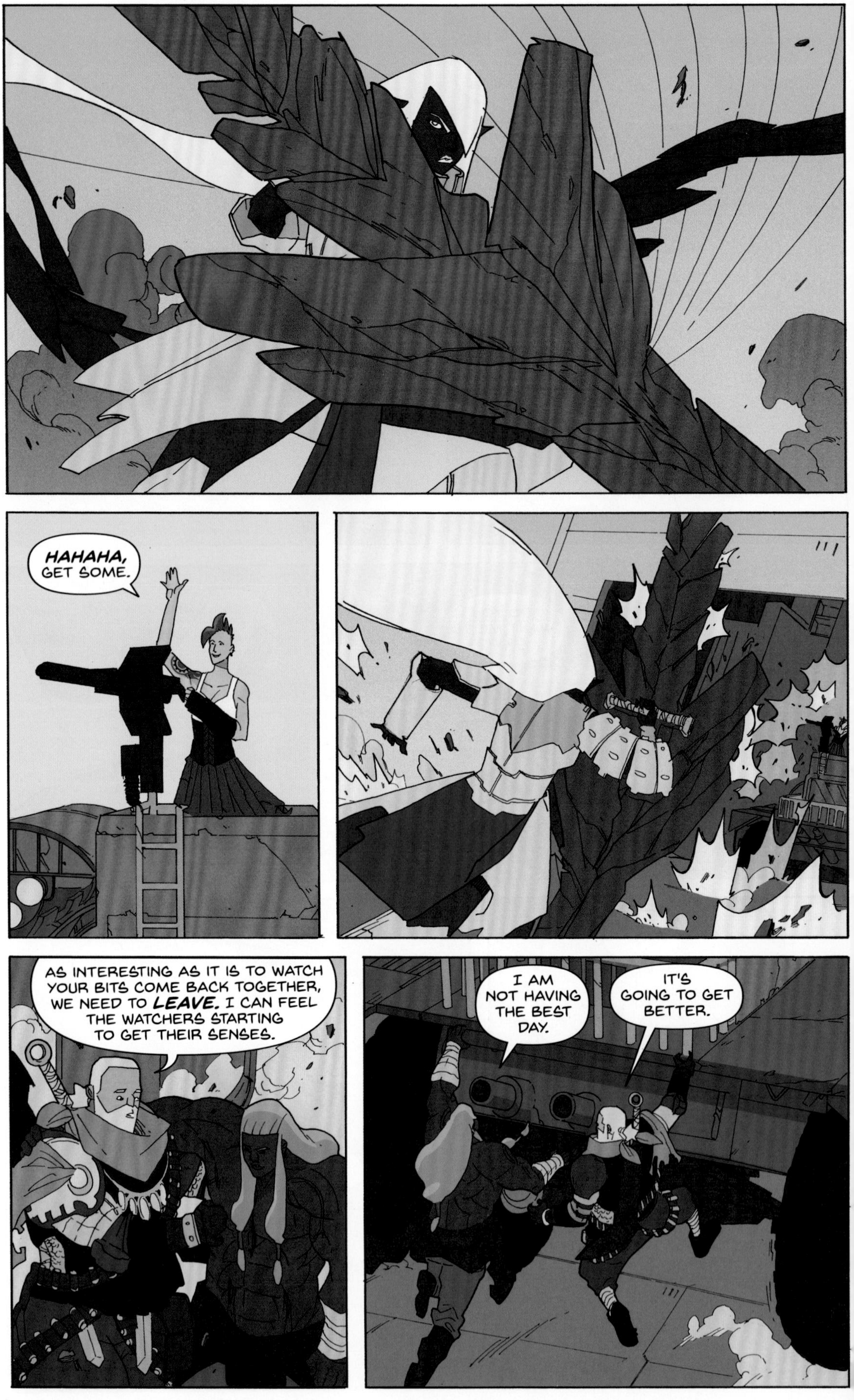
HAHAHA, GET SOME.
AS INTERESTING AS IT IS TO WATCH YOUR BITS COME BACK TOGETHER, WE NEED TO LEAVE. I CAN FEEL THE WATCHERS STARTING TO GET THEIR SENSES.
I AM NOT HAVING THE BEST DAY.
IT'S GOING TO GET BETTER.

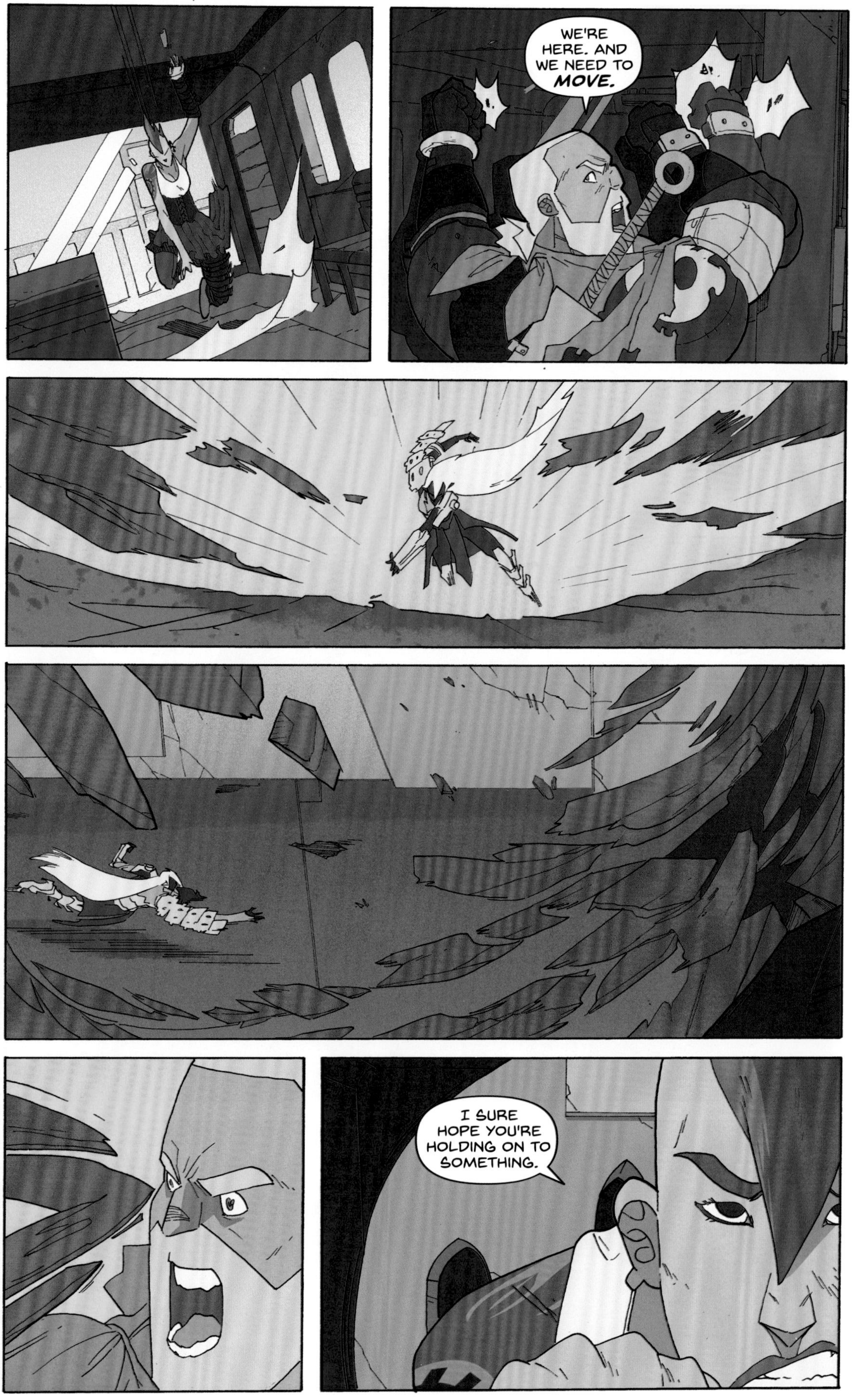
WE'RE HERE. AND WE NEED TO **MOVE.**
I SURE HOPE YOU'RE HOLDING ON TO SOMETHING.

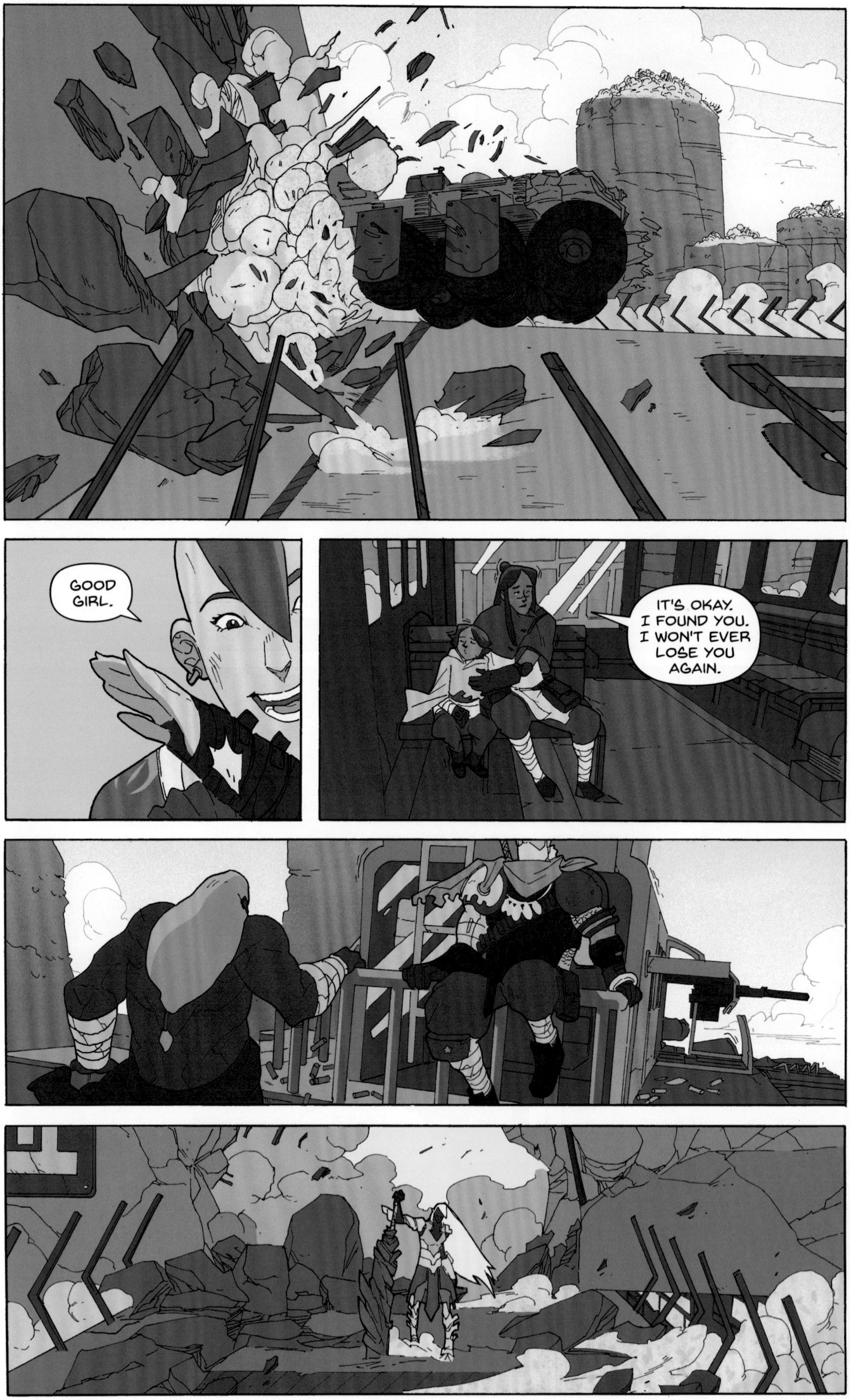
GOOD GIRL.
IT'S OKAY. I FOUND YOU. I WON'T EVER LOSE YOU AGAIN.

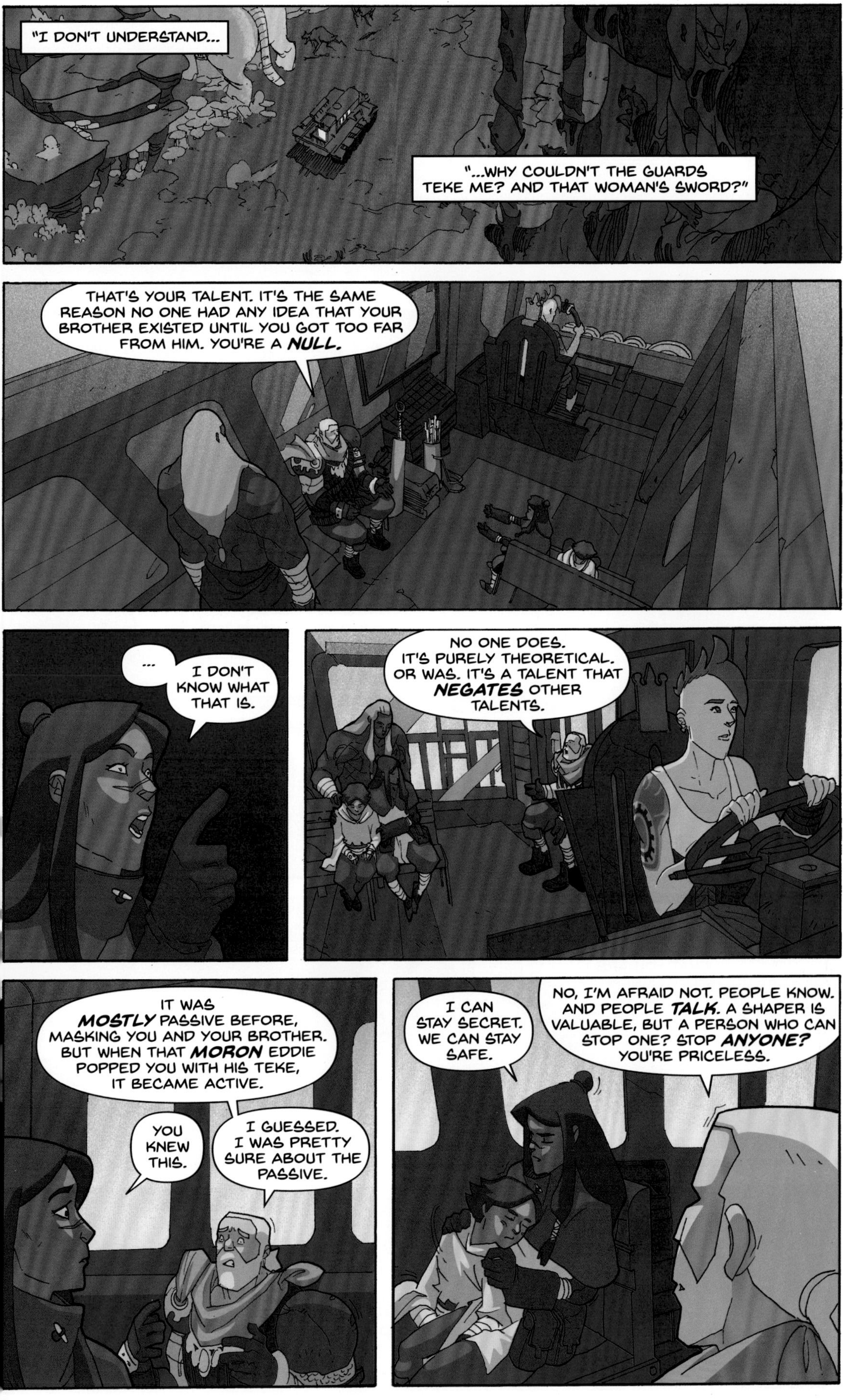
"I DON'T UNDERSTAND...
"...WHY COULDN'T THE GUARDS TEKE ME? AND THAT WOMAN'S SWORD?"
THAT'S YOUR TALENT. IT'S THE SAME REASON NO ONE HAD ANY IDEA THAT YOUR BROTHER EXISTED UNTIL YOU GOT TOO FAR FROM HIM. YOU'RE A NULL.
...
I DON'T KNOW WHAT THAT IS.
NO ONE DOES. IT'S PURELY THEORETICAL. OR WAS. IT'S A TALENT THAT NEGATES OTHER TALENTS.
IT WAS MOSTLY PASSIVE BEFORE, MASKING YOU AND YOUR BROTHER. BUT WHEN THAT MORON EDDIE POPPED YOU WITH HIS TEKE, IT BECAME ACTIVE.
YOU KNEW THIS.
I GUESSED. I WAS PRETTY SURE ABOUT THE PASSIVE.
I CAN STAY SECRET. WE CAN STAY SAFE.
NO, I'M AFRAID NOT. PEOPLE KNOW. AND PEOPLE TALK. A SHAPER IS VALUABLE, BUT A PERSON WHO CAN STOP ONE? STOP ANYONE? YOU'RE PRICELESS.

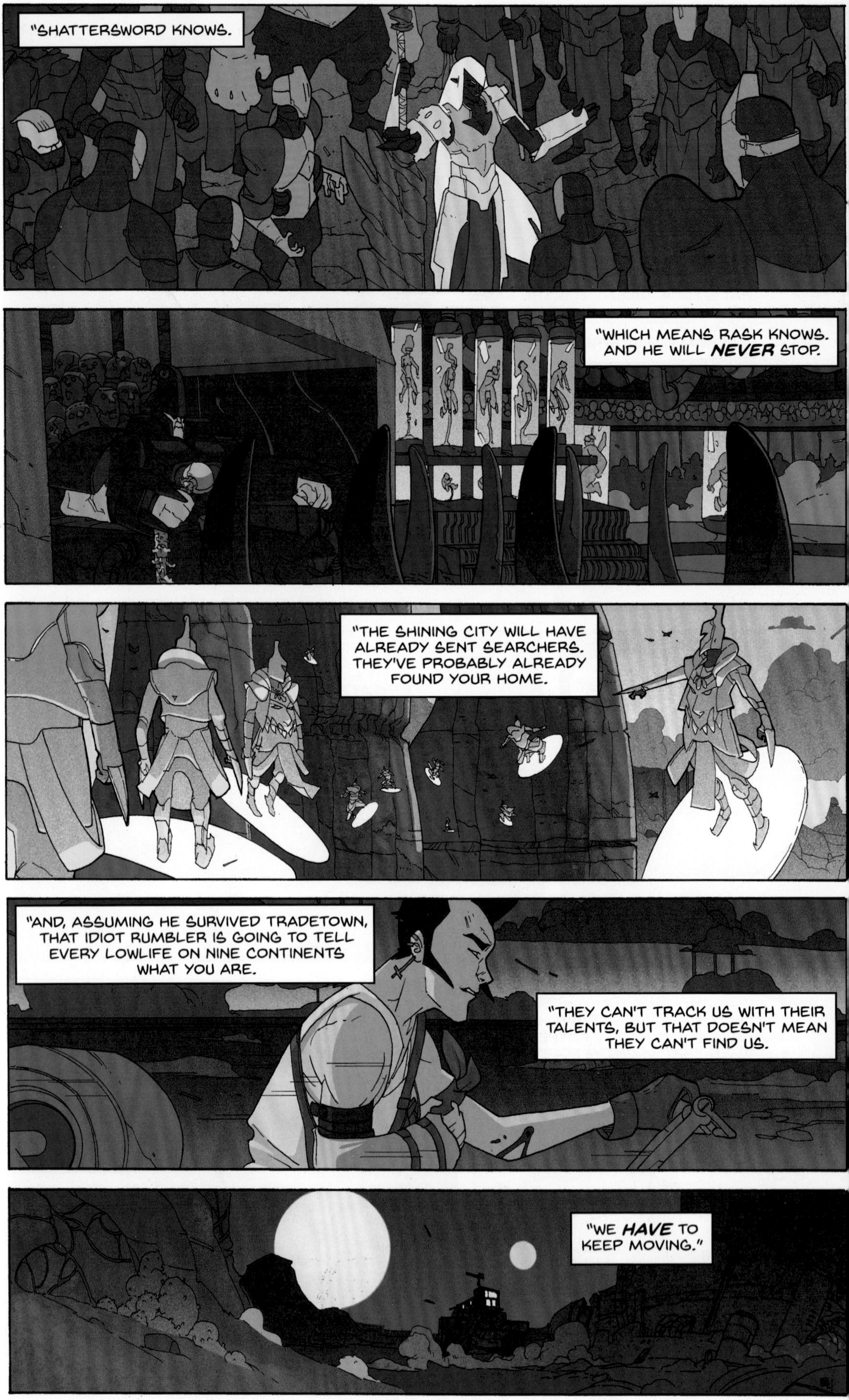
"SHATTERSWORD KNOWS.
"WHICH MEANS RASK KNOWS. AND HE WILL NEVER STOP.
"THE SHINING CITY WILL HAVE ALREADY SENT SEARCHERS. THEY'VE PROBABLY ALREADY FOUND YOUR HOME.
"AND, ASSUMING HE SURVIVED TRADETOWN, THAT IDIOT RUMBLER IS GOING TO TELL EVERY LOWLIFE ON NINE CONTINENTS WHAT YOU ARE.
"THEY CAN'T TRACK US WITH THEIR TALENTS, BUT THAT DOESN'T MEAN THEY CAN'T FIND US.
"WE HAVE TO KEEP MOVING."